PERGAMON INTERNATIONAL LIBRARY
of Science, Technology, Engineering and Social Studies
The 1000-volume original paperback library in aid of education,
industrial training and the enjoyment of leisure
Publisher: Robert Maxwell, M.C.

Spatial Dimensions of Public Policy

THE PERGAMON TEXTBOOK
INSPECTION COPY SERVICE

An inspection copy of any book published in the Pergamon International Library
will gladly be sent to academic staff without obligation for their consideration for
course adoption or recommendation. Copies may be retained for a period of 60 days
from receipt and returned if not suitable. When a particular title is adopted or
recommended for adoption for class use and the recommendation results in a sale
of 12 or more copies, the inspection copy may be retained with our compliments.
If after examination the lecturer decides that the book is not suitable for adoption
but would like to retain it for his personal library, then a discount of 10% is
allowed on the invoiced price. The Publishers will be pleased to receive suggestions
for revised editions and new titles to be published in this important International
Library.

PERGAMON OXFORD GEOGRAPHIES
General Editor: W. B. Fisher

Other Titles in the Series

Other Titles of Interest

The terms of our inspection copy service apply to all the above books. Full details of all books listed will gladly be sent upon request.

Spatial Dimensions of Public Policy

Edited by

J. T. COPPOCK
University of Edinburgh

and

W. R. D. SEWELL
University of Victoria, British Columbia

PERGAMON PRESS
Oxford · *New York* · *Toronto* · *Sydney*
Paris · *Frankfurt*

U.K.	Pergamon Press Ltd., Headington Hill Hall, Oxford OX3 0BW, England
U.S.A.	Pergamon Press Inc., Maxwell House, Fairview Park, Elmsford, New York 10523, U.S.A.
CANADA	Pergamon of Canada, Ltd., P.O. Box 9600, Don Mills M3C 2T9 Ontario, Canada
AUSTRALIA	Pergamon Press (Aust.) Pty. Ltd., 19a Boundary Street, Rushcutters Bay, N.S.W. 2011, Australia
FRANCE	Pergamon Press SARL, 24 rue des Ecoles, 75240 Paris, Cedex 05, France
WEST GERMANY	Pergamon Press GMbH, 6242 Kronberg/Taunus Pferdstrasse 1, Frankfurt-am-Main

Copyright © Pergamon Press 1976 J. T. Coppock and W. R. D. Sewell

First edition 1976

Library of Congress Cataloging in Publication Data

Main entry under title:

Spatial dimensions of public policy.

(Pergamon Oxford geographies) (Pergamon international library)

Based on papers presented at the annual meeting of the Institute of British Geographers, held at the University of East Anglia, Jan. 1974.
1. Regional planning—Congresses. 2. Geography, Economic—Congresses. 3. Coppock, John Terence. II. Sewell, W. R. Derrick. III. Institute of British Geographers.
HT391.S65 1976   309.2'5   76–10989
0–08 –020629–8

Printed in Great Britain by A. Wheaton & Co. Exeter

CONTENTS

ACKNOWLEDGEMENTS

The inspiration for this volume came from the annual meeting of the Institute of British Geographers, held at the University of East Anglia in Norwich, in January, 1974. Adopting as its theme "Geography and Public Policy", the Conference featured several special sessions designed to stimulate discussion of the past, present, and future role of geographers and geographical analysis in the field of public policy. These discussions covered the broad relationships of geographers to the policy area as well as inputs to specific topics, such as resource management, urban development, regional development and the alleviation of poverty.

Some of the chapters in this volume are based upon papers presented at the I.B.G. meeting and a number of others were invited from geographers in the United Kingdom and elsewhere who have been involved in research, administration, or other activities relating to public policy. The main emphasis is upon policy-making in the United Kingdom, but papers by geographers from Canada, the Netherlands, New Zealand, Nigeria, and the United States not only provide an assessment of the role of geographical research in policy formulation in those countries, but also a perspective on such research in the United Kingdom.

Several people made very useful contributions to preparation of the volume for publication and the editors wish to acknowledge this assistance. In particular, they wish to thank Mrs. J. T. Coppock who prepared the Index; Mr. C. Clark, Mr. R. Harris and Mr. A. Bradley who drew the maps and diagrams, and Mrs. C. Cumming and Miss S. Smith who typed various drafts of the manuscript.

J. T. COPPOCK,

Department of Geography,
University of Edinburgh,
Edinburgh, Scotland.

W. R. DERRICK SEWELL,

Department of Geography,
University of Victoria,
Victoria, B.C., Canada.

GEOGRAPHY AND PUBLIC POLICY

CONTRIBUTORS

J. T. COPPOCK is Ogilvie Professor of Geography in the University of Edinburgh and Director of the Tourism and Recreation Research Unit. His main fields of interest are in rural land use and in geographical information systems, and his research has had an increasing public policy content over the past 15 years. He has been a member of numerous government committees in these fields, including the England Committee and Land Use Panel of the Nature Conservancy, the Land Use Research Grants Committee of the Natural Environment Research Council and the Departmental Committees on Tourism in Scotland and on Information Systems for Planning, and in 1971-2 he acted as Specialist Adviser to the Select Committee on Scottish Affairs in their investigations into Land Resource Use in Scotland.

W. R. DERRICK SEWELL is Professor of Geography at the University of Victoria, Victoria, B.C., Canada. His main fields of interest are in decision-making in resources management, particularly with respect to the role of professionals and of the public, and the impact of natural hazards. Prior to his present appointment he was on the faculty of the University of Chicago, and previously was an economic advisor to the Canadian Government on the negotiation of the Columbia River Treaty. He has written widely on resources management issues, particularly on techniques of evaluation, the role of perceptions and attitudes, and the development of policies and institutions. He has been a consultant to various bodies, including the United Nations, the federal governments of Canada and the United States, and various provincial and State governments in those countries. Currently he is also a member of the International Council of the Man and the Biosphere Programme.

C. I. JACKSON is Executive Director of the Canadian Participation Secretariat in the Ministry of State for Urban Affairs, Ottawa. This Secretariat is responsible for Canadian participation in Habitat: the United Nations Conference on Human Settlements, Vancouver 1976. Prior to this he was Director of Priorities and Planning in the Ministry. After graduate studies in climatology at McGill University, Montreal, (which included 12 months as a member of the Canadian International Geophysical Year

Expedition to northern Ellesmere Island), he was a Lecturer in Geography at the London School of Economics from 1959 to 1969. His research during that period included a critical assessment of British water supply policy and pricing. After joining the Canadian public service in 1969, Dr. Jackson worked on geographical and resource management problems in the Department of Energy, Mines and Resources and the Department of the Environment before moving to Urban Affairs in 1971.

F.. KENNETH HARE is Professor of Geography and Physics at the University of Toronto, and is Director of the Institute for Environmental Studies there. He has been involved in public resource and environment policy issues in three countries. In Canada he was a member of the National Research Council, and later served as Science Advisor to the Federal Department of the Environment. He is a present member of the Canadian Environmental Advisory Council. In the United Kingdom (where he was formerly Master of Birbeck College) he served on Sir Dudley Stamp's Advisory Committee on Natural Resources, and was a founding member of the Natural Environmental Research Council. In the United States he is a Director of Resources for the Future. He is currently Chairman of the Ecosciences Panel of the North Atlantic Treaty Organisation. When asked how he does all these things he answers "the trick is superficiality; never do anything really well."

EDWIN BROOKS is senior lecturer in Geography at Liverpool University and Dean of College Studies. His main fields of interest lie in social and political planning in Great Britain, East-Central Europe and Brazil. In 1972 he led an enquiry into the conditions of tribal Indians in the Amazon. From 1958 to 1967 he was a councillor in Birkenhead, chairing the Works and Building Committee and the Youth Employment Committee. From 1966 to 1970 he was a Labour Member of Parliament for Bebington and a member of the Committee of Public Accounts. As a private Member he promoted the National Health Service (Family Planning) Act of 1967. He was the first President of the Conservation Society from 1966 to 1967.

MICHAEL CHISHOLM is Professor of Economic and Social Geography at the University of Bristol; in October 1976 he becomes Professor of Geography at the University of Cambridge. His main research work has been in the field of locational economics and regional development, with special reference to the United Kingdom. He was a member of the South West Advisory Committee to the Land Commission, and for 5 years served on the Social Science Research Council. He is currently a member of the Local Government Boundary Commission for England. In addition, he had acted as consultant, mainly with Economic Associates Ltd., on a number of problems concerned with development, both in the United Kingdom and abroad.

J. W. HOUSE is Halford Mackinder Professor of Geography in the University of Oxford and a member of the Northern Economic Planning Council. His research in applied geography has had a particular emphasis on social and economic problems in both urban and rural North-East England. From 1969 to 1971 he was a member of the Northern Pennines Rural Development Board, and for some years served on the Northumberland Rural Community Council. Between 1964 and 1968 he was Director of the then Ministry of Labour sponsored research programme into "Migration and Mobility in Northern England".

J. B. GODDARD is Henry Daysh Professor of Regional Development Studies in the Department of Geography of the University of Newcastle-upon-Tyne and was formerly a lecturer in Geography at the London School of Economics and Political Science. His main field of research is on office communications and office location. He has participated in research on this topic for the South-East Economic Planning Council, the Location of Offices Bureau, the Department of the Environment, the City of London Corporation and the Swedish Government. He has developed close links with Swedish researchers in this field, most recently as a Leverhulme Fellow at the University of Lund. His international work has also included a study for the Economic Development Committee of the European Free Trade Association on National Settlement Strategies. This work has been associated with a widening interest in the role of information flows in organisational and urban systems development.

DAVID STARKIE is lecturer in the Department of Geography, University of Reading, and is currently on leave as Director of Transport Planning and Research and Acting Deputy Director General of Transport, Government of Western Australia. He served as the Specialist Adviser to the Environment Sub-Committee of the House of Commons Expenditure Committee for a number of investigations between 1971 and 1975, and has acted as Transport Adviser to the Government of Argentina. His main fields of interest are transport and environmental appraisal. He has published widely in both aspects and has conducted research for the Department of the Environment into the environmental effects of transport.

PETER R. ODELL has been Professor of Economic Geography and Director of the Economic Geography Institute in the Netherlands School of Economics—now a part of the Erasmus University, Rotterdam—since 1968. Prior to that he was on the staff of the London School of Economics where he commenced his research interests in the field of energy problems, on which he has published extensively. Most recently he has been much involved in public policy debates—both at national and the European level—on the reshaping of energy policies following the post-1971 changes in the international oil industry and has been a firm proponent of the idea of European self-sufficiency in energy based essentially on the full and rapid exploitation of the off-shore oil and gas reserves of the continent.

R: G. LISTER is Professor of Geography in the University of Otago, New Zealand. He has been closely concerned with regional planning and environmental policy during the past decade, serving on many regional and national bodies that have been developing public involvement in these fields in New Zealand. He has been a member of the New Zealand Environmental Council since its inception in 1970 and attended the Stockholm Conference on the Human Environment as a government representative in 1972. He is a member of the Clutha Valley Development Commission, serves as chairman of the Technical Advisory Committee of the Dunedin Metropolitan Regional Planning Authority and is a frequent radio commentator on local and national affairs in New Zealand.

AKIN L. MABOGUNJE is Professor of Geography at the University of Ibadan and Co-Director of the Planning Studies Programme of the Faculty of Social Sciences of that University. His main interest is in information systems and quantitative techniques as they relate to the field of urbanisation and regional planning. He was Census Adviser to the Western Nigerian government for the 1962 Census and to the Federal Government for the 1973 Census. He has served on a number of Government Commissions and Committees. He was a member of the Western Nigerian Land Utilisation Committee (1960-2), member of the Western State Economic Advisory Council (1968-72), Chairman of the Committee investigating into Forest Policy and Management in Western Nigeria (1966-8) and Chairman of the Western State Forestry Advisory Commission (1968-74). More recently, he has served as a member of the Public Service Review Commission (1972-4) that was set up by the Federal Nigerian Government to advise on the reform of its public services.

RICHARD MORRILL is Professor and Chairman of Geography, and Associate Director of the Institute for Environmental Studies at the University of Washington. His main fields of interest include regional planning and development, and theory and models of spatial organisation and interaction. In addition to involvement in political and school redistricting, he is enmeshed in local and regional issues of growth, metropolitan transportation and administrative organization. In 1970 he visited the University of Glasgow as a Sir John McTaggart Fellow.

T. HÄGERSTRAND holds a research chair in the University of Lund in Social and Economic Geography under the Swedish Council for Social Science Research. He has been working on population geography (migration in particular), spatial diffusion, geo-coding and space-time budgeting. The nature of his studies has brought him into close contact with the planning policy as well as with future-oriented research. He served on the Commission for Local Government Reform, the Commission for Regional Administration Reform and the Advisory Group for National Physical Planning, and is a member of the Expert Group for Regional Research. He has also contributed to regional policy studies in the European Free Trade Association. He took part in the formation of the Swedish Cabinet's Secretariat for Future Studies and holds the position as chairman of the Joint Committee for long-term interdisciplinary research of the nine major national research councils.

PREFACE

In nearly all countries the public purse is now the major source of university funds and accountability and relevance are increasingly the watchwords of the politicians who control these funds. It is true, of course, that one of the earliest roles of universities was the provision of trained manpower for the professions—the Church, the Law and Medicine; but while professional training continues to be an important task for universities, many disciplines in the modern university are not directly concerned with such training and their practitioners cannot escape the question: "What are you contributing to the good of the society which supports you?" In part, the answer is the provision of minds trained to think logically and critically about complex topics, and the enlargement of human knowledge and understanding, and for many subjects this may be sufficient. But geographers, whose field of study is the contemporary world, increasingly seek to understand the public policies which affect its human (and, indirectly, its physical) characteristics and, through their professional expertise, to make some contribution to shaping such policies, particularly those which have important spatial and environmental dimensions.

This book is a selection of such contributions, chosen to give some indication of their variety and in no way intended to be comprehensive. It had its origins in the Annual Conference of the Institute of British Geographers in 1974 which had, as its theme, "Geography and Public Policy". The authors are distinguished geographers who have played various roles, as politician, civil servant, adviser, consultant, researcher and critic, in a wide range of issues. By their very nature, such contributions are often not readily observable, nor without breaches of government security or undue immodesty can the participants themselves disclose their roles; nevertheless, sufficient can be indicated to reveal something of the nature of each contribution. The nature of the topic and the role of the authors also largely control the degree to which professional expertise as geographer can be directly applied; for, as several contributions show, the nearer the point at which policies are decided the more general must the contribution be.

The chapters fall broadly into four groups. The first comprises a set of views about the geographer's actual and potential contributions to public policy. The opening chapter is based on the author's presidential address to

xiii

the Institute of British Geographers and examines, primarily in a British context, both the nature of the contributions and the reasons why they have not been as effective as the relationships between geographers' interests and important issues of public policy might suggest. The second chapter, by Ian Jackson, once an academic but now a senior civil servant in the Canadian Ministry of State for Urban Affairs, describes how policy decisions are made in Canada and reviews the nature of disciplinary contributions to governmental decision-making at the highest level. In the following chapter, Kenneth Hare, from his long background in scientific research and administration, shows how his experience as a science policy adviser in the Canadian Department of the Environment has modified his views about the nature of such contributions. Finally, Edwin Brooks, a former elected representative in local government and in Parliament, where he was a member of the powerful Public Acounts Committee, discusses his views as a backbench member on two aspects which have been neglected by geographers-regional policy and broad issues of world strategy.

The second section examines specific contributions to public policy, with particular reference to experience in the United Kingdom. Michael Chisholm, as a member of the Local Government Boundary Commission for England, discusses the achievements of the Commission in drawing the new district boundaries according to the terms of reference given by the government. John House, as the only academic member of the Northern Pennines Rural Development Board, evaluates a geographical contribution to the making and implementation of policies during the Board's brief existence. Terry Coppock then reviews the experience of the Tourism and Recreation Research Unit at Edinburgh University in undertaking research for a wide variety of government agencies and its contribution to their emerging policies. The last two contributions in this group provide a convenient link to the third group, for they put British experience in a wider setting. John Goddard describes research he has undertaken for the Department of the Environment and the Location of Offices Bureau into the relocation of offices from central London and compares this with Swedish research on the dispersal of the Swedish civil service, while David Starkie, from his background of research into economic aspects of pollution and as Specialist Adviser to the Select Committee on Estimates, reviews three spatial aspects of pollution policy, one of which at least has an international component.

The third group of chapters is devoted to policies outside the United Kingdom. Peter Odell, on the basis of experience as an employee in the oil industry and subsequently as a consultant and researcher in the field of energy, reviews energy policies for Western Europe, with particular reference to oil and natural gas. Ronald Lister examines a geographer's contribution to environmental problems in New Zealand, especially from the viewpoint of his membership of the Environmental Council and as a New

Zealand delegate to the Stockholm Conference on the Human Environment and the Bucharest Conference on World Population. Akin Mabogunje describes the difficulties of achieving an accurate population census of Nigeria from his viewpoint as Census Adviser in charge of the demarcation of enumeration areas for the 1973 census, a role which was at least in part a consequence of pressure on government by university geographers. Richard Morrill, from a background of research with a strong policy content, describes the context and results of the task which he was asked to undertake in 1972, the reshaping of the legislative and congressional districts of the State of Washington. Finally, Torsten Hägerstrand, the doyen of geographers working in the field of applied geography, analyses the contributions of Swedish geographers to the development of an effective administrative structure at both communal and regional level, the latter in particular involving close collaboration between civil servants and university researchers.

In the last chapter, which forms the fourth section of the book, the editors review this wide and varied range of experience and points several important lessons and conclusions which are relevant to contributions which geographers will be able to make in the future.

CHAPTER 1

GEOGRAPHY AND PUBLIC POLICY: CHALLENGE, OPPORTUNITY AND IMPLICATIONS

J. T. COPPOCK

University of Edinburgh

The present is a time of great challenge and opportunity for the geographical profession. The challenge lies in the fact that topics with which geographers have been concerned throughout the existence of geography as a university discipline have now become matters of great public importance, above all, those relating to their central theme of the earth as the home of man, or in its modern dress, the environment. This challenge provides an opportunity for geographers to demonstrate both to the academic community and to government and the public that they have the necessary skills and concepts to contribute effectively to the solution of some of the major problems facing Society. Moreover, if geographers do not respond, they will find that others adopt a role which they have traditionally regarded as theirs. This chapter will review what geographers have achieved, identify the weaknesses and the reasons why this contribution has not been more widely appreciated, examine the implications for teaching and research, and suggest ways in which the challenges can be more adequately met. The discussion will be conducted largely in the context of the United Kingdom, though reference will frequently be made to North American experience.

The time could hardly have been more opportune for a discussion of geography and public policy. In the world at large the Stockholm Conference on the Human Environment has provided a reminder of the problems posed by the way in which the earth's resources are used and of the interdependence of life on this planet, while the current energy crisis has given dramatic evidence of the fact that mankind inhabits one world and shares a closely-knit world economy. In their domestic affairs, the British are faced with the task of creating an urban environment of high quality in the cities they have inherited from the nineteenth century, of devising a structure of local and regional government which fits the facts of modern geography and of meeting the increasing demands upon limited land resources in ways which are economically efficient, politically acceptable, ecologically sound and aesthetically pleasing. For many of these problems freedom of action is limited by legacies of the past, but, with the discovery of massive new resources of oil and natural gas in the North Sea, there are both the challenge of major new developments and the opportunity to avoid the mistakes of the past, and it is timely to ask what light geographers can throw on these and similar problems.

THE GEOGRAPHER'S CONTRIBUTION

Geographers have contributed in numerous ways towards the understanding and, less frequently, the solution of such problems. Indeed, as John House (1973) has effectively demonstrated, the growing volume of such contributions has been a marked feature of the past 25 years, in parallel with the growth of the subject itself. This contribution is widely diffused and its importance is perhaps underrated for that reason; for it embraces teaching, research, professional employment and advice to government.

Teaching has probably been the geographer's most important role, especially in the schools, where geography has been the principal source of awareness about both the local and the world environments. In the universities and colleges, too, there is increasing evidence of changes of focus in teaching which have given greater attention to environmental problems and to the contribution of public policies in the use of resources. This contribution of teaching is difficult to evaluate, for much is absorbed unconsciously and helps to shape the thinking of a future electorate and of future policy makers. What seems quite clear is that students themselves are increasingly receptive to approaches to teaching which emphasize real problems and attempt to offer solutions.

Perhaps because of the way in which modern geography evolved as a university discipline and because the main outlet for geography graduates was for long in teaching, research has tended to have a less important place in the geographical profession than in many of the science-based disciplines which share the geographer's field of interest; yet, as John House's review and those which have appeared in the pages of *Progress in Geography* (Board *et al.,* 1969-) and elsewhere have shown, there has been a very considerable increase in the volume of geographical research. While relatively little of this research has been policy-oriented, there have been several fields of inquiry in which geographers, notably in North America, have not only made effective contributions, but have provided intellectual leadership to those in other disciplines. There are illustrations in several branches of geography, notably in the urban, transport and resource management fields. These include the studies of natural hazards undertaken by Gilbert White and his colleagues (1965 and 1974), research on highway development by William Garrison

(1956), investigations of problems of urban ghettoes by Richard Morrill and studies of human dimensions of weather modification by Derrick Sewell (1973). In addition, geographical research has assisted the appraisal of views about various public policies in both the urban and the resource management fields. Here the work of Gilbert White (1966) on the formation and role of attitudes, investigations of perceptions of various natural hazards by Ian Burton (1964) and Robert Kates (1962) and others (Sewell and Burton, 1971), and studies of influence of perceptions and attitudes of various groups of specialists (Sewell, 1971, M. Barker, 1972) are especially relevant. In addition, geographers have also studied the efficiency of various types of public involvement in planning and policy-making, and have helped shape policies in this connection, as in the work of Timothy O'Riordan (1971), Jonothan O'Riordan (1975), and Derrick Sewell (1975) in Canada. In this country, perhaps the most effective contributions have been those of Peter Hall (1973) in the urban and regional fields, but much of the research outlined by John House has served to inform policy.

Perhaps more influential than research has been the contribution of geographers in a professional role as servants of both central and local government. Canada, where geographers have long held posts in various government departments, as well as in planning agencies, provides an interesting illustration. At the federal level there was formerly a Geographical Branch, devoted principally to studies of the physical environment (particularly the nature and magnitude of glaciation) and the mapping of various phenomena. More recently Canadian geographers have been able to take a much more direct role in planning and policy making in several different types of agency. In the Department of Environment, for example, numerous geographers are involved in appraisals of policies for water resources and in the organization of programmes of public participation. Several geographers are employed by the Ministry of Urban Affairs in the development of policies for urban renewal and population redistribution. The Department of Northern Affairs also employs geographers in research relating to the development of Northern resources. In provincial and regional government agencies, too, more posts are being occupied by geographers. Their numbers at all levels are increasing, and as in the United States, geographers are most commonly employed as "social scientists", "specialists planners", or "research assistants", rather than as geographers. Most geographers in the United Kingdom also appear in other roles, especially as planners. One estimate has indicated that as many as 40 per cent of a recent intake into the planning profession had taken first degrees in geography (House, 1973, p. 285), and smaller numbers appear as conservationists and in other guises. The contribution of geographers in the planning profession in Great Britain has been the subject of appraisals by Geoffrey Powell (1970) and Christie Willatts (1971), and it seems likely that the geographical training of planners has contributed in no small measure to the creation of an increasing awareness of the spatial dimension in major public policies affecting the environment.

Perhaps the most important contribution by geographers to the understanding and solution of major problems in the field of public policy has been as advisers to government departments and official committees, or as members of committees of inquiry and of those which advise on policy. This contribution, too, has been reviewed by John House and need not be elaborated further. Of course, by their nature, such contributions, like those of serving professionals in central and local government, cannot always be identified and, once identified, cannot easily be measured. Both the processes by which policies are formed and the subject matter of environmental policies are highly complex and would be difficult to evaluate even if no problems of confidentiality arose. In this connection it would be instructive for members of the profession to examine the Reports on Land Resource Use in Scotland (Select Committee on Scottish Affairs, 1972) and on Sport and Leisure (Select Committee of the House of Lords, 1973) to see whether they can detect any geographical influence by the specialist advisers (all geographers).

There is no doubt that the contributions of geographers have increased both in amount and in range, but, particularly in respect of research and advice, they remain small by comparison with those of other disciplines. In the United States, for example, expenditure on geographical research by the National Science Foundation was less than a sixth of that on anthropology or economics or sociology (Taafe, 1970 p. 117); in that funded by the Social Science Research Council (1973) in the United Kingdom, geography's share was only 14 per cent of that of economics. Nor is the claim of geography to have a primary interest in environmental and resource problems widely accepted outside the profession. Today, "environment" is more likely to be associated in the public mind with ecology and "resources" with economics.

A PARADOX OF LONG-ESTABLISHED INTEREST AND LIMITED AWARENESS

While it is obvious that not all questions concerning public policy and the environment are matters for the geographer, it seems clear that geographers are not being asked to make the contribution of which they are capable. There is thus a paradox between the existence of a long-established area of interest and a growing contribution in research, on the one hand, and a widespread lack of awareness of that contribution outside the profession on the other.

There are several reasons why this should be so, for some of which the profession must accept the blame. Thus, much of the relevant research, though falling broadly within the applied field, has not been designed to answer questions which are relevant to public policy and frequently cannot be adapted to this end; where it has been concerned with policy, it has evaluated past policies and has generally failed to offer alternative strategies for the future and predictions of their likely effects. Equally important are causes outside the profession. In general, policy-makers in the United Kingdom do not seem to be aware of (or, if they are aware, to be interested in) the spatial dimensions of their problems or policies. The reasons may in part lie in its relatively small size, though the United Kingdom contains a great diversity of environments and there is an increasing concern in the constituent countries, especially in Scotland and in Wales, at the attempts to apply policies conceived in London uniformly throughout the Kingdom. This question will, of course, become of increasing importance as attempts are made to find European solutions; the preliminary definition of hill areas in the European Economic Community by reference to a single measure of height, despite its vastly different significance throughout the Community, is an interesting contemporary example.

Solutions to both these internal and external constraints lie to a large extent in the hands of the profession, particularly through a growing volume of research of good quality which is oriented to policy questions, and a flow of suitably-qualified and able graduates in geography to work in these areas. Even those geographers who do not wish to participate must surely recognize that there is virtually no aspect of contemporary geography which is not affected to some degree by public policy. Understanding policies and processes of decision-making is thus essential to an understanding of the contemporary geography of a country.

There are also more general reasons why the profession should be concerned with such research and with its contributions to the making and implementation of effective policies. Universities in the United Kingdom are now largely funded from the public purse and are subject to an increasing degree of central direction, though in many ways this is due to a failure by politicians and their advisers to appreciate the true role of the universities which have a duty to look beyond the immediate problems, to consider the long-term implications and to offer dispassionate criticism. Whatever the reasons, geographers are increasingly likely to be judged, not only by the intellectual standing of their subject, but in relation to the need for trained manpower and by geography's usefulness to the community at large. It is interesting to consider why there is a much stronger sense of involvement in public issues in universities in North America; in large measure, no doubt, it is due to the different place of the universities in society, to the origins of many of them in the needs of the community, as in the Land Grant Colleges, and to the much greater mobility of staff between universities, government and the private sector.

Yet these are all negative reasons for advocating a greater concern with policy-oriented research; much more important from the point of view of the profession is what geographers have to offer. This contribution is of two kinds. First, at a general level, is a broad awareness of the way in which aspects of present problems of the environment and the use of resources fit together in particular contexts, a contribution which stems from the geographer's role as general practitioner in a world of specialists. This is not to suggest a role for the geographer as the great synthesiser; his contribution is a much humbler, but none the less increasingly difficult one of attempting to see problems in context and to avoid unnecessary blinkers, a need that is increasingly acute in problems which affect both men and nature. Taking the broader view is both difficult and requires conscious effort; it is also essential to the making of good public policy.

There is an equally important contribution, the ability to analyse the spatial dimensions of environmental problems and, more particularly, to handle, analyse and interpret spatially-distributed data. The hand-drawn map was for long the main tool available to geographers and T. Hägerstrand (Chap. 14) shows that such maps may still have an important role to play; but geographers are now provided with techniques and methods of increasing versatility. This awareness of, and facility in handling, the spatial dimension, which is a major ingredient of all problems of environmental and resource management, is something not generally provided by those in other disciplines and tends to be overlooked if the geographer does not provide it.

RESOLVING THE PARADOX

.Even if it is accepted that much greater involvement by geographers in policy-oriented questions is desirable, nothing very much will happen merely by such acceptance. At least three developments are necessary. The first task is one for the profession, to identify the contributions which geographers can make, both with the skills that are widely available now and with those which seem relevant to the solution of policy-oriented problems and which might be encouraged in various ways, whether they arise from technical developments, as in remote sensing, or from advances in theoretical geography, as in the study of spatial statistics.

Secondly, having identified the contributions, research must be encouraged in projects which will illustrate the methods and approaches that geographers use and provide a demonstration that such approaches are capable of extension to the solution of the large-scale problems which policy-makers face. Such differences of scale are of considerable practical importance, for inefficiencies which may be tolerable at a small scale are not acceptable when large quantities of data must be handled.

The third necessary development is a dialogue between the profession and those who advise on, make and implement official policy (whether at national, regional, or local levels), so that the latter can be aware of the significant contributions that geographers are capable of making towards the solution of environmental and resource problems, in ways that can be used to help devise, implement or monitor policies. Clearly this role will be greatly affected by the changes arising from the British government's acceptance of the broad principles outlined by Lord Rothschild for the funding of government research and development (Lord Privy Seal, 1971, 1972); but the application of these principles is in its infancy and government departments are still identifying their research requirements and developing machinery for the commissioning of the necessary research. Geographers should accept the invitation to a dialogue with the customer departments and should raise, as an important ingredient of such discussions, the nature of available data; for geographers are more dependent than most scientists on data provided by others (especially official agencies) which both constrain and shape their research.

THE FEASIBILITY OF POLICY-ORIENTED RESEARCH

These three developments inevitably pose a number of questions about the ability of both the universities and the geographical profession to undertake such research and the desirability of their doing so.

The first question is whether the universities, as at present organised, are competent to undertake such research. The development of contract research faces universities with commitments of a kind they have not previously undertaken on any scale. Much of the research undertaken in the past with public funds or with support from foundations has been fairly open-ended and, while reports have generally been required, it is widely recognised that such research, often undertaken by those who have recently graduated under the general supervision of a member of staff, contains a substantial component which can properly be classified as learning. A research contract, on the other hand, requires a defined product by a specified date. More important is the fact that, while teaching understandably and rightly has priority in universities so that the time which teaching staff can devote to research tends to be a residual legatee, experienced senior staff are required for the successful prosecution of contract research. Even where full-time research staff are employed, there may be conflicts over access to resources, such as computers, which may be required for student records, or printing equipment, on which priority must be given to committee papers. It is not therefore surprising that universities should have a bad reputation for not producing reports on time.

There are several solutions to these difficulties. Full-time research workers can be recruited, though it is generally difficult to recruit staff of sufficient seniority owing to the absence of any career structure. In this respect, as in a number of others, geography is at a disadvantage compared with other disciplines interested in the environment and in resource management where there are research or professional institutions of various kinds to provide a parallel career structure, as with the research stations of the Agricultural Research Council for agriculturalists, the Natural Environment Research Council and the Nature Conservancy Council for biologists, and the National Institute of Social and Economic Research and units of applied economics for economists.

An alternative solution is the secondment of teaching staff to work on such projects, but this does not seem to be popular in the United Kingdom; secondment is not recognised as desirable by universities, and academic staff, too, seem to feel that it will harm their careers. Although there has been much discussion of interchanges between government and industry and the universities, such exchanges seem to happen only on a small scale and to have involved moves in one direction only, from government agencies to universities. Greater mobility all round would have a number of advantages, by bringing fresh experience and critical thinking to bear on the problems of both government departments and universities, by facilitating closer liaison between them and by making it easier for centres of excellence to emerge.

Even if these difficulties are disregarded and it is assumed that universities are competent to undertake such research, it is not at all clear whether they wish to do so or whether the government favours such research. Government statements on university policy have increasingly stressed their teaching function and implied that, as staff/student ratios worsen, the time available for research is likely to diminish. At the same time, the University Grants Committee has urged universities to ensure that research pays its way, and has suggested that an average figure of 40 per cent should be added to research costs to meet overheads. Such an approach is quite appropriate if contracting bodies have the resources to provide such overheads, but much research is undertaken on quite inadequate budgets and it is clear that research in subjects which have yet to make their mark would make little progress if such a policy were rigorously applied. Moreover, government departments and agencies seem very unwilling to provide such contributions and the research councils, as a matter of policy, do not. Paradoxically, governments draw heavily on academic time for advisory work in many fields, a function which itself conflicts with teaching and which can hardly exist without an adequate research base.

Even if both universities and the profession are able and willing to undertake such research, it is debatable whether the government wishes the universities to do so. In view of the Rothschild philosophy of encouraging in-house research, it remains to be seen whether departments will be willing to commission needed research in neglected aspects, especially if these are in politically sensitive areas or if funds for research are much less than is required. Government departments generally have tended to neglect the monitoring of policies and, in the face of political pressures, to take short- rather than long-term views of their responsibilities, a situation which, while understandable in the light of political pressure, is not helped by the complex nature of many problems in the environmental field and the lack of clear government goals and policies. It may also be doubted whether departments will commission research which is likely to be critical of their policies, although evaluations of present and past policies, which must depend on the co-operation of the responsible department, are essential.

Fears have also been expressed that applied research which is policy-oriented will be harmful to the profession, distorting academic judgments and prostituting the profession. Yet such research is both necessary and beneficial. Not only will geography tend to decline in importance vis-à-vis other disciplines if the profession does not interest itself in such questions, as Brian Berry (1970) has argued, but contract research can bring compensatory benefits; for without resources many such investigations are simply not possible. Contract research may offer an opportunity of obtaining data which are much more satisfactory than those normally available; for example, as a result of work on outdoor recreation, the Tourism and Recreation Research Unit at Edinburgh has acquired an unrivalled set of data on recreational journeys, which is capable of much more extensive use in academic investigations into the nature of recreational travel (Duffield, 1973). Secondly, such applied research may similarly provide opportunities to test ideas and concepts under demanding operational conditions and thereby to qualify and develop them in ways more appropriate to the observed reality which (presumably) it is intended to explain; in particular, such work may provide insights into the real world which may be helpful in the development of theory. Thirdly, such research provides an opportunity to devise and test new techniques of measurement, as in the recording of caravan traffic by means of ciné cameras linked to traffic counters (M. L. Owen and Duffield, 1971), or in the monitoring of recreational sites by cameras suspended from tethered kite balloons (Duffield and J. Forsyth, 1973). Fourthly, contract research provides experience in the management of large-scale projects, especially in handling large data sets and in undertaking analyses under conditions which place a premium on cost-efficiency. Lastly, although the need to keep to deadlines and to produce reports has been advanced as a criticism of such research, it can, in fact, be an advantage; for academia is rich in unwritten books and uncompleted research, and the need to produce a report by a specified data may thus be a useful discipline.

There is, however, one aspect of commissioned research which needs constant vigilance, for there is a real danger that constraints will be imposed over publication, especially if a report contains criticisms of the sponsors or explores politically sensitive areas. There appears to be an increasing unwillingness to give unconditional permission to publish in academic journals, and phrases such as "permission to publish will not be unreasonably withheld" are increasingly used. Whatever leaders of political parties may say in opposition, British governments have never been very keen to publish the results of official research or enquiries, though this is not a problem peculiar to geography, but one for the academic world as a whole.

Despite these dangers, problem- and policy-oriented research within the broad field of applied geography is both good and necessary. Although this chapter emphasises rural themes, these comments apply equally to urban geography; indeed it could plausibly be argued that geographers with urban interests are not only much more numerous but have also made more policy- and problem-oriented contributions, both through the development of theoretical concepts and analytical tools, and through empirical studies (Berry and F. E. Horton, 1970). These conclusions are also valid for physical geography and there is an increasing interest among physical geographers in policy-oriented and publicly important problems (Gregory, 1974); among geomorphologists, for example, in land classification, in studies of the effects of erosion on water management and in the use of gravel and other superficial deposits, and among climatologists in studies of urban climates, of pollution and of weather modification. In this connection the distinction between human and physical is increasingly meaningless, both because of technical, methodological and theoretical developments within geography, and because most important policy questions lie at the interface between the two. Geographers have shown strengths and leadership in various kinds of research, notably in the study of outdoor recreation, in the use of water resources and in urban studies, and are demonstrating a useful competence in the development of geographical information systems; environmental impact, too, seems a natural field of inquiry for geographers and increasing numbers are involved. Yet there are weaknesses which have implications for pure research, for teaching and for academic and professional organisation, each of which will now be briefly explored.

IMPLICATIONS FOR PURE RESEARCH

The Rothschild distinction between pure and applied research is not very appropriate to subjects such as geography, though there is no doubt that the attempts to develop a body of theory have made the distinction more real than in the past. Furthermore, there are several areas where conceptual and technical developments can contribute to the effectiveness with which applied research is undertaken. Perhaps the most important area lies in developments in spatial statistics, in devising statistical procedures which are appropriate to the handling of spatially-distributed data. Those working in the applied field have been all too ready to seize on any statistical tool that comes to hand, even though it was conceived in the context of aspatial, independent and normally-distributed observations. There are real dangers of what Brian Berry (1973, p. 3) has called "the mindless use of inferential statistics", and Richard Cormack (1971, p. 321) has commented that few things have been more harmful to statistics than the availability of computer package programmes of multivariate analysis. Theoretically-minded geographers need to develop, in conjunction with sympathetic statisticians, spatially-oriented statistical procedures and to explore more fully the implications of analysing the aggregated statistics on which geographers must often depend.

There are two other areas where theoretical work is needed, viz., behavioural studies and prediction. Much policy-oriented research involves, and will increasingly involve, firstly, the evaluation of policies and their impact, and secondly, predicting the likely effects of alternative policies. Both imply an understanding of human behaviour in general and of processes of decision-making and of perception in particular, fields which are generally recognised as of increasing importance to geography as a whole. Most policies are intended to shape the future and must inevitably look forward, but geographers, with a few notable exceptions, have been primarily concerned with the past or the present. All forecasts have spatial dimensions and spatial implications, yet forecasting, as practised by econometricians and others, has largely been aspatial. Geographers need to develop their competence in spatial forecasting and in modelling systems which represent sections of the real world and which can then be used to estimate the likely effects of change in policy (M. Chisholm, A. E. Frey and P. Haggett, 1971).

In addition to requiring conceptual work of this kind, geographers interested in applied research need the help of other colleagues in the development of skills and competence in the handling of various kinds of data. One of the most urgent needs is for critical appraisals of sources of information which are all too readily accepted at their face value.

Secondly, there are developments in automated cartography, over which the profession as a whole seems to show a curious lack of concern, considering the geographer's dependence on the map as a tool and the flexibility and speed of analysis that can result from automation. Much work in this area is currently at an early stage of development, resembling in many ways the early stages of automation in agriculture in that attention has been primarily directed at doing by machine what has hitherto been done by hand. As yet there has been relatively little fundamental thinking about what geographers require of automated cartography in an ideal world. There is now the opportunity to escape from the tyranny of the conventional map which, Torsten Hägerstrand (1973) has argued, shapes the way geographers see problems by its emphasis on static and permanent features, and a need to think hard about multi-dimensional maps, about the representation of change and movement, and about the place that maps might have in the making and monitoring of policies. Exploratory investigations of this kind undertaken at Edinburgh make it clear that both technical advances and modifications to processes of policy formation will be necessary.

The third area in which research and development are urgently needed if geographers are to make their potential contribution to policy-oriented research is remote sensing, both through the use of conventional panchromatic air photography, which is likely to remain the principal source for some time and whose potential has only partly been exploited by geographers, and by other sensors from other platforms. With the development of satellite imagery, geographers will be faced with problems not only of interpretation but also of handling large quantities of data and of analysing change. There are now exciting possibilities of monitoring movement and change which may have considerable implications both for the problems we examine and for the ways in which we handle them. There is urgent need for work by geographers in evaluating the comparative usefulness of the various techniques which are becoming available.

Lastly, there are applications of computers in geographical research (Haggett, 1969). The advent of the large digital computer is one of the most important developments for the practice of geography, providing geographers with a potential flexibility which they lacked when the sheer labour of manual methods left them with little time or energy to undertake analyses of their data, let alone to consider alternative strategies. Of course, there are equally dangers in the mindless use of computers, which are not a substitute for thought, but there is also a clear need for work with computer scientists on the efficient handling of spatial data which will overlap that in automated cartography.

IMPLICATIONS FOR TEACHING

This emphasis on techniques might more appropriately come under the heading of implications for teaching, for, as Geoffrey Powell (1970) has reminded geographers, they need to develop their technical competence if they are to play the part in the analysis of real world problems of which they are capable; but there is important fundamental work to be done here also. It is possible only to touch briefly on the many important implications of this theme for the teaching and training of undergraduates, of graduates and, perhaps most important of all, of existing members of the profession.

In the teaching of undergraduates geographers face a dilemma of which they have long been aware and which their colleagues in related science departments have generally not had to face, the conflict between the educational needs of potential professionals and of those for whom geography is merely part of a general education, a problem which is particularly acute in Scotland where geography is taken as part of the Ordinary degree by large numbers of students, for whom courses in geography provide one contribution to environmental awareness. The requirements of applied research imply a more rigorous theory-, technique- and problem-oriented geography, such as has recently been outlined by Peter Gould (1973) in his paper "The Open Geographical Curriculum". In the short run, it is doubtful if this solution is feasible, in part because of the antipathy of many good students to the mathematisation of geography, but it is also clear that a focus on problems facing society is one that appeals to many students and that this motivation makes both the development of theory and the application of techniques in the search for solutions more acceptable than if these are treated in isolation. There is also a need to experiment in ways in which undergraduate students can be involved in the study of real problems, as is commonly done in planning and environmental courses.

For the present, at least, it seems that efforts to provide such skills should be concentrated on the graduates, who are potential professionals; for many of them are imperfectly equipped to undertake research and their topics often lack a sufficiently clear focus. There is certainly a case for reconsidering, in respect of both course work and group projects undertaken in collaboration with members of staff, the approach to graduate work which has been characteristic of most British geography departments. Such group projects are a frequent feature of laboratory sciences and are particularly appropriate to policy- and problem-oriented topics where a range of skills is required; such an approach would also result in much closer supervision and direction, which might be highly beneficial for the weaker student, though the freedom of the traditional approach still has many advantages for the very able or imaginative student. A larger degree of formal professional training at this level would also help to provide suitably qualified staff to work on contract research or to take research posts in government.

IMPLICATIONS FOR UNIVERSITY ORGANISATION

Thirdly, the development of policy-oriented research, especially that funded through contracts, has implications for universities themselves.

Universities are not organised for the efficient pursuit of contract research; in particular, they lack expertise in managing and costing such research, in finding the staff and in carrying it out. In some universities research teams or units have emerged, as in Edinburgh and London, but these have arisen without any encouragement from university administrations and lack security and a proper career structure. Some universities have met these problems by establishing companies to undertake such research, as at Cambridge, Lancaster and Norwich, and the results of these experiments need to be monitored and disseminated. Another approach is the establishment of research institutes, as has been widely done in North America, where faculty members often hold joint-appointments in a department and a research institute.

An alternative idea, which has also been canvassed, is that there should be specialisation by universities, both as between teaching and research, and in respect of fields of research. The first proposal, that some universities should be primarily teaching establishments and that others should have a major emphasis on research, runs entirely contrary to the whole philosophy of university teaching in this country, but it might provide a better approximation to reality, where the bulk of research is done by a small proportion of the profession, though no discipline can survive merely as a teaching subject and its health in the long run must depend on the quality and quantity of its research. The second, that there should be specialisation by fields of research, seems both inevitable and desirable. Most departments have only one member of staff in each branch of the subject and, while there is merit in this breadth, each member tends to work in isolation and lacks the stimulus of constant discussion and debate with others working in the same field. The fact that every department tries to cover the whole range of geography, so that expertise is thinly spread, may be a contributory reason why the profession is continually being taken by surprise by new developments in the subject and suggests that there would be advantages if departments recognised a number of strengths and specialised in those, shaping their research, teaching and recruitment accordingly. Of course, given the limited mobility of academic staff in the United Kingdom and the slow growth likely over the next decade, such a change could be effected only slowly. There has already been some tendency in this direction, and Robin Best (1970) has drawn attention to the strength which the Rural Studies degree at Wye draws from its focus on a single area of study where there is already a well-developed research interest. There is also a long-established precedent of this kind in North America. Thus, the Department of Geography in the University of Chicago, on the basis of a broad training in physical and economic geography, statistical analysis and cartography, has specialised in urban and resource studies, with some attention to the Far East. What is clear from the evidence of such specialisation is that these departments have tended to attract good staff and good students, as well as abundant research funds, and to have received numerous calls from public bodies for professional advice.

Specialisation by departments raises the wider question of specialisation and collaboration by disciplines. Many of the skills which geographers require depend on close collaboration with other disciplines, notably with statisticians, mathematicians and behavioural scientists. Consideration of how far it is possible to acquire competence in more than one discipline has implications for training, for geographers are needed who have sufficient understanding for other fields to appreciate their methods, approaches and limitations, and can carry on an effective dialogue with specialists in such disciplines. Geographers have often been good at seeing what needs to be done, as in perception studies, but have tended to lack the professional competence to undertake such work, and it is still an open question whether such topics can best be tackled by individuals with competence in more than one field or by collaboration between specialists. A range of skills is certainly required for the solution of problems which recognise no disciplinary boundaries, yet evidence of collaboration within or between academic departments is not encouraging. There are relatively few examples of collaboration in research between colleagues within the same geography department, and even fewer of research involving collaboration across departmental boundaries, though this situation is partly due to the fact that there are major administrative obstacles in most universities in the way of achieving such collaboration.

This dilemma of specialisation is not peculiar to geography. One solution which has been adopted is the development of multi-disciplinary departments or schools, particularly within the environmental and resource fields, as in the School of Environmental Sciences in East Anglia, the Department of Forestry and Natural Resources in Edinburgh and the Countryside Planning Unit at Wye, in each of which there has been effective inter-disciplinary collaboration. The desirability of such an approach to environmental resource problems is increasingly felt and is shown by the growing number of interdisciplinary journals concerned with the management of resources, to which geographers have made numerous contributions, as in *Regional Studies,* the *Natural Resources Journal,* the *Journal of Leisure Research, Environment and Behaviour,* and the *Journal of Environmental Management.* Similar developments are apparent in the urban field. There is also an increasing convergence both of approach and of the skills required in different disciplines, many of which, notably in computing, statistics and modelling and in such fields as decision-making and game theory, might be provided by some common training. It should be remembered in this connection that no subject boundaries are sacrosanct and that none is apparent in any of the problems which are the concern either of citizens or of policy makers.

In many ways, this concept of specialisation is the antithesis of the holistic approach which geographers have advocated and which has been shown to represent a valuable contribution in their professional and advisory roles. One implication is that specialisation should not come too early. The general aim should be competence within a wider awareness; perhaps, if we try hard, we can both have our cake and eat it.

IMPLICATIONS FOR PROFESSIONAL ORGANISATION

Discussion of the contribution of geographers to policy- and problem-oriented research in the environmental and resource fields has focused so far on individual geographers, departments and universities, but geographers are part of a wider profession, and these developments have implications for the geographical profession as a whole. There is clearly a need for some continuing organisation with the task of reviewing research needs and of identifying and grasping opportunities as they occur. In part, this is a role for the Research Councils, and one which the Social Science Research Council has valiantly tried to fulfil. The reviews of research by Michael Chisholm (1971) and others represent a valuable contribution to the debate.

A contribution from the profession is also necessary. In part, the Council of the Institute of British Geographers has tried to achieve this by giving the Institute a more professional face and by altering the committee structure to ensure that the Institute is anticipating rather than reacting to events. The reconstructed British National Committee for Geography also has a role to play and its Standing Committee has been established to meet the need for quick reactions. These are steps in the right direction, but some machinery for a continuing dialogue with government agencies is also needed. One possibility is the establishment of an Institute of Geographical Research, on the lines of, say, the National Institute of Social and Economic Research or the Institute of Geological Sciences. It was suggested by the author to the Natural Resources Advisory Committee of the short-lived Ministry of Land and Natural Resources that they should establish a Land-Use Data Unit, which would receive, map, analyse and interpret all appropriate data bearing on the use of land and collected by government departments and other agencies, and B. E. Coates and E. M. Rawstron (1971) have advocated the establishment of a Geographical Survey, which would keep under continuous review and analysis all geographical data. Such a body could provide a focus for the continuing review of research needs, but agreement seems unlikely, given the strength of feeling in government departments about the custody of the data they collect. The proposal for a Land-Use Data Unit has, to a large extent, been overtaken by developments in data banking.

For example, the Canada Geographical Information System is capable of far more ambitious analyses, though it is interesting to note that its current role is that of a potential source of information, staffed mainly by technicians who respond to such requests as are made to them, rather than an initiator of inquiries. In any case, the geographical profession should not be too strongly identified with survey, for it has suffered from the widely-held misconception that geographers are merely collectors and mappers of information. For similar reasons the proposal by Kenneth Hare and Ian Jackson (1972), that geographers should at least in the short run make a contribution by assembling and mapping the data relevant to particular environmental problems, needs to be treated with caution. Nevertheless, it is time to reconsider all possibilities, including a multi-disciplinary institute, with a focus on environmental questions, in which geographers could play a leading part.

CONCLUSION

This review has largely been concerned with asking questions, in the context of growing public concern about the environment, the Rothschild report and changing university attitudes towards research, about the contributions which geographers could and should be making to policy- and problem-oriented research in fields of the environment and of the use of the earth's resources. It has tentatively suggested a number of changes which could be made to ensure that such contributions are both larger and of better quality than in the past. Making them would, in turn, require some change of attitude on the part of the geographical profession and, if fully implemented, some change in the role that universities play in society. If they are implemented, they will give students a training which will enable them to play a more effective role and meet the need for men and women who combine breadth of vision with technical competence and a skill in formulating and providing answers to the right questions. Such developments, in so far as they are reflected in an increasing volume of good research, will also help to improve the standing of geography, both in the academic world and in the world of affairs.

ACKNOWLEDGMENT

This chapter is based upon the author's presidential address to the Institute of British Geographers, published in *Trans. Inst. Brit. Geogr.,* **63**, pp. 1–16.

REFERENCES

Barker, M. (1972) *The Structure and Content of Environmental Cognitions,* unpublished Ph.D. dissertation, University of Toronto.

Berry, B. J. L. (1970) "The geography of the United States in the year 2000", *Trans. Inst. Brit. Geogr.,* **51,** pp. 21-53.

Berry, B. J. L. (1973) "A paradigm for modern geography", in Richard J. Chorley (ed.), *Directions in Geography,* Methuen, London, pp. 3-21.

Berry, B. J. L. and F. E. Horton (1970) *Geographical Perspectives on Urban Systems,* Prentice Hall, Engelwood Cliffs.

Best, R. H. (1970) "Rural environment studies", *Area,* **1,** pp. 22-3.

Board, C., R. J. Chorley, P. Haggett and D. R. Stoddart (eds.) (1969-) *Progress in Geography,* Arnold, London.

Burton, I. and R. W. Kates (1964) "The perception of natural hazards in resource management", *Nat. Res. J.,* **3,** pp. 412-41.

Chisholm, M. D. I. (1971) *Research in Human Geography,* A Social Science Research Council Review, Heinemann, London.

Chisholm, M. D. I. and H. B. Rodgers (eds.) (1973) *Studies in Human Geography,* Heinemann, London.

Chisholm, M. D. I., A. E. Frey and P. Haggett (eds.) (1971) *Regional Forecasting,* Colston Papers, No. 22, Butterworths, London.

Chorley, Richard J. (ed.) (1973) *Directions in Geography,* Methuen, London.

Coates, B. E. and E. M. Rawstron (1971) *Regional Variations in Britain,* Batsford, London.

Cormack, R. M. (1971) "A review of classification", *J. Roy. Stat. Soc.,* Series A, **134,** pp. 321-67.

Duffield, B. S. (1973) *Outdoor Recreational Traffic Patterns in the Edinburgh Area,* Tourism and Recreation Research Unit, University of Edinburgh.

Duffield, B. S. and J. Forsyth (1973) "Assessing the impact of recreational use on coastal sites in East Lothian", in Countryside Commission, *The Use of Aerial Photographs in Countryside Research,* Report on a Conference, London.

Dury, G. (1970) "Merely from nervousness", *Area,* **1,** pp. 29-32.

Garrison, W. L. (1956) *The Benefits of Rural Roads to Rural Property,* Washington State Council for Highway Research, Seattle.

Gould, P. R. (1973) "The open geographical curriculum", in Chorley (ed.), *op. cit.,* pp. 253-84.

Gregory, S. (1974) "The geographer and natural resources research", *South African Geographer,* **4,** pp. 371-82.

Hägerstrand, T. (1973) "The domain of human geography", in R. J. Chorley (ed.), *op. cit.,* pp. 253-84.

Haggett, P. (1969) "On geographical research in a computer environment", *Geog. J.,* **135,** pp. 597-607.

Hall, P., R. Thomas, H. Gracey and R. Drewett (1973) *The Containment of Urban England,* 2 vols., Allen & Unwin, London.

Hare, F. K. and C. I. Jackson (1972) *Environment: a Geographical Perspective,* Geog. Paper 52, Dept. of the Environment, Ottawa.

House, J. (1973) "Geographers, decision-takers and policy makers", in M. D. I. Chisholm and H. B. Rodgers (eds.), *op. cit.,* pp. 272-305.

Kates, R. W. (1962) *Hazard and Choice Perception in Flood Plain Management,* Research Paper 78, Dept. of Geography, University of Chicago.

Lord Privy Seal (1971) *A Framework for Government Research and Development,* Cmmd. 4814, H.M.S.O.

Lord Privy Seal (1972) *A Framework for Government Research and Development,* Cmmd. 5046, H.M.S.O.

Morrill, R. L. (1965) "The negro ghetto: problems and alternatives", *Geographical Review,* **55,** pp. 339-61.

Natural Environment Research Council (1974)

O'Riordan, J. (1975) "The Canada-British Columbia Okanagan Basin Study", *Nat. Res. J.,* **16,** forthcoming.

O'Riordan, T. (1971) "Public opinion and environmental quality—a reappraisal", *Environment and Behaviour,* **3,** pp. 191-214.

Owen, M. L. and B. S. Duffield, J. T. Coppock (ed.) (1971) *The Touring Caravan in Scotland,* Scottish Tourist Board, Edinburgh.

Powell, A. G. (1970) "The geographer in regional planning", in R. H. Osborne, F. A. Barnes and J. C. Doornkamp (eds.), *Geographical Essays in Honour of K. C. Edwards,* University of Nottingham, Dept. of Geography, pp. 224-32.

Saarinen, T. C. (1966) *Perception of the Drought Hazard on the Great Plains,* Dept. of Geography, Research Series, No. 106, University of Chicago.

Select Committee of the House of Lords on Sport and Leisure (1973) *2nd Report, Minutes of Evidence and Appendices,* 3 vols., House of Lords Paper 193, H.M.S.O.

Select Committee on Scottish Affairs (1972) *Land Resource Use In Scotland,* Report, Minutes of Evidence and Appendices, 5 vols., House of Commons Paper 511, H.M.S.O.

Sewell, W. R. D. (1971) "Environmental perceptions and attitudes of engineers and public health officials", *Environment and Behaviour,* **3,** pp. 23-59.

Sewell, W. R. D. and I. Burton (eds.) (1971) *Perceptions and Attitudes in Resources Management,* Information Canada, Ottawa.

Sewell, W. R. D. *et al.* (1973) *Modifying the Weather,* Western Geographical Series, University of Victoria, Victoria.

Sewell, W. R. D. (1975) "Public involvement", in *A Manual on River Basin Planning,* Information Canada, Ottawa.

Taafe, E. J. (ed.) (1970) *Geography,* the Behavioural and Social Sciences Survey, Prentice Hall, Englewood Cliffe, N.J.

White, G. F. (1965) *Choice of Adjustment to Floods,* Department of Geography Research Series, No. 93, University of Chicago.

White, G. F. (1966) "Formation and role of public attitudes", in H. Jarrett (ed.), *Environmental Quality in a Growing Economy,* Johns Hopkins Press, pp. 105-27.

White, G. F. (ed.) (1974) *Natural Hazards,* Oxford University Press, Oxford.

Willatts, E. C. (1971) "Planning and geography in the last three decades", *Geog. J.,* **137,** pp. 331-8.

CHAPTER 2

POLICY PLANNING IN THE GOVERNMENT OF CANADA

C. I. JACKSON*

Ministry of State for Urban Affairs

> Our community assigns the responsibility for taking decisions to a collection of action-oriented individuals, people who have run for sheriff—who spend their life running for sheriff—and who are acutely aware, in a general manner, of where the country ought to go, but lack the detailed itinerary and the choice of means to go there.
>
> These individuals in turn are served by an elaborate committee structure, a support staff largely paralyzed by the newly-discovered inter-relatedness of it all, and an over-worked layer of deputy ministers who generally exercise their judgement on the backs of envelopes or the fronts of table napkins (C. M. Drury, 1974).

These remarks by a Canadian Cabinet Minister were, as he admitted, a caricature of the Ministerial process of decision-making, but they were, as all caricatures must be, founded on reality. Presumably they apply with similar truth to the governments of the ten Canadian provinces and, substituting for "deputy ministers" the equivalent term "permanent secretaries", they may also be a reasonable caricature of the process by which Ministerial decisions are made in the United Kingdom.

The main purpose of Mr. Drury's remarks was to inject a note of earthy realism into a discussion on "Mathematics and Policy Analysis", in which he was the keynote speaker—and almost the only non-mathematician. In the nineteenth century his address might have carried a more elaborate title: "On the Role that the Mathematician should play in the Policy Development Process, with some Observations on the Inadequacy of the Past Performance of this Profession in that Regard." His remarks apply in most cases with equal force to geography, and indeed to most disciplines. Drawing on some years' experience as President of the Treasury Board, the group of Cabinet Ministers that monitors federal government expenditures, Mr. Drury (1974) was in an excellent position to evaluate the contribution that such specialist assistance had made.

> I want to challenge the article of faith, the unexamined prejudice, which underlies the planning for this conference: that mathematics helps in the process of policy planning. I know that systems consultants represent a sink of unbelievable scope for pouring money down. I

* The views expressed in this paper are those of the author and are not necessarily those of the Government of Canada.

know that planning and evaluation activity of a mathematical and esoteric sort now represents an immense overhead burden on our system of government. The first question I hope this conference will seriously consider is whether in fact this undeniable capacity delivers anything, contributes, to the process of policy formation, anything of value commensurate with its costs.

If there is indeed a real difficulty in bringing mathematical, or geographical or any other type of analysis and expenditure to bear on the major policy decisions of the day, it is surely not because such expertise is irrelevant. As the present writer (C. I. Jackson, 1972, p. 351) has observed elsewhere, for example,

There are few major national or regional issues in Canada which do not have significant geographical aspects. This is inevitable in a country where two provincial capitals are separated by six time zones and by a Trans-Canada Highway which is 8050 kilometres in length; where the length and severity of the winter are almost everywhere a major factor in economy and society; where a predominantly youthful population lives mainly in a few major urban areas which are expanding rapidly while most of the 9,000,000 square kilometres of Canada are either uninhabited or settled by a scattered and declining population. Geographical problems in Canada tend to be fundamental, exciting and very relevant to national and regional needs.

If both geography and geographers are potentially useful in the development of public policy, why then is not more use made of them? It might be worth questioning the implicit assumption here: that this potential remains largely unrealised. A reasonable case can be mounted that, in Canada at least, geographical insight and the contributions of individual geographers do illumine the public policy planning process in a way that is more deserving of self-satisfaction than mortification. Despite this, it probably is true that geographers could play a much larger role than they do.

One difficulty—in the eyes of the individual specialists—seems to be the fact that the closer one comes, in either intellectual or institutional terms, to the fundamental issues with which public policy is concerned, the less scope one has for being a geographer and nothing else. Or, for that matter, the less scope for remaining solely a mathematician, an economist, a biologist or an engineer. Such issues are simply too complex to be conveniently docketed as "geographical", "economic" and so on. If they are to be tackled effectively, they require solution in their own terms, not on the basis of a disciplinary subdivision of knowledge, a subdivision which is itself demonstrably arbitrary, though convenient and useful, since knowledge is a continuum.

This line of argument is not intended as a defence of the democratic process, in which Cabinets or other final decision-makers are traditionally more lay than specialist; the principle probably applies with as much force in autocratic or totalitarian societies as in a democracy. There is probably no question of public policy worth answering that is best answered by a specialist, because a specialist response is by its nature one that will emphasise some issues and neglect or ignore others of comparable significance. The task of public policy-making is to establish the objective and the general way to attain that objective. If the specialist can make a contribution, so much the better, but helping to implement policy is not the same as helping to formulate it. Generals may be permitted to decide the time for a battle, the targets to be attacked and the resources to be employed, but they are not entrusted with the decision on whether to declare war.

The military metaphor is useful in the present context, since from the military arena comes the notion of a *general staff.* While a military officer is identified with his specialism—infantry, armour, transport, and so on—his contribution is essentially limited to the exercise of that professional function. Only when he rises beyond this specialist training to the general staff does he take part role in the resolution of fundamental strategic issues. Although his previous training, specialist knowledge and loyalties will no doubt continue to illumine his advice and decisions as a general, they must recede into the background if he is not to be crippled in the execution of his new role.

The notion of policy-making as essentially that of a general staff or, in civilian parlance, of generalists, is surely not difficult to accept. A university departmental staff meeting, or any other similar group, can only make progress on basic issues if the members come with a willingness to suspend their specialist interests in favour of a broader view of the general good. *Microcosmographica Academica* (F. M. Cornford, 1953) and innumerable other texts have been written to demonstrate just how difficult it is for otherwise reasonable men and women to achieve this broader view, but it remains a necessity.

In a period when interdisciplinary and multidisciplinary activities have (justifiably) established themselves as an essential approach to the solution of complex problems, some further words on the role of the generalist in public policy-making may be necessary. Cannot the problem of providing adequate treatment for all the dimensions of a problem be solved by a multidisciplinary approach by a number of specialisms? Is this not a better approach than one that is deliberately non-specialist? It is undeniable that a multidisciplinary project, if it is well managed, can progress very much further in analysing a problem, developing tentative solutions and devising alternative objectives and strategies, than is possible for any individual, be he generalist, specialist or anything short of a genius. The most impressive illustration of this in the author's experience came from a university rather than from government, when the Greater London Group was formed as a cooperative venture by half a dozen departments at the London School of Economics (F. Smallwood, 1965). The members of the group had the rare experience of seeing their assembled conclusions on the desirable future government of London adopted by the Herbert Commission and, with inevitable omissions and alternatives, translated into fact through the London Government Act. That was, however, exceptional: successful enterprises of this kind are probably more frequent in government than in academe, mainly because of the existence in government of hierarchical sanctions that help to prevent the natural drift towards anarchy among the members of such interdisciplinary teams. In both government and academe the failure rate remains considerable, and even the successes probably owe much to the ability of participants to ensure that the result of their activities is more than the sum of its parts. Without minimising the value of such activities in any way, it seems reasonable to assert that such multidisciplinary group approaches to policy planning, with the emphasis on specialist contributions, will only rarely provide an appropriate mechanism. Apart from any other considerations, they usually require a considerable time to develop and mature, time which is frequently not available before decisions have to be taken.

A notion that seems even less tenable is that because spatial considerations have been and continue to be of great importance in many questions of public policy in Canada there is therefore inevitably some special role for the geographer that he alone can play. It might be possible, with hindsight, to look back on some of the major themes of Canadian history, the fur trade, the building of railways to the Atlantic and Pacific, the settlement of the prairies, the development of an industrial state and the opening up of the Canadian North, and identify occasions when geographical or spatial factors were recognised and times when they were ignored. But it would be difficult to distil from such an historical approach much that would help to ensure a greater concern for geographical factors now and in the future. The Canadian framework for policy development and decision-making is continuously evolving, and the influence of distance, climate, population distribution and similar factors is also subject to continuous change. It is still 5000 miles (8000 km) from the capital of Newfoundland to the capital of British Columbia, and the constitution of Canada is still based essentially on the 1867 British North America Act of the Westminster Parliament. But governments use different techniques and different sets of values in a society where television is coast to coast, where radio talk-shows can set a resident of St. John's arguing with someone in Victoria, and where a bureaucrat can leave his Ottawa office after a day's work, fly to Vancouver, participate in a meeting the next morning, have a long working lunch and be back in bed in Ottawa that night.

If the geographer is to contribute to the development of public policy, it is clearly necessary that he should understand the *structure* of government and the nature of the government *process*. This is arguably one of the greatest gaps in the training of most geographers. As the present writer remarked some years ago (Jackson, 1970, p. 11):

> Researchers often seem willing to spend years on the details of their investigations but get impatient after a few minutes, days or weeks trying to get through with their results. They also

seem reluctant to read the British North America Act or, at least, to recognize that different governments and different departments have different jobs and that it is only slightly more moral for a department to spend money on a project which does not form part of the task for which Parliament voted those funds than it would be to blow the lot at the race track. I am not suggesting that, to be effective, individuals must become experts in constitutional law or in government organization. . . . But obviously there is a system, which has different structures, tasks and work patterns to those of universities or research institutes. It does not seem unreasonable to expect that persons who accept the need to learn how to drive, understand library classifications, operate electronic field equipment and so on in order to do their research should put a similar amount of effort into understanding the nature of the organization which they hope will use the results of that research.

THE STRUCTURE AND PROCESS OF POLICY PLANNING IN THE FEDERAL GOVERNMENT

1. Federal-Provincial Concerns

Since this essay is mainly based on the author's own experience, it naturally focuses on the governmental structure and the process of policy development and decision-making in the Government of Canada. Nevertheless, Canada is a federal state, and the existence of eleven sovereign legislatures and governments is fundamental. The question of jurisdiction is something of a Canadian obsession, probably much more so than in the United States, though possibly not more so than in Australia. The keyword, of course, is "sovereign": the legislatures in Charlottetown, Fredericton, Regina, Victoria and the other six provincial capitals have powers that cannot be altered or reversed by Ottawa, and vice versa. The question of jurisdiction—competing, conflicting, concurrent or obscure—runs as a thread through Canadian history since 1867; it will no doubt do so in the future even if the Canadian constitution is "patriated" from Westminster and a new division of powers among federal and provincial governments emerges.

Although this is not a treatise on federal-provincial relations, three features need emphasis in the present context. The first is that jurisdictional difficulties may be, temporarily or permanently, significant barriers to the achievement of optimal solutions to particular problems. These difficulties are as likely to arise in areas where the division of powers is well-defined as in those where it is not, as illustrated by two current examples. One of the products of the 1973-4 energy crisis was a confrontation between the Government of Alberta and the Government of Canada over the exploitation of Albertan oil and gas resources. Oil and gas are resources, and resources have been matters primarily within the field of provincial jurisdiction. But one of the questions at issue concerned the volume and price of oil and gas exports from Alberta to the United States (and, incidentally, also to eastern Canada). Responsibility for the management and control of international trade is clearly a matter primarily for the federal government. The same energy crisis helped to sharpen another dispute, this time in an area where jurisdiction is less obvious. There are hopes that the Atlantic Provinces of Canada, especially Nova Scotia and Newfoundland, lie adjacent to off-shore resources of oil and gas comparable to those of the North Sea. Is jurisdiction over resource development on the adjacent continental shelf primarily an extension of terrestrial jurisdiction (more plainly, do oil and gas royalties come to the adjacent provinces) or are these resources to be considered part of the coastal zone of Canada as a whole?

The second significant feature is that, despite the complexity of such issues, there is a long tradition of accommodation and compromise between federal and provincial governments in achieving workable solutions, and both the frequency and the novelty of these solutions is increasing. Neither of the two disputes described in the previous paragraph has yet been finally resolved, but there seem reasonable prospects that solutions will be devised. One recent example of the way in which such jurisdictional problems can be overcome is the Canada Water Act 1970, a piece of federal legislation that was designed to tackle the problem of water pollution and the need for comprehensive water resource management. Here again the federal government was intervening in resource matters but it could claim that many of the water bodies affected are of international or interprovincial significance: these include the Great Lakes, the Ottawa-St. Lawrence, Saskatchewan-Nelson and the Peace-Athabasca-Mackenzie systems, and the Saint John-St. Croix drainage basin. The mechanism used in the Act is one that enables the federal government to negotiate agreements with one or more provincial governments, with provision for joint funding for the planning and implementation of comprehensive water management systems. The legislation does contain residual federal government powers, for use if such agreement is impossible, but it is not expected that these powers will be needed. After initial doubts and suspicions on the part of some provincial governments, a growing number of such agreements has been signed and the Canada Water Act may be a model to be used in other areas of mixed jurisdiction.

The third feature that seems worth emphasis is that these examples concern matters of considerable interest to the geographer. Other relevant issues could have been chosen in such fields as urban affairs and transport. Federal-provincial disagreements and agreements are essential elements in any adequate study of such matters in Canada, yet there seem to be many geographers and others who are ignorant of their significance. There are others who regard such controversies, and the devices to resolve them, as annoying distractions that indicate the inadequacy of government or that must be consciously disregarded if the problem itself is to be investigated scientifically. It should go without saying that attitudes of this kind are not merely incapable of contributing to the development of realistic public policy, they are also likely to inhibit even an academic and objective study of the problems.

If the criticism contained in the preceding paragraph seems too strong, it can surely be agreed that geographers and other specialists in the natural and social sciences have seldom been actively interested in such institutional devices as federal-provincial agreements. The novelty of the Canada Water Act, however, arose from a recognition that water problems were extremely diverse, spread over all governmental jurisdictions, and could be effectively solved only if the powers and resources of different governments were integrated and applied to the problems in a way that also took account of the spatial aspects of the problem. The result was legislation providing for intergovernmental comprehensive planning of water basins. If this seems an obvious solution to those who have a specialist knowledge of water resources or water pollution, this merely reinforces the argument that such specialists should concern themselves with institutions and with such things as legislative agreements: the solution is not immediately obvious to a political scientist or a drafter of legislation. If the latter must learn something about water resources to provide a workable device, why should not the geographer or engineer know more about legislation institutions and similar matters?

2. The Cabinet Process

Nowhere has the evolving character of governmental processes been more evident than in the operation of the primary decision-making body of the Canadian government: the Cabinet. Gordon Robertson, who was Secretary to the Cabinet from 1963 to 1974, has described the general practice up to 1940 (R. G. Robertson, 1971, p. 489).

> There was no agenda, no secretariat, no official present at meetings to record what went on, no minute of decisions taken, and no system to communicate the decisions to the departments responsible to implement them. Subjects to be discussed at each meeting were settled by the Prime Minister with no advance notice to Ministers. As Ministers had no notice of what was going to come up, they were normally quite unprepared for the discussion or for the decisions expected of them . . . it was a singularly inefficient and unfair way for a collective executive to reach decisions for which all would share responsibility. After a meeting few knew precisely what had been decided; there could be no confidence that all relevant information had been available or considered; and the accurate transmission of decisions, if it occurred at all, was a happy accident.

Such a system, or lack of it, might well be regarded as inadequate for staff meetings in a university department, though it may not be completely unknown in such an environment. The pressures of war and the post-war growth of government responsibilities forced a series of changes in the Cabinet process which would not have pleased Prime Minister Mackenzie

King; he, in Robertson's words (p. 488), "preferred to hold everything close to his chest to be brought out as, when and how he preferred, with his Ministers taken by surprise and at maximum disadvantage." There gradually emerged a formal Cabinet agenda, standard rules for the preparation and submission of Cabinet Memoranda, a formal method recording and circulating Records of Cabinet Decisions to those who "need to know", and a series of standing Committees of Cabinet.

Most of these innovations are fairly obvious and straightforward, but the structure and methods of Cabinet Committees are particularly important elements in the mechanism of decision-making. Although the number, names and methods of operation of these Committees have changed over the years, and will no doubt continue to evolve in the future, the present structure is one that has existed since 1968 and, in general outline, since 1964 (Robertson, pp. 490-1). Nine standing committees of the Cabinet handle the vast majority of Cabinet Memoranda; other special purpose committees meet on an "as required" basis, or are created and dissolved to meet specific short-term needs. Five of the standing committees deal, in Robertson's words, with "areas of government activity": External Policy and Defence, Economic Policy, Social Policy, Science, Culture and Information, and Government Operations. The other four are coordinating committees: Priorities and Planning, Federal-Provincial Relations, Treasury Board, and Legislation and House Planning.

The titles of these committees are less exclusive than they may appear. Some committees do have well-defined areas of responsibility: External Policy and Defence, Treasury Board, and Legislation and House Planning are of this kind. Some Memoranda coming to Cabinet may be clearly in the field of economic policy, or social policy or science, culture and information, or they may concern a specific aspect of government operations. Very many, however, are less obviously identifiable with a single committee. For example, a Memorandum may have social as well as economic implications; it may have implications for federal-provincial relations; and it may also be of such importance or urgency that it has a claim to the agenda of the Priorities and Planning Committee. The titles of the Cabinet Committees thus serve primarily to describe general areas of responsibility, but there are no rigid boundaries. This, among other advantages, enables individual Memoranda to be routed through the committee where they can be handled most expeditiously as well as most effectively.

This flexibility is evident also in the membership of Cabinet Committees. Each of the 27 Ministers in the Cabinet (in the Canadian government, unlike its British counterpart, all Ministers are members of Cabinet) is named to a number of committees, but Ministers also have the rights to attend meetings of most of the other committees, so that they can participate in discussions of particular importance to them.

The importance of these committees is based on two things. First, since 1964, virtually all Cabinet Memoranda go to a Cabinet Committee *before* going to full Cabinet; prior to that date matters were referred by Cabinet to Cabinet Committees when necessary. Second, and more important, in 1968 this shift was supplemented by the delegation of power to Cabinet Committees to take specific decisions. In practice, a Cabinet Committee can do one of three things: it may refuse to endorse a Memorandum, because it requires further work or because the principles it contains are unacceptable; it may accept the recommendations in a Memorandum, with or without modification; or it may decide that the topic requires to be discussed by full Cabinet. Since the number of Cabinet documents has averaged 818 for the last three years (i.e., to 1971, Robertson, 1971, p. 492), and since this total inevitably tends to increase rather than to decline, it is desirable that as many memoranda as possible should be dealt with by Cabinet Committee rather than by Cabinet. Robertson describes the safeguard built into the system which ensures that Cabinet Committee decisions are formally ratified by Cabinet; this provides an opportunity for a topic to be re-opened by a Minister who might not have been able to attend the relevant committee meeting, but who, as a member of the Cabinet, would share collective responsibility for the decision.

The feature of the Cabinet Committee system which has greatest significance for the broader process of policy development throughout the government is the fact that senior officials may participate in Cabinet Committee discussions, although they are never present at meetings of the full Cabinet.

> Ministers in general carry the discussion but officials participate actively, especially on factual and operational aspects. They are conscious that policy decisions, and therefore the main aspects of policy assessment, are for Ministers. . . . There are times when the responsible Minister lets the deputy explain: there are times when the deputy remains silent while the Minister explains. Both normally participate in active discussion. It is a blending of roles that requires mutual confidence and an awareness of their differences. . . . The advantages in decision-making are clear. There are equally advantages in administration. The exposure of senior officials to the thinking and policy concerns of Ministers help them to explain to their departments the logic of decisions that might otherwise seem wrong, incomprehensible or "petty politics" (Robertson, 1971, p. 500).

Although Robertson (p. 489) admits that "briefing papers . . . based on a meticulous recording by officials of discussions by ministers in cabinet committees" would have disturbed Mackenzie King, the advantages of this practice seem undeniable, and may be more far-reaching than Robertson indicated. The growth in importance of the role of Cabinet Committees since the mid-1960s, and the presence of senior officials as well as Ministers, seem to have had a strong influence on the development of a policy planning capability within individual departments and ministries.

The Policy Planning Process at the Bureaucratic Level

It is probably necessary to begin this section by making clear that the Canadian governmental system is, like the British, based on the firm principle that Ministers, not officials, determine policy. From personal experience, it is possible to affirm that this principle is understood and accepted by the vast majority of officials; those who do not understand or accept it either come to do so or they do not reach a level in the public service where their lack of understanding or agreement begins to matter. In Canada, as in the United Kingdom, public servants are scrupulous in observing this principle both in letter and in spirit.

This declaration is essential because there are some, outside government, who would regard the subheading to this section as evidence that the principle is ignored. If policy determination is a matter for Ministers, they might argue, how can there be a policy planning process at the bureaucratic level? The answer ought to be obvious: it is one thing to assemble the resources to investigate a problem, to identify possible solutions, cost the various strategies, examine the legislative requirements, and suggest possible implications of the strategies for other policies or the actions of other governments; it is quite another to review the digested wisdom of such a process and to take a decision in favour or against particular courses of action. Policy planning is not the same as policy determination.

A more sophisticated objection to this might be raised by the cynic; he might claim that the principle may be observed in form, but ignored in practice. Officials, simply because they command such intellectual and technical resources, can arrange that they present to a Minister a policy option that is in fact no option, since the Minister lacks the capacity to evaluate the proposal adequately and to offer an alternative of his own. Those who firmly believe that this technique is prevalent are unlikely to be convinced otherwise, and it is remarkably difficult to disprove the contention. One reason for this difficulty is that there is likely to be a similar degree of commitment on the part of a senior official, whether a policy proposal emerges as a result of a long objective process involving a large team, or whether it is one of his own bright ideas: enthusiasm that derives from the former process can easily be mistaken as evidence of the latter by the cynic. All one can say is that, firstly, the system of policy development and presentation includes checks and safeguards to limit or prevent such abuse. For example, Memoranda to Cabinet not merely require the signature of the responsible Minister before they go to Cabinet Committee, they must include an explicit evaluation of alternatives to the recommended action, and it is relatively easy to spot those alternatives that have been put up merely as "straw men". Secondly, the right of Ministers to be the arbiters of public policy is one that is jealously and justifiably guarded by ministers individually and collectively, and they are sensitive (though not hypersensitive) to

attempts to limit this right. Lastly, there is the sense of responsibility of
senior officials; not merely are most public servants aware of the limitations
on their roles, but their commitment to the rules of the game is tested well
before they get to the stage where they can do serious damage. Policy
planning at the bureaucratic level is a legitimate activity.

The creation of groups in individual federal government departments that
are specifically charged with the task of planning policy is, however,
something that has occurred on any scale only within the last 10 years. The
need for them can be traced to two principal sources, the first of which was
the general spread of more formal management practices, including
"management by objectives" and PPBS (Planning Programming Budgeting
Systems) and especially their adoption by Treasury Board Secretariat. In the
late 1960s Treasury Board Secretariat began to insist that departmental
estimates and programme forecasts be developed in a more policy-ordered
framework than in the past. The second stimulus was the changes in the
Cabinet Committee system already described: if Cabinet was changing its
methods in order to deal more effectively with basic issues of policy development and policy changes, it was clearly necessary that individual departments
of the Government should develop the capability to meet Cabinet's needs in
this direction.

It is difficult to underestimate the importance of the greater emphasis on
policy and policy planning that has been required of individual departments
of the federal government (although, since he has been involved in meeting
this requirement for the last 5 years, the present writer may be guilty of some
personal bias). Departments have been forced to operate in a way that
involves a constant re-evaluation of their activities "Why are we continuing
with this programme? Has it outlived its usefulness? Should we recognize
that the objectives we had for it are either fulfilled or that this programme is
the wrong way to achieve them? Can we recast this programme so that it
contributes to new objectives that are more relevant to contemporary
Canadian needs? What changes—of resources, methods, personnel,
location, finance and the like—will be necessary if we do alter the objectives
of the programme?" Such critical self-examination is one of the tasks
normally assigned to policy planning groups, and it has led inevitably to a
situation where such groups become as concerned with the broader
objectives of the federal government (and, in a federal state, with national
objectives also) as they are with the more circumscribed objectives of their
individual departments.

This ambivalence is an almost inevitable consequence of the sequence of
questions in the previous paragraph. If we are to bring about major changes
in the activities of a government department—activities which may directly
involve hundreds or even thousands of public servants, and millions of
dollars of annual budget annually—then we have to be sure that the

objectives we are abandoning are indeed obsolete or inappropriate, and that the new ones that are set for the department are both realistic and in accord with national needs and the wishes and priorities of the Minister, Cabinet and Parliament. Policy planning groups therefore find themselves intimately involved in communicating such needs and priorities to their own departments, and in assisting their departments to adjust policies, programmes and other activities to changing objectives of the government. By a logical extension, they also often become involved in the identification of the broader objectives and goals themselves, if only in the form of options which may sooner or later be presented to Cabinet by an individual Minister or group of Ministers.

If this role seems heady and exciting, it should be borne in mind that such policy planning groups may more frequently be frustrated by their inability to awaken departmental colleagues to changed needs and new horizons than they are exalted by their ability to assist nascent ideas germinating in their departments to become translated into policy or programme proposals that may win Ministerial, Cabinet or intergovernmental assent.

This awareness of broader objectives and activities than those of an individual department seems to have led to improvements in interdepartmental coordination and cooperation, no small factor in a world where, for example, it has been estimated that over 25 federal government departments and agencies administer over 120 programmes that directly affect urban areas. Policy planning groups tend to be well-informed about the activities of other departments as well as their own, and able to anticipate the type of bureaucratic confrontation that occurs when large agencies develop their own ideas with minimum contact with each other. Since policy planners tend, almost by definition, to be generalists, this development of a common purpose and a common frame of reference is aided by the fact that individuals find it relatively easy to change departments and thus to share and extend their experience. There exists, it is true, the danger that such policy planning groups in different departments will ultimately form a close fraternity whose members understand each other and "the problem" perfectly, while having no significant influence on their departments or the development of public policy. It seems fair to say that such a situation is not imminent.

The roles described in these paragraphs also constitute one of the most important tasks of the Deputy Minister of an individual department, and his immediate colleagues in senior management. Policy planning groups in line departments are therefore normally established as staff groups serving the Deputy Minister directly, or they may be organised under an Assistant Deputy Minister whose primary role is that of policy planning. The groups tend to be small (often not more than a dozen, including support staff), and to be composed of officials who have a deep commitment to the policy planning process and the general objectives of government, but who can be reasonably dispassionate about their own specialisms or departmental interests. They tend to know what is feasible at a particular time; desirably also they should be able to sense when their Deputy Minister, the Minister or Cabinet are looking for new ideas.

This survey of the present system for broad policy development, and for policy-making and decision-making in the federal government would not be complete without some mention of the role of the so-called "central agencies" and of the Ministries of State. Both these have responsibilities that are "horizontal" rather than "vertical": they are concerned with the coordination and integration of federal policy and programmes in major fields or across the whole system, rather than with the implementation of government activity in a particular area such as defence or transport.

There are four central agencies whose activities are closely related to the policy planning process described above: the Privy Council Office, the Treasury Board Secretariat, the Department of Finance and the Department of Justice. A fifth, the Prime Minister's Office, is in many respects a parallel organisation to the Privy Council Office that is concerned with political matters that arise outside rather than within the Public Service; its role up to 1971 has been described by M. Lalonde (1971). Of the four other agencies, the Privy Council and Treasury Board Secretariat are of primary importance; the Departments of Finance and Justice play a more indirect role related to their frequent contact with other departments. The Department of Finance is primarily concerned with maintaining the economic prosperity of Canada as a whole: it is neither a "bureau of the budget" (the main role of Treasury Board Secretariat) nor is it concerned with the actual collecting of revenue (performed by the Department of National Revenue). Since, however, approximately 38 per cent of Canada's Gross National Product is in the public sector, and 19 per cent represents activities of the federal government, Keynesian economics and common sense dictate that the Treasury Board Secretariat and the Department of Finance should act in concert. The Department of Justice has a similar "central" role because of its function as the legislative drafting agency of the federal government.

The Privy Council Office and the Treasury Board Secretariat occupy central places in the policy planning process, though, as will be emphasised later, this central position is not a dominating one. A primary function of the staff of the Privy Council Office is to provide the secretariats for all Cabinet Committees except the Treasury Board. Inevitably, therefore, the Privy Council Office acquires considerable influence on the policy planning process, through its knowledge of the continuing evolution of the concerns, priorities and needs of each group of Ministers in a Cabinet Committee. The Privy Council Office (PCO) is in a good position to see "the whole picture". Until the development of the policy planning groups within individual departments, the PCO was one of the few bodies with any capability for policy development. Since the emergence of these groups, staff of the PCO are in frequent, sometimes almost daily, contact with them, in order to keep in touch with policy development activities in individual departments, especially those that are likely to result in Memoranda to Cabinet. Such liaison is again an extension of the regular contact that did and does take place between the Secretary of the Cabinet and Deputy Ministers.

The Treasury Board Secretariat exercises a similar function, since it provides the secretariat to the Ministers who constitute the Cabinet Committee that is the Treasury Board. The influence of the Treasury Board Secretariat is also important because of its budgetary role, in regard to the annual estimates of individual departments, the requirement that departments provide annual 5-year programme forecasts, and so on. Once again, the Treasury Board Secretariat is in a position to see the whole picture, though it has to be remembered that neither agency is solely one person; the picture is in fact being seen by a number of different eyes in both the Privy Council Office and the Treasury Board Secretariat, eyes which must be carefully coordinated within these agencies if a recognisable image is to emerge.

Lastly, and more briefly, there are the Ministries of State. The Government Organization Act 1970 gave the government the power through Order-in-Council, to create up to six Ministries of State at any one time. These might be Ministries designated to deal with a particular problem that was both urgent and short-lived. They might be, like the present Minister of State for Fisheries, responsible for an area of concern to the federal government that does not require the establishment of a full department (although the Minister may be given responsibility for relevant programmes housed in one or more federal departments). Thirdly, there have been created two Ministers of State, for Science and Technology and for Urban Affairs, each of whom is supported by a Ministry whose officials are specifically charged with the task of policy planning (including research, policy development and policy coordination) but who do not have responsibility for the implementation of programmes. It should be noted that Ministers of State, whatever the function they perform, are not to be equated with Ministers of State in the British Government. Canadian Ministers of State, for example, are members of the Cabinet on an equal basis with their colleagues who are in charge of line departments. What distinguishes a Ministry of State from such a department is the absence of responsibilities for programmes and the concentration on policy development across a broad area of governmental concern and activity. Ministries of State are naturally much smaller than programme departments: for example, the Ministry of State for Urban Affairs has about 300 employees, the Department of the Environment over 11,000. This, however, tends to mask the fact that a

Ministry of State represents a much greater capability for policy planning than is found in most operating departments in Ottawa, at least at the present time.

Although the present writer has been associated with one of these Ministries of State almost from its inception, this is not an appropriate place to attempt an evaluation of its work or its success (see, for example, P. Avcoin and R. French, 1974). What is important, however, is the increased emphasis on *integrated* and, if possible, *comprehensive* approaches to matters of public policy in broad fields such as urban affairs. A similar emphasis can be observed in the United Kingdom in the creation of the Department of the Environment, which brought together the central government agencies responsible for many of the key sectors of the human environment: housing, local government, transport, public works and others. This development cannot be overemphasised; it is a recognition that sectoral approaches are inadequate for those problems that are by their nature not capable of simple resolution into sectoral elements.

The system of policy planning just described, involving Cabinet, individual Ministers and Deputy Ministers, central agencies, ministries of state and policy planning groups in line departments is one that is extremely complex, difficult to understand or follow from the outside, and one that is in any case highly dynamic and changeable, in terms of personnel, institutions and relationships. The cynic may say on the one hand that it is so complex that nothing can ever get done, on the other that the events of the last few years have created an élite group of policy planners who are capable of distorting government priorities, following their own individual biases, or who are just too powerful. These two criticisms are, of course, mutually exclusive. If the system is complex, no one has yet devised a better one: the federal Cabinet does seem to be in a better position to fulfil its main role of setting priorities, determining priorities and taking decisions than it was in the past; and the opportunities for abuse of the system by individual policy planners (or a group of them) are constantly monitored by an elaborate system of checks and balances. The activities of the central agencies are carefully (and occasionally even suspiciously) watched by policy planning groups in individual departments; the latter are kept on track by Deputy Ministers and by central agencies who are constantly in touch with the preferences of different Ministers, different Cabinet Committees, or the Cabinet as a whole. Behind both of these are individual Ministers and the Cabinet, sensitive to the wishes of Parliament and of the electorate, aware of the realities of federal-provincial and other constraints, and rightly concerned that their decision-making and policy-determining functions shall not be taken from them by officials, however well-meaning the latter's motives.

In the final analysis, government—the work of what in the United States would be termed the Executive Branch—is done by individuals, whether

Ministers or officials, and the system of policy planning that has been described is, in the present writer's opinion, one that does enable individual abilities to be marshalled and oriented towards the development of public policy in an efficient, equitable and positive manner.

What scope for geography?

If this, in broad outline at least, is the policy planning process at the federal level, where does this leave the geographer or the mathematician? How can their skills be utilised most effectively, and how can spatial and other concerns be taken into account in the process? It seems evident that the recent evolution of the policy planning process has implied a rejection of the notion that the main requirement for the solution of major problems of public policy is the application of specialist skills. Such skills are often *essential* for problem resolution, but they are far from *sufficient*. As the links and interrelationships between economy and society become ever more complex and as the role of the government similarly increases in importance and becomes more complex also, it seems inevitable that the problems which require the skills only of one major branch of knowledge, or that require one type of expertise will not be those that are most important or most interesting. The more we place emphasis on integrative and comprehensive approaches rather than searching for sectoral solutions, the less scope there is for identifying a specific field of policy development where spatial or similar factors are most important, and where the experts in such matters can take the leading role in problem-solving.

Conversely, however, it is equally evident that this increasing awareness of the complexity and interdependence of problems has led to a recognition that spatial factors cannot be neglected in the development of public policy as they frequently were in the past. Urban regions, for example, have ceased to be geographical concepts primarily of interest to the geographer; they have become often the most important element in the restructuring of local government that has taken place in the United Kingdom, Canada and other countries during the last decade.

What is true of the subject-matter is surely also true of those who practise the subjects. If there is no clear and specific role for the mathematician or the geographer in policy planning—or, for that matter, for any particular specialist—then neither can it be claimed that there is a particular form of training that makes the best policy planners. Mathematicians, geographers, political scientists, engineers and so on may prove to be good or bad at contributing to the development of public policy, but the proof relates to the individual, not his background or approach. One's training is seldom a handicap, let alone a disqualification.

The mathematician, for example, may find it easier than others do to think about a problem in abstract (or, better, basic) terms, without becoming obsessed by detail. He may be able to divorce the problem more easily from its traditional assumptions, or to look at existing programmes and their objectives and ask the questions: "What are we trying to do? What are the elements of the resources we are utilising in the attempt, and are our intentions being realised?" Or, put another way, "Does the equation add up?"

Similarly, a geographical training is no disadvantage in policy planning. Some of the writer's colleagues in Ottawa have, fixed to their office windows, transparent plastic on which neat lettering constantly reminds them that beyond the window lies "the real world". That is a reminder that the geographer should not need—though it is also apparent that many geographers do need it. Just as the historian should be constantly aware that events take place in a time continuum, and that what is right now is not necessarily right in the past or in the future, so the geographer should be more readily aware than others that events take place, and policies are implemented, in a real world which is spatially separated into very different human and natural environments. It used to be a valid criticism of a motion picture that "it won't play in Peoria". Nowadays both motion pictures and public policies are designed with the knowledge that something which does not suit Peoria may well be ideal elsewhere, and that Peoria itself is not so homogeneous a society as it may have been in the past. Geographers have no monopoly of such insight, but its provision is part of a geographer's training. The geographer should also find little difficulty in accepting the fact that many of the most interesting problems facing society are complex, closely interrelated with other problems and are basically insoluble: improvement, yes, elimination, no.

If geographers are no worse, and no better, qualified to become generalists and to try to grapple with such matters, they should at any rate find many issues to absorb their energies. The big issues of public policy in Canada are still, as in the past, ones in which geographical factors demand attention. The list of issues includes environmental quality; the management of renewable and non-renewable resources; regional economic disparities; the debate on whether transportation is a utility that should cover its costs, or whether it is an essential requirement for national unity and social and economic prosperity; cultural differences, between francophones and anglophones, between immigrants and native-born Canadians, between Indians, Eskimos and Metis on the one hand and white on the other; the urban and especially the metropolitan concentration of population and economic activity; and many others. What is true of Canada is presumably true of other countries, though the list of issues will naturally vary in content and in relative priority.

The Future: Crystal Ball, Projection or Normative?

Policy planning, which is the theme of this chapter, is based on the assumption that governments and public policy should be concerned with the future: that is why we plan. It assumes also that not merely should we be ready for the future when it happens, but that we have the ability consciously to shape that future in ways that would not occur if the planning did not take place. This normative view of policy planning becomes all the more important if we accept the notion of society as in a state of accelerating change—the view profounded fairly convincingly by Alvin Toffler (1970) in *Future Shock*. The need for normative as well as anticipatory planning is also strengthened by the arguments of Daniel Bell (1973) and others that the advanced industrial countries, including Canada and the United Kingdom, are approaching or in the midst of a transition from an industrialised society to a post-industrial society.

We need to plan, then, in order that the economy, society, environment—and the geography—of Canada, the United Kingdom and other countries change in a manner that is acceptable to or desired by the populations of these countries. Those who are excited by "futures" often, however, seem to prefer a crystal ball to a real plan. They are concerned with identifying an hypothetical end-state—in 1990, 2000, 2050 or some such date—but they seldom think in programmatic terms about the way that end-stage is to be reached. Will it happen inevitably, or do we have to take firm steps in certain fields in order to divert present trends to the desired goal? If so, which are the important fields and what steps are necessary: legislation, administrative action, public information and motivation, or what? What do we have to achieve in the next 5 years, and what can we afford to leave until a later date?

In order to answer such questions—in order to make future planning less like crystal ball gazing and more programmatic—we need constantly to balance projections against normative views of the future. Projections of present trends are notoriously unreliable predictors of future events, especially in such a basic fact as population. The principal use of extrapolation, however, should not be to provide a basis for a plan that takes the extrapolated value as the anticipated future state. We do not, for example, extrapolate the population of Canada to the year 2000 solely or even primarily in order to adjust our policies and programmes to anticipate the requirements of that "expected" population. The primary objective of extrapolation should be to identify those areas in which present trends seem to need correction, in terms of our current values and of our aspirations for the future. If present trends suggest a Canadian population of, say, thirty millions in 2000, is this good or bad in terms of its impact on Canadian society and economy as we see these evolving? If some other population figure seems preferable, what options are open to us now and in the future, to bring it about, and at what cost and with what prospects of success can we exercise these options? In only slightly more geographical detail, what do present demographic trends indicate about the rural-urban balance, the growth of metropolitan areas or urban regions at the expense of isolated urban centres, the balance of population and economic activity among major regions? Is this what we want?

Physical planning of this kind has been with us as a major activity in the United Kingdom at least from the 1940s. Sir Patrick Abercrombie and his colleagues provided a series of normative visions of Greater London, the Clyde Valley, Edinburgh and elsewhere, based on a 25-year time-scale. Subsequently that normative vision seemed to fade, as planners became engrossed in the more day-to-day and year-to-year responsibilities that were suddenly thrust upon them. When normative visions reappeared in the 1960s—as for example in the Lothians Study (Scottish Development Department)—there was a new emphasis, less on physical planning and more on social and economic influences. In Canada that reawakening was probably more economic in outlook than in the United Kingdom. In part this economic emphasis was due to a growing recognition of the trend towards regional economic inequalities and the divisive national character of such disparities; in part it reflected work of the Economic Council of Canada which, since its creation in 1963, has been preoccupied with the future of the Canadian economy and of the Canadian society that is dependent on that economy.

Although normative planning is becoming popular again, it is astonishing how little those who are not directly involved in such planning seem to take into account the probability of rapid change in our social and economic future, let alone see the opportunity that this represents for conscious improvement. There are too few people prepared to gaze into a crystal ball, let alone go beyond crystal balls to programmatic, step-by-step identification of future change. There are very few who feel the need to look at extrapolated trends in major social and economic parameters for the rest of the decade or century and to examine the implications of these trends for their own field of activity, let along go beyond projection to advance some normative views of the way in which present trends should be altered. There are, finally, very few people who seem interested in disaggregating national trends, national projections or national aspirations to the level of regional or local impacts, dangers and opportunities.

If the message for geographers is not clear by now, further insistence on it is probably pointless. Instead, an example of one current problem of public policy that seems to cry out for geographical attention seems worth mentioning. It is taken from Canada, but it has implications for the United Kingdom and other advanced industrial countries that are probably no less significant.

One characteristic of the post-industrial society that seems to be inadequately recognised is the growing separation of industrial policy from employment objectives. Since the 1930s governments in many countries have been preoccupied with creating and maintaining full employment, and of attracting industry to areas of high unemployment. Industry has usually meant manufacturing industry, and it has also meant jobs. This easy equation seems increasingly obsolete. The Ninth Annual Review of the Economic Council of Canada (1972) contained a table (reproduced as Table 2.1) in which the projected growth of output and growth of employment during the present decade are compared across the major sectors of the Canadian economy.

TABLE 2.1. *Output and employment changes and distribution of employment, by industry group*

	Real domestic product[1]		Employment		Share of total employment		
	1960-70	1970-80	1960-70	1970-80	1960	1970	1980
	(Average annual percentage change)				(Per cent)		
Agriculture	1·2	2·3	—3·1	—2·1	11·4	6·5	4·1
Forestry	3·9	5·0	—1·6	1·2	1·6	0·9	0·8
Fishing	1·9	1·9	1·1	—[2]	0·3	0·3	—[3]
Mining, oil and gas	5·8	6·3	4·9	2·1	1·6	1·6	1·5
Manufacturing	6·1	5·6	2·5	0·2	23·8	22·7	17·1
Construction	5·0	6·5	2·7	3·7	6·5	6·0	6·3
Electric, water, and gas utilities	7·6	6·4	3·0	—0·8	1·2	1·1	0·8
Transportation, storage and communication	6·3	5·7	2·2	2·0	8·4	7·7	7·1
Wholesale and retail trade	5·5	5·3	2·9	3·0	17·1	16·8	16·5
Finance, insurance, and real estate	5·1	5·5	5·0	4·3	3·8	4·6	4·9
Community, business, and personal services	6·6	6·2	6·4	6·1	18·6	25·7	34·4
Public administration	2·8	2·7	3·8	3·4	5·8	6·2	6·5
Total economy[3]	5·4	5·5	?·1	3·1	100·0	100·0	100·0

[1] Calculated in 1961 dollars.
[2] The numbers here are too low to form a basis for reliable projections.
[3] Includes the value of imputed rent on owner-occupied dwellings, not shown separately. Sources based on data from Statistics Canada and estimates by Economic Council of Canada.

From the bottom row of the table, it can be seen that the real Domestic Product in Canada is expected to grow at about 5·5 per cent per annum between 1970 and 1980, as it did in the previous decade. Manufacturing *output* is projected to grow at approximately the same rate as the expansion of the national economy. *Employment growth* in manufacturing, however, is expected to show a very sharp fall from the 4·9 per cent per annum of the sixties to virtually zero in the seventies. In other words, Canada no longer needs extra people to produce more manufactured goods. Manufacturing seems destined to follow primary activities like agriculture into a situation where we habitually produce more goods with fewer people. By the end of the 1970s, manufacturing industry is projected to account for only 17·1 per cent of total employment in Canada, as compared to 22·7 per cent at the beginning.

These are, of course, projections, not predictions. They are derived from the first results of CANDIDE, a large-scale econometric model of the Canadian economy developed by the Economic Council, and it is already evident that there are weaknesses in the model that require correction. Nevertheless, the implications contained in that single row of figures against "Manufacturing" seem profound even if they are out by an order of magnitude or by a decade. They are particularly profound in a country such as Canada, which is in the midst of a period (1965-80) when more people, in absolute numbers, are expected to enter the Canadian labour force than will be added to the labour forces of the United Kingdom, West Germany and Italy *combined*. But the implications are profound for the latter countries also. Already about two out of three jobs in Canada are in the tertiary and quaternary sectors of the economy. Is the British economy likely to move in the same direction, and if so, should employment policies be less oriented towards attracting manufacturing industry and more designed to create service employment? If a high level of employment in manufacturing industry is foreseen for some decades to come, what implications do rising labour costs have in terms of competition in a world economy where output by competitors is based on automation? More specifically geographical, what implications do that row of figures have for the regional policies pursued by governments in Canada, the United Kingdom—or, for that matter, in less developed countries?

REFERENCES

Avcoin, P. and R. French (1974) *Knowledge, Power and Public Policy,* Science Council of Canada Background Study No. 31, Information Canada, Ottawa.

Bell, D. (1973) *Coming of Post-industrial Society: a Venture in Social Forecasting,* Basic Books, New York.

Cornford, F. M. (1953) *Microcosmographica Academica,* 6th Edn., Bowes and Bowes, Cambridge.

Drury, Hon. C. M. (1974) *Speech* to the Conference on Mathematics in Canada, March 4th, Ottawa.

Economic Council of Canada (1972) *Ninth Annual Review* (The Years to 1980), Information Canada, Ottawa.

Jackson, C. I. (1970) *Crustal Gazing: for Fun or Profit?* Discussion Paper No. 70-6, Policy Research and Coordination Branch, Department of Energy, Mines and Resources, Ottawa (limited distribution).

Jackson, C. I. (1972) "Wide open spaces on the map of Canada", *Geographical Magazine,* **44,** 5, pp. 342-51.

Lalonde, M. (1971) "The changing role of the Prime Minister's Office", *Canadian Public Administration,* **14,** 4, 1971, pp. 509-37.

Robertson, R. G. (1971) "The changing role of the Privy Council Office", *Canadian Public Administration,* **14,** 4, 1971, pp. 487-508.

Scottish Development Department (1966) *Lothians Regional Survey Plan,* H.M.S.O. Edinburgh.

Smallwood, F. (1965) *Greater London: the Politics of Metropolitan Reform,* Bobs-Merrill, New York.

Toffler, A. (1970) *Future Shock,* Bodley Head, London.

CHAPTER 3

GEOGRAPHY AND PUBLIC POLICY ISSUES IN CANADA

F. K. HARE

University of Toronto

Twelve years ago, when I was President of the Canadian Association of Geographers, I compelled a polite and sceptical audience to listen to my version of a policy for geographical research in Canada (F. K. Hare, 1964). At that time it was I, and not the membership, who was convinced that the discipline ought to have a great deal to say about public policy, and that it should choose its research topics with this in mind. I was roundly criticised for what were then unpopular views, and was taken to task in the *Canadian Geographer* by Hans Carol (1964).

Geographers are obviously still worried about their failure to make much impact on public policy, resource management, environmental design and other concerns of the moment. I am always happy to write about this theme. Yet I am also embarrassed, because I have become sceptical about the relevance of scientific disciplines in the policy domain. Once again, therefore, I am a bit out of step with the profession—and with the scientific community as a whole, because geographers are not alone in their desire to cut a better figure in public affairs. I hear the same complaints from discipline group after discipline group. Journals such as *Science* and *Nature* show by their editorial policies that this unease is widespread in the western world. My embarrassment comes not from a rejection of the sense that there is something wrong in the relations between science and government—that much is obvious—but because I cannot see any easy way to put matters right.

The word "policy" is itself ambiguous. It means, broadly speaking, the courses of action (or inaction) adopted by any group that has the power to make its action stick. At the senior level it means those public actions or attitudes sustained by the government of the day. Slightly lower down it covers the tactics of the senior public and private bureaucracies, such as those of the federal and provincial governments, and of the larger private corporations. Some policy is codified by legislation, or by constitutions and by-laws. Much of it is unwritten, but not the less effective as long as it is consistently employed. Thus it is the policy of the Canadian Federal Department of the Environment that environmental quality in air and water should be protected by means of national standards, rather than by assessments of local assimilative capacity. This policy is fully applied by the Environmental Protection and Environmental Management Services. Yet other administrations in other countries take the opposite view, showing that policy does not rest simply on cool-headed science, but must also involve political judgment. At a more mundane level, the boards of various airlines applied for decades the policy that stewardesses could not marry—a policy now quite properly in the waste-paper basket. Obviously the word lacks precision—but the English language is notable for getting large mileages out of ambiguity.

The term *science policy* is even more fuzzy. To the Canadian academic witnesses who appeared before the Senate Sub-Committee on Science Policy, it seemed to mean "How does one get more money for academic research?" Learned society after society got up on its collective feet and argued that too little was being spent on their little bailiwick. Some of them tried to show that it would be socially useful to spend more, but there were many who seemed to feel that research was self-justifying, even when it pressed hard on the lay tax-payer. The Canadian Association of Geographers was an exception. Having, in fact, no collective opinion, the Association asked me to prepare and present a brief on its behalf. In it I argued that geography was a socially useful discipline, which had an especially useful role to play in Canada; but I said nothing about money. I assumed, as I still do, that science policy has to do with the most effective use of science in support of public objectives. Undoubtedly one of these was, and is, the support of pure research for its own sake. But the public has many other pressing concerns, some of which can be helped by applied science. Science policy should clearly be that branch of *public* policy that sees to it that publicly-supported science serves these objectives. It is not a policy to serve the needs of science, important though they may be in their own right.

All unwittingly, when I transplanted myself from the University of Toronto to a federal post in Ottawa in 1972, I stepped into the middle of a controversy about science and policy making. I had certain fixed beliefs that made me align myself with one of the schools of policy-making theory. I know now, but did not then, that this school is called by some political scientists the root method of policy making (C. Lindblom, 1959). The theory holds that policy should be based on a thorough knowledge of the system that one seeks to conserve or modify. One must understand the background of the situation in all its complexity. One must try to foresee the consequences of policy change a long way ahead, and in terms of indirect as well as direct consequences. Obviously this root method has a system ring about it. It asserts, in fact, that policy making depends on a sort of simulation modelling of a complex situation, and some modern economic modelling more or less does this.

I have publicly asserted the truth of this view. It has seemed to me obvious that environmental and resource policy should always be based on the most sophisticated possible scientific analysis of the actual situation. I have been inclined to say, along with many ecologists, that one can only plan the future of an environment if one can know and account for its past, and cope knowledgeably with its present. I was convinced, in fact (and the switch to imperfect tense is deliberate), that ecosystem analysis in its most fundamental form was a necessary preliminary to good environmental policy making. In the geographical realm I am likewise on record as believing that land-use planning should be based on a long, hard look at existing land use and on the history that makes it what it is, a view I learned from Dudley Stamp (F. K. Hare, 1968).

The root theory of policy making is very satisfying to scholars and scientists, because it makes them indispensable to good government. It is also gratifying to the systems analyst, the computer scientist and the econometrician. The more politicians believe that policy should be based on profound academic analysis, the more secure is the academic stake in government, the more lush the consulting pastures. In Canada it has created a unique industry—that of permanent and indestructible Royal Commissions, whose lives prolong themselves, like those of Laputan scholar communities, into epochs in which no one can recall what the Commissions were set up to advise on, or what their staffs are supposed to find out.

But policy is rarely made this way. At the national and provincial level it is made by ministers, cabinets and parliamentary majorities who want to be re-elected. They listen to their officials, but they listen more to what they can detect of public dissatisfactions, and of what the media amplify these into. They know that elaborate new policy structures nearly always contain hidden traps. They know, too, that a very large *per saltem* changes in the *status quo* shock the electorate and produce unexpected tremors in previously stable seismic realms. So in practice they move slowly, changing policy by small incremental steps (often announced in dramatic language) chosen from a very small number of possible courses. The best bureaucrats know this, and serve up these possible courses in a highly pragmatic and deliberately short-term framework. A familiar lesson for the scientist in government is to serve up an elaborate draft policy and then to watch it progressively simplified and sharpened in focus by those who really know the art of the feasible.

This is the *branch* theory of policy making, and it is one that I have learned to appreciate, without being able to master it. The British, and Charles Lindblom, call it *muddling through*. Those who accept it say that they do so because the complex system, the complex whole that they want to modify, is fundamentally unknowable, beyond comprehension. A major figure in ecological modelling (with human action included), C. S. Holling (1972), puts it as follows:

> Traditional approaches plan on the presumption of knowledge—knowledge that is certainly not complete, but is presumed to be sufficient. . . . We now need a planning philosophy that explicitly recognizes the area of our ignorance rather than the area of our knowledge.

Of course, Holling is not making a virtue of ignorance. He is instead arguing that the levels of understanding considered minimal in the disciplines are rarely attainable in the domain of planning—and, I would add, policy. He argues further that we must "replace the lost resilience in our social and ecological system with a resilience in our approach to planning, and, in this way, eventually return flexibility and stability to the total system".

Hence I have been forced to conclude that the traditional academic disciplines, and the disciplinary skills of their exponents, may have little to say about policy making. Even economics, which sets out to do just this, often misses the mark, and in any case rarely yields unequivocal advice. Of course, I am not ruling out a useful role for the disciplines. I am only saying that the systems of thinking represented by policy making on the one hand and academic disciplines on the other are very different, and that technical skill in the one system is unlikely to confer practical skill in the other. Resilience in the presence of uncertainty, the capacity to act incisively on the basis of highly imperfect understanding, is a necessary quality in the policy maker. I doubt if it is desirable in an academic and, as an academic, I admit that I do not have it myself.

How does geography rate in this state of affairs? I think of it as a different kind of discipline, one where bringing together disparate things is root *and* branch. In the days when we thought of ourselves as synthesisers this was obvious, and the tools were literary and philosophical. More recently we have seen ourselves as more concerned with spatial organisation and interactions and hence with analytical procedures. Essays in multivariate analysis, however, are not substitutes for synthesis; eigenvector loadings may tell us more about ourselves than they do about the functioning of natural or man-made systems. I am not decrying the new geography. On the contrary I would say that the introduction of quantitative methods of analysis *and* synthesis was long overdue; it was a duty incumbent upon us as upon all scientists. But I am saying, and believe, that the fundamental objectives of geography remain the same, and that these are closer to policy making than those of most other disciplines. Some of the best policy writers I know are geographers, though I must admit that they function more as pragmatic generalists than as geographers when they are at work.

What are these objectives? I would say that they include the comprehension of the earth's surface as the human habitat in physical and biological terms (*not* biophysical, which means something else); a full knowledge of the pattern and function of human settlements, including trade and communications within and between them; the system of exploitation of the physical and biotic elements within the environment to support the human economy; and the various historical, behavioural and accidental considerations that one takes into account in tying these disparate things together. I am not offering this as the latest definition of geography. But it is the range of subjects dealt with in our journals, and is hence empirically what geographers do.

It might also serve as a definition of things over which public policy must be extended. The latter has to go into each subject on the foregoing list except comprehension of the natural environment. In other words, there is a distinct resemblance between my list of geographical objectives, and my idea of what policy makers need. As long as we do not shunt ourselves into long-forgotten sidings by undue specialisation we ought to be able to be useful in the policy domain even if we stick to our discipline.

Let me list a few major issues in which further public policy will have to be established in the next few months or years. First, energy policy. How should Canada plan to meet her future energy needs? Should she attempt to reduce these needs by economy measures? Should she begin to exploit northern gas and oil resources, or accelerate the use of the Athabasca tar sands? How should she transport them? And how should she relate these domestic supplies to imported materials? How should she balance gas, oil, coal, nuclear, biomass and new forms of energy? Ought she to conserve oil and gas for petrochemical use? What environmental protection measures are needed in the various options? Who should own Canadian energy resources?

Second, population and urban policy. Is Canada over- or under-populated? What changes in immigration policy should Canadians envisage in either case? If we decide to accelerate or to discourage immigration, what consequences can we foresee for our future demography? Urban growth and its problems are already with us. What measures should we take, for example, to deal with urban transportation? Do we advocate a cessation of expressway building, a softening up of downtown areas, a policy of rigorous land-use control to keep population and traffic densities, as well as the social and ethnic balance, near some desirable norms? How do we advance towards regional government in a city dominated world? What forms of recreational access should we seek to guarantee, and how do we cope with alien ownership?

Which leads to the third area, land policy. Do we need a national land policy? What does national mean in this context? A policy for federally-owned or controlled lands? A federal-provincial concord of some kind? Or an assemblage of provincial policies? Is controlled land use a proper public objective outside urban areas, where zoning already exists and often wider planning powers? Why control land use? To protect good farmland? To achieve better environmental management? To keep land out of foreign ownership.

And fourthly, water policy. What measures should we take now to guarantee adequate water quantity and quality for the foreseeable future? Should we countenance the export of water? How do we achieve suitable measures of multiple use? How do we combine power development, industrial and domestic use, with navigation and sewage disposal?

Obviously I could go on like this all day, and so could every publicly aware person. They are the sort of questions that arose in my federal office every day of the year. It was my job to suggest how science can be put to use in solving such problems, or in generating sound policy. The technical side was, of course, well looked after before I got near a problem: we had excellent technical services who can harness science and engineering in the everyday management job. But the large policy issues were often wide-open, and I often found myself trying to put forward answers.

I found that my training as a geographer, and as an academic administrator, had created within me a healthy curiosity about all these issues. I had not been narrowed down, or taught that wisdom comes from wearing blinkers. On the other hand, I rarely if ever had a chance to apply any specific technique derived from my research or from any other geographers. I have recently been very interested in relating Canada's energy budget to the annual water yield of the surface (Hare and J. E. Hay, 1971). Clearly this is closely related to water supply. Yet the present active interest in national water policy never seems to give me a chance of using my results. Policy issues, as I said earlier, are in practice of a different kind. They are simpler, less intellectually demanding, and at the same time call for more wisdom, than the things I do when I want to get a paper published in a learned journal.

Ottawa has certain public think-tanks called Ministries of State. These exist in order to generate public policy and to influence opinion in areas of broad national concern, especially where federal jurisdiction is a bit limited. Science policy has its own Ministry of State for Science and Technology (MOSST). A ministry of critical importance to geography is that for Urban Affairs, and geographers are playing a key role in that Ministry. Ian Jackson (Chapter 2) runs planning and evaluation, Harry Swain is deep in research and the Director of Research, Len Gertler, is himself a near-geographer. I am curious to know whether Gertler and Swain find the formidable body of research into urban geography useful in their new roles. How often do they refer to the learned journals of geography and other disciplines? To what extent do they find, as I do, that it is what their disciplines have made of them, as men, that is their real resource, rather than their technical skills?

Because, of course, Osbert Sitwell claimed that he was educated in the vacations from Eton College, and others have said that culture is the state of mind engendered by the things that one has forgotten. I think one profits in skill and in wisdom from a geographical training. I only hope that the discipline will evolve in such a way that geographers will always feel this way.

CONCLUSION

I seem to have come to a pessimistic conclusion about the role of formal academic disciplines in policy making. But I am not really pessimistic, because I believe that people trained in some of these disciplines can adapt more readily to the policy framework than people from narrower traditions.

Economists, for example, find less opportunity than they would wish to apply their theory, their econometric modelling, and their views on fiscal policy, welfare and resource development. Yet they play a key role in policy formation, because they are trained to have a broad familiarity with the complex details of the social and economic system. They have established their right to be heard. Political scientists are also in a strong position, and their comparative studies—integrally part of their discipline—are of great value to the policy writer. If I have any conviction it is that the older tradition of geography, that in which personal synthesis and literary craftmanship played major roles, resembles much of modern political science in its usefulness. It is something we simply must not lose.

I believe that the real role of the disciplines is in aiding management and effectuation, rather than policy formation. Branch methods work better for the latter, but root methods can and do contribute heavily to good management practices all the way from planning to post-evaluation. You may muddle through in policy, but in management you do try to use complex "root" techniques.

The scholar and scientist must always ask himself "do I want to affect public affairs?" Many say "no", and that is clearly their right. Those who say "yes" must then ask "how?" One way is to become a political activist, like my brilliant Toronto colleague Donald Chant. Without such scientist-activists I suspect that we should have made little progress in environmental protection. People who are impelled by their consciences to do this incur a lot of hostility from their own colleagues, and make a real sacrifice in their careers; we should value them highly. Many United States geographers have done just this. The other way, if one says "yes", is to ask constantly "how can I, as a trained specialist, and how can my academic discipline, contribute most effectively to good public affairs?" The answer, I suggest, is to try—however hard it may be in practice. If one tries one soon finds that it is one's own personal and intellectual qualities, and one's capacity for persuasive generalisation, that count most. I hope that we can make sure that the discipline, as it bears down on us as scholars, does something to enhance these qualities.

ACKNOWLEDGMENT

This chapter is a modified version of an address given to the Canadian Association of Geographers on 28 July 1973, at Lakehead University, Thunder Bay, Ontario.

REFERENCES

Carol, H. (1964) "Open letter to Professor Kenneth Hare", *The Canadian Geographer,* **8,** 203-4.

Hare, F. K. (1964) "A policy for geographical research in Canada", *The Canadian Geographer,* **8,** 113-16.

Hare, F. K. (1968) "The conservation of resources", in *Dudley Stamp Memorial Volume,* Special Publication No. 1, Institute of British Geographers, London, pp. 43-51.

Hare, F. K. and J. E. Hay (1971) "Anomalies in the large-scale annual water balance over northern North America", *The Canadian Geographer,* **15,** 79-94.

Holling, C. S. (1972) "Ecological models: a status report", *Proceedings, International Symposium on Modelling Techniques in Water Resource Systems,* Environment Canada, Ottawa, pp. 11-20.

Lindblom, C. (1959) "The science of 'muddling through'", *Public Administration Review,* **19,** 1959, pp. 155-69.

CHAPTER 4

THE GEOGRAPHER AS POLITICIAN

E. BROOKS

University of Liverpool

Whatever his geographical pretensions, the new Member of Parliament finds his mental map of Westminster becoming as distorted as a mediæ Orbis Terrarum, with the Division Lobby instead of Jerusalem domina as the first-order central place. Periodically he will advance from the Ultima Thule of the backbenches to combat the monstrous beings on the Other Side, but it is unlikely that such crusades ever help him map the real corridors of power and communication. These remain unobserved on the blessed isles of Whitehall, where mandarins converse with multi-nationals in an ecumenical rather than a Manichaean spirit.

The analogy need be pursued no further to make the central point that politics is the theology of a secular society, and that the role of the professional politician serving a mass party is different in kind from that of the professional scholar loyal only to truth. The distinction implies no necessary dishonour, for students of the *science* of the possible are not invariably best fitted to practise the *art* of the possible; but an incessantly gladiatorial confrontation may ultimately undermine the rationality upon which democratic consensus rests. An excessive sense of righteousness, in other words, is ultimately as damaging to the political arena as it is to the academic cloisters.

It would be comforting to hope that the academic in politics would thus be doubly insulated against the simplicities of a two-dimensional moral world, but there is unfortunately no such guarantee. Nevertheless, if the geographer-politician does not invariably behave as befits a dispassionate academic geographer, this is not to say that his professional training does not influence his political perceptions or that there are not spatial dimensions to public policy. This chapter will therefore concentrate upon two sensitive issues which have not received the critical treatment they merit from professional geographers: first, the policies of regional subsidisation conducted by successive British governments after 1945 to combat high unemployment in the Developing Areas; and secondly, the geostrategic pattern which followed the Second World War and which has decisively changed the United Kingdom's status as a world power.

Geographers would not dispute that these are legitimate areas of concern for their profession, and indeed they have published many valuable studies of regional policy in Great Britain and elsewhere (G. Manners *et al.,* 1972; J. W. House, 1973). However, it seems fair comment that most geographers have neglected the role of geopolitics and military geography in the post-war world. The imperial Diaspora of the British, the results of which lie thick in vintage copies of the *Geographical Journal,* has retreated to more introverted and domestic concerns. The United Kingdom has lost an Empire and her geographers seem to have lost interest in imperialism, whether of the past or of the present. Indeed, we often seem to abandon any historical perspective, rarely feeding into our models the likelihood that the recent outbreak of succession states upon the Earth's surface will prove to be as ephemeral as that other rash of succession states which appeared in the East European shatter-belt in the wake of an earlier episode of imperial collapse.

British geographers may show less complacency at home towards the political *mores* and basic strategy of regional policy, but only cautiously, and with excessive politeness, is any fundamental critique advanced, and exceptions to the rule stem from the Marxist rather than the liberal democrat. Yet the latter has a no less urgent need to be iconoclastic, and to ask the embarrassing political questions.

UNEMPLOYMENT AND THE SCALE OF DELIMITATION OF PRIORITY AREAS

During the last 15 years the role of government in the United Kingdom, at national and also local level, has become increasingly decisive in physical and economic planning. At the national level there was elaboration of regional development policies which first became powerful in 1945, and which had as their primary aim the elimination of serious unemployment in any region of the country. In the 1960s State intervention in industrial location policy gained much greater impetus and massive injections of public finance to private industry came to be regarded (particularly by the Labour Party) as a perfectly proper way for central government to shoulder its responsibilities to the national economy.

At the local level the role of government became no less crucial in physical planning, particularly within the urban areas of each authority. Although comprehensive planning was discouraged, or alleged to be hindered, by the anachronistic boundaries inherited from the nineteenth century, there was nevertheless a major programme of land-use planning, such as slum clearance and highways development, which steadily transformed the landscape of both town and countryside.

In short, the national emphasis on an areal approach to factor deficiencies in the economic field was paralleled at the local level by an areal approach to factor deficiencies in the social field. But the functional link between these two aspects of government was weakly recognised and co-ordination was seldom attempted. Instead, policies have been like ships passing in the night, with little departmental pressure to form convoys.

A particular casualty of this fragmented policy-making was unemployment, which in many crucial respects (especially during the 1960s) arose more from social than from economic causes. It is true that there are semantic problems involved in this distinction, but it can also be claimed that Whitehall's structure of government responsibilities—the separate bureaucratic hierarchies of decision-makers—rests upon a deep-seated and almost automatic assumption that social and economic policies can be visualised and planned separately. Furthermore, the traditional delegation of powers to local authorities itself ensures a marked difference of emphasis and focus—as well as personalities—at the national and local scales of planning respectively.

However, such executive duality is daily confronted with the unitary responsibility of the Treasury for overall fiscal and monetary management as expressed through the major spending Departments of State. These, such as the Department of Education and Science or the Department of the Environment, in turn shape priorities and the allocation of resources at local government level. Against this background of ultimate financial stranglehold from the centre, a more explicit liaison between decision-makers at the two levels of government in the formulation of a common and social strategy would seem sensible, if only to test the extent to which classic economic problems such as unemployment might respond to unconventional social remedial treatment.

Yet in our crude regional approach to the eradication of unemployment, we have, for years, been chasing a mirage. Industrial policies for the regions should devalue unemployment statistics, and even forget them altogether in many instances. Alternatively, governments should stop trying to introduce jobs fit for workers into the regions, and instead ensure that the workers are made fit for the jobs cajoled into their locality. Regional unemployment is often less a matter of economics—of structural adjustment, say—than of sociology and psychology; it is a problem of human resources, especially educational and cultural, measured in behaviour and social attitudes.

The emphasis should thus be switched to the individual or the small social group rather than to large regions; that is, we need a "pointillist" technique for dealing with poverty and unemployment rather than the broadbrush regional strokes of post-war British policy. The latter, with all its simplistic anachronism, was probably a key factor in producing the crisis of stagflation which gripped the country in the early 1970s and which by mid-decade paradoxically threatened unemployment on a more serious scale than at any time since 1945. These matters need to be put provocatively if only to dislodge the inertia of political orthodoxy (especially on the Left) towards regional policy.

Disenchantment with the conventional regional remedy in no sense implies that unemployment and poverty are unimportant. On the contrary, it is the continuing (often concealed) waste of human talent which should make us sceptical towards the policies of the last 30 years.

Let us consider the conventional wisdom about regional industrial policy. Basically it affirms that locational liberty must be constrained in the interests of regional equality and national fraternity. Inequality in Great Britain is conceived broadly in terms of a poor Palaeozoic North and West and a rich post-Palaeozoic South-East. The economic geography of the country is thus a modern version of the old cultural dichotomy between Highland and Lowland, with an income gradient falling steadily and sometimes steeply towards the Celtic fringe.

This peripheral poverty in the British Isles is seen as part of a wider West European pattern, with a rough symmetry between the British gradient of poverty and that which falls away to the south-east, towards the Mezzogiorno. In other words, the perimeter of the European Economic Community (E.E.C.) tends to concentrate the poor, and the embryonic European regional policy has been conceived via a juxtaposition of a rich core and a poor periphery. So a model well known to students of Third World countries underlies (somewhat ironically) our approach to regional imbalance within the developed world of the European Communities. Moreover, the close correlation between the regional concentration of the poor and that of the unemployed seems to confirm this core-periphery pattern, and policies of regional assistance, including central government subsidies, are concentrically emphasised outwards.

Seen in this way, the regional problem of the E.E.C. is not unlike that of modern Brazil. In both cases there is a relatively rich and affluent core, in the E.E.C. along the Birmingham-Milan axis and in Brazil along the Rio-Sao Paulo axis, with a hinterland of relative poverty to which growth industries are unlikely to go without persuasion or coercion. As an extension of the analogy, Merseyside would therefore correspond to an Indian Reserve in the Amazon basin, given protected status for the sake of its impoverished, culturally backward and unemployed or underemployed natives. Regional policy is in both cases a form of income redistribution, involving a horizontal transfer territorially rather than (as with a progressive tax system) a straightforward vertical transfer between social classes. Again, there is a parallel between the Brazilian paternalistic wish to bring assistance which might launch poor Indians upon sustained economic growth and the expressed intention of successive British governments since the war that the

Development Areas should eventually succeed in sustaining themselves independently after the period of infant industry protection.

However, any analogy between Merseyside and the Xingu Indian Park has several flaws. In particular, the Indians are ethnically homogeneous, with all members of the group facing similar cultural handicaps in coming to terms with the rich Brazilian core. Merseyside, by contrast, contains internal zones of affluence which compare favourably with those in the more prosperous regions of the European industrial heartland; and this sub-regional diversity should make us question whether blanket regional subsidies and other protective devices are the right way to help the "poor Indians" within the wider Merseyside community.

The Whitehall apologist might reply that the planned diffusion of affluence from the growth region to the non-growth region via broad national strategy should trigger off a secondary impulse and encourage local diffusion of wealth and job opportunity to the weaker members of the assisted region as a whole. But we might legitimately be sceptical of any such benign outcome; there is too much friction hindering the transmission of wealth and opportunity within a society of manifestly unequal members. Instead of subsidies filtering down to the deprived, or benefiting them in the long run by social osmosis, the spoils tend to go to the rich sectors within the assisted region, thus reinforcing the earlier plea for a more pointed rather than a broad-brush treatment in remedying economic inequalities.

At the heart of the Government's problem is the explanation of unemployment itself, and of the poverty and degradation which it provokes. Why are people unequal in this index of social success, and what can be done by environmental measures to overcome their possibly related handicaps of inequality, including those of heredity?

When politicians discuss the eradication of unemployment, they often seem to have an image of a pool of mobile labour in which float individuals of identical specific gravity. An investment in a region generates ten thousand jobs, say, and since all men are presumed to be equal this is held to off-set unemployment of similar size. This naive approach was seen during the early 1960s on Merseyside, when local politicians equated the number of jobs about to be introduced by the motor industry with the number of those unemployed. Presumably the only difference they detected between the employed and the unemployed was that the former happened to be in work and the latter out of work, and they assumed that the dole queues would contract in direct ratio to the expansion of jobs. This proved an extremely glib assumption.

But before examining why some people remain unemployed, we should critically examine the familiar statistics of "unemployment". Are the published figures of people out of work a meaningful scientific indicator of regional economic imbalance, distress or poverty? Indeed, what precisely does measured unemployment show? Here admittedly there has been a dawning realisation by some decision-makers that published unemployment statistics are a very imperfect indicator of economic malaise; for the figures omit concealed unemployment and fail to reveal the short-time working or lack of opportunities for overtime which play havoc with family incomes (D. Metcalf and R. Richardson, 1972). They are equally useless in revealing the extent to which workers are in jobs which offer them, even in the best of times, a miserable wage little better than the State benefits they might draw as recruits to the army of the unemployed. In any case, poverty and frustration are not simply the product of lack of work as such but rather of the absence of jobs which are enriching in the fullest sense.

But any academic quibbles about the meaning of unemployment pale into insignificance compared with the passions aroused by that term which politicians refuse to utter in polite company—the "unemployable". It is understandable that social workers should be reluctant to use the term and flay those who lack similar scruples; for once we label a person in this derogatory fashion, his self-image may become so downcast and defeatist that the label is retrospectively validated. Nevertheless, we must recognise that there are people within our society who are incapable of holding down jobs (at least of the sort which modern technology creates) for more than a short time at best. We have no difficulty in adjusting to this disconcerting fact when we consider those overtly handicapped, physically or mentally. The autistic adolescent or the youngster suffering from spina bifida clearly fall into the category of unemployable, or employable only in a sheltered environment. In such cases it is seen as "progressive" for local authorities to provide sheltered workshops, special transport facilities, or one-to-one ratios between the handicapped children and their teachers. In short, we admit the reality of a class of people for whom paternalistic policies are a pre-requisite of survival itself. The analogy drawn earlier between our own society of inequality and that of the Brazilian Amazon remains valid. "Backward" Indians also require protection if they are not to be swept aside by those with greater competitive skills.

But in our society we do not create such "reserves" for other than the overtly handicapped or the anti-social. We then call them hospitals for the sub-normal, H.M.Prisons, Borstals or Approved Schools. Such places of refuge or incarceration are part of the fabric of our society, but we rarely see them as a particular territorial version of the old socialist precept, "to each according to his needs". Yet when people in all their rich variety respond to free locational choice, a general sifting mechanism manifests itself territorially in terms of individual propensity. We are familiar with this process in migration studies, where we expect to find that the typical migrant is younger, more ambitious, more able and more risk-taking than the non-migrant. Equally we know about worsening dependency ratios and the growing proportion of the elderly, the infirm and the ill-educated within the areas from which the more mobile have fled.

This process of territorial sifting is also taking place within sub-regions, conurbations and, particularly, the inner city, which is generally being abandoned by the mobile and foot-loose owner-occupier.

In other words, social vertical sifting is translated into geographical horizontal sifting. This phenomenon is common to those societies such as the British which have no legal restrictions upon social and/or territorial mobility of the sort found in the rigidly stratified societies of antiquity or those of contemporary communist states such as the Soviet Union or China. In democratic open societies where equality of opportunity has become a political canon, any real community of the unequal is made impossible by a process which encourages those with superior skills to escape the unwelcome proximity of their less well-endowed neighbours. Areas evacuated by the socially mobile eventually become the preserve (rather than the statutory Indian reserve) of the socially immobile, a territorial sump for the rejects of meritocracy.

In the United States this process has gone even further than in the United Kingdom, with the inner city relegated to the bottom of the intra-urban hierarchy as the refuge (or tacit concentration) camp for the drop-outs, drug addicts and various others—not least the unskilled Blacks—perceived to be "inferior" by the pace-setters of society. Thus the core-periphery contrast which, at the macro-regional level, is common to both Western Europe and Brazil, has become inverted at micro-regional level within the cities of the developed western world; the residential core is surrendered to the poor while the suburbs become the home of the rich. Of course, this is a highly simplified and schematic depiction of a complex urban reality, but it is not misleading to identify such a broad pattern of intra-urban sifting within a conurbation such as Merseyside.

Closer inspection shows that the inner city "sump" is but one example of a set of deprived sub-regions of which others may be found severed and possibly quite remote from the inner city proper. The council estates bordering Liverpool are akin to Indian Reserves in that a paternalistic authority has created a legally distinct environment of rented and subsidised housing for those too poor or insecure to move into the world of owner-occupation. Within such areas of the initially deprived further sifting occurs once the educated children of formerly disadvantaged parents climb the social ladder. In time this continued winnowing of social chaff within decaying neighbourhoods produce the urban equivalent of the astronomer's black hole—a region of total collapse. For example, in the North End of Birkenhead a group of high rise council flats, built in the late 1950s to replace the former slums, had themselves degenerated by 1975 to the point of no return and were having to be evacuated completely.

In this urban situation a version of Gresham's Law operates. Bad families drive out good, making it more and more difficult to attract the type of tenant who could improve the squalid neighbourhood image. Such cycles of degeneration have already run their course (to eventual demolition) in several American cities, e.g. St. Louis, and they seem likely to remain endemic to liberal meritocratic societies.

Growing awareness of this problem led in the 1960s to the creation of Educational Priority Areas in the inner parts of various cities in Great Britain (A. H. Halsey, 1972, Ch. 4). Again, this is not unlike the special help given by the Indian Foundation in Brazil for education within tribal reserves. The difference, however, is that in Great Britain such areas of social priority have emerged as a consequence of territorial withdrawal by the more affluent, whereas in Brazil the reserves occupy areas which are penetrated by rich interests anxious to develop natural resources (E. Brooks, 1974).

But before pursuing this train of thought, let us return briefly to the measures used to tackle unemployment in Great Britain. The growing scale of state intervention and subsidy was defended by the argument that the under-used labour resources of the assisted areas would, when fully mobilised, encourage higher national production. Full employment policy was integral to the re-structuring of regional economies which would eventually lead to a maximising of economic growth.

Unfortunately this optimism has not been vindicated. Post-war unemployment has remained far below the level of this inter-war period but there has demonstrably been no British equivalent of the "German miracle". Instead, a disappointing rate of economic growth steadfastly accompanied "full employment" (in the sense understood by Keynes and Beveridge), suggesting that central government had a poor return on the regional subsidies and locational restraints deployed to hold the unemployment rate below the level of 3-4 per cent.

The situation in the early 1970s became dangerously worse, combining a Keynesian rate of full employment with (at best) zero economic growth and unprecedented inflation (W. A. P. Manser, 1974). The sharp deterioration reflected global conditions to some extent and was found in all industrialised countries, but its exceptional severity in the United Kingdom marked the culmination of a process of economic decline extending over decades and even generations. It seems likely that the gathering post-war crisis in the United Kingdom was due less to minor fluctuations in a full or overfull employment rate than to the overmanning, the gross inefficiencies, the managerial incompetence, the built-in overtime working and the antiquated adversary confrontations which beset the country. To put it bluntly, and to paraphrase a Labour politician who committed hara-kiri by so accusing the farmers, governments have too long feather-bedded senile industrial invalids and given a particularly cosy and enervating bolster to the Development

Areas in particular. Unwillingness to accept so-called high unemployment in the regions has enabled inefficient sectional interests to pull out the begging bowl rather than to set their own houses in order and, by political blackmail, to perpetuate their failings at the expense of the taxpayer and consumer. This action remained politically realistic as long as the latter could nevertheless expect rising real income each year, but vanishing national buoyancy will inexorably shrink disposable income. The resulting "scissors" crisis of penal (and politically impracticable?) taxation will undoubtedly be a challenge to the art of the democratically possible.

In this deteriorating situation a redoubled call for increased regional subsidies will doubtless be heard. But before treading that beguiling path, we should consider whether intensification of past policies may make the underlying condition worse rather than better. At the very least, we should ensure that there are parallel changes in labour's ability to respond to the new job opportunities which such subsidies and intervention stimulate.

The frictional problem involved was seen on Merseyside with the arrival of the motor industry. Far from the new jobs mopping the unemployed, the labour was mainly poached from old industries incapable of offering such high wages. One example was the Liverpool Corporation bus service, which was permanently weakened by the haemorrhage suffered (J. Salt, 1967). Such denuded enterprises were henceforth unable to carry on efficiently, incapable as they were of offering the high wages which the motor industry could pay good "employable" labour. The arrival of the motor industry in effect shuffled the available hands, leaving the registered unemployed—particularly the unskilled—facing an even worse situation than hitherto in that potential employers were increasingly hard hit by the income expectations generated locally. In short, the multiplier effect was upon wage inflation rather than the unemployed.

If this is the effect of subsidising growth cuckoos in the regional nest, one is tempted to suggest that money might be better spent subsidising the unemployed to stay on unemployment benefit. Less cynically perhaps, could we extend the concept of sheltered workshops to the long-term unemployed and/or the unemployable? Protective segregation has become a method of helping the overtly handicapped (e.g. the Remploy system or the Grenfell formula) and it might offer constructive help to the more insidiously handicapped who would otherwise stay on the scrap heap permanently.

But the problem is more deep-seated than simply coping with the so-called unemployables. Even more fundamental is providing jobs fit for human beings. In other words, the need is not simply for jobs as such, like the dead-end employment which so many children enter after school (National Youth Employment Council, 1974) but for jobs which permit spiritually satisfying as well as materially affluent lives.

It is appropriate in this connection to recall the Educational Priority Area concept, which seemed to offer a promising approach to the wider social and environmental problems of which unemployment statistics may be only a crude symptom. In short, politicians should aim for the protection and rehabilitation of vulnerable human beings, particularly in those areas where the socio-economic problems of tomorrow are daily being nurtured in the homes of today. Delinquent parents create delinquent children, while a delinquent peer group can equally deform the children of a neighbourhood throttled by the pressures of anti-social conformity. Sub-cultures of the socially alienated form and grow like malign tumours. What constructive thought arises is quickly stifled by the squalor, the frustration and even the depravity of social situation in which child, family and community are debased.

Politicians tend to minimise this problem of the urban ghetto, perhaps because of its highly sensitive implications, genetic and racial as well as social and economic. As an example of current coyness, we may recall the decision of the Labour Government of 1966-70 to defer the higher school-leaving age, a socialist "betrayal" which led Lord Longford to resign from the Cabinet in disgust. Yet when the age was eventually raised it provoked such a breakdown of discipline in many schools that compulsory attendance has since been honoured more in the breach than in the observance. Hordes of children now roam the streets of Liverpool when they should be at school, and truancy has reached epidemic proportions in some neighbourhoods. As a result of this breakdown of the legislative intention (notably in the very areas where its benefits were mainly intended) we have a situation worse than before. At least in the bad old days children who left school at 15 could go into a new job legally, whereas today an employer is unable to hire them until they reach the statutory age of 16. As a result many semi-literate and anti-school youngsters wander the streets, virtually encouraged to drift into a criminal sub-culture because they see how easy it is to break the law. Yet few politicians have yet faced up to the disciplinary implications of collapsing law and order in the gang patches of their constituencies.

Earlier reference has been made to the tax payer's subsidy to industries moving into the Development Areas to rectify marginal and often unimportant inequalities in unemployment rates. Meanwhile, as this money continues lavishly to be poured into company coffers, social rehabilitation in the cities is starved for funds from both national and local sources. Expenditure on the scale current in regional industrial subsidies would, if spent on social development within our cities, transform the economic situation in a decade. Instead of a few hundred pounds being doled out for an urban aid scheme, we should be thinking of expenditure running into tens of millions of pounds to revitalise the battered neighbourhoods and derelict sub-regions of the conurbations.

The reality is parsimony and a grudging attitude to the quality of urban life. Expenditure on new housing in down-town areas has often been nullified by the persistence in adjacent streets of vast tracts of desolation, dereliction and squalor, hardly calculated to lift the spirits or the expectations of the children growing up in such so-called renewal areas.

This advocacy of social priority spending is not just a sentimental plea. On the contrary, much of the answer to unemployment itself should be sought in the inner city and other islands of the deprived. A zonal approach to welfare may have some defects, in that areal remedies risk missing the strictly deserving. But if the areal approach to rehabilitation is open to objection within the relatively small urban sub-region, it is far more objectionable when applied in a blanket fashion to regions on the scale of current Development Areas.

In advocating a "pointillist" approach to government subsidies the aim is to find a more effective, individually refined approach to social and economic planning. Local government, despite its reform in the mid-1970s, still fails to meet this challenge adequately, for the new Metropolitan Districts are too big for the voice of the deprived (and often inarticulate) communities to be heard effectively. Nevertheless, it would help if the planners and politicians could be persuaded to see the linkages between varying endowment, opportunity, educational status and income within their recognised "problem areas". Geographers have an instinct for such synthesis, and the techniques devised for showing the multi-dimensional spatial geometry of the city might yet have political value in discouraging the single-factor approach. But as the Marxist might ruefully say, a grasp of the dialectic does not automatically produce a steeled revolutionary, and it is equally likely that principal components analysis will not by itself promote the egalitarian society. That, however, raises a quite different sort of principle.

GEOSTRATEGY AND POLITICAL PERCEPTION

The theme of protecting the vulnerable which has been examined in terms of domestic policies will serve as an appropriate text for the second theme. Alliances between nation states have been a recurrent *motif* of the last few hundred years and have obviously had a profound impact on the economic and social fortune of the communities involved. Such systems of collective security respond to a political perception of military hazard, or, to put it more bluntly, the wish to be on the winning side in the event of conflict. Constructing military alliances is therefore a process similar to farmers devising schemes of insurance or promoting co-operative marketing in order to minimise risk in their conflict with the fluctuating elements. Yet, despite the seeming appositeness of the theme, geographers have been slow to examine the political perception of risk in the post-war years and its effect upon the complex systems of alliance which have festooned the world during that period.

To stake a claim for military geography to be part of the perception studies now commonly carried out by geographers is merely to revive an older tradition, which was expressed most effectively by an earlier geographer member of Parliament, Sir Halford Mackinder. To those who regard Mackinder's writings on the Heartland as unworthy of scholarly attention, an appropriate comment is that the perception of risk by the military decision-maker is not always a function of academic appraisal. In other words, the importance of the Heartland concept to students of geostrategy lies less in its scientific claims to historical validity than in the acceptability of its imagery by the combatants of the contemporary world (R. E. Walters, 1974).

The Christian and the Marxist would both affirm that ideas can move mountains, particularly when they are invested with the magic of historical inevitability, and Mackinder's famous triad of geopolitical aphorisms, progressing from the control of the Heartland via the World-Island, to the world itself, should strictly be seen as members of a family of potent prophecies which, from their moment of utterance, exist as an independent force in human affairs (H. J. Mackinder, 1904, 1919). In other words, those who dismiss geopolitics because of its subjective and allegedly unscientific basis have missed the whole point. Geopolitics is the way politicians perceive the global power struggle, and academics seeking to understand diplomatic behaviour must try to enter imaginatively into that specialised world of geostrategic interpretation in which literally deadly decisions are taken about overseas bases, nuclear submarines, orbiting satellites or lunar bases. The bogy of the menacing Heartland may be just as riddled with misunderstanding as the bogy of unemployment, but if we are to understand, let alone seek to influence foreign policy, it is necessary to recognise that the bogy *as perceived* can dominate the waking hours as well as the nightmares of senior statesmen.

Whatever the impact of Mackinder's thinking upon the execution of British policy, there seems little doubt that it had a profound impact upon post-war geostrategic thinking in the United States. The spread of communism in the 1940s outwards from the socialist Fatherland seemed to be vindicating Mackinder's second aphorism, with peripheral countries such as Czechoslovakia and China enlarging in turn the already formidable and monolithic power which straddled the Heartland. Furthermore, there is evidence that the Marxists themselves during that period regarded the path of world communist transformation as most likely to follow such a process of contiguous revolutionary expansion, with the Soviet Union providing the military core and bastion from which diffusion of the creed could safely take place (P. M. Sweezy, 1942). Even much later, in 1968, it is possible to locate the so-called Brezhnev Doctrine in the direct lineage of such arguments.

Thus the invasion of South Korea in 1950, or the externally supported efforts to extend communism to South Vietnam in the 1960s, could all be genuinely seen as a process of steady enlargement of the Heartland at the expense of the relict post-colonial succession states of the Eurasian perimeter. The sea-based European empires having collapsed, the United States took upon itself the task of "containing" communism by an encircling ring of military alliances and bases. As the map of 1959 illustrates (Fig. 4.1.) this electronic and military girdle around the Heartland was by then almost continuous. The only major gap in the interlocking system of alliances, ranging from the North Atlantic Treaty Organisation (NATO) through the Central Treaty Organisation (CENTO) to the South East Asia Treaty Organisation (SEATO), occurred where an avowedly neutralist India refused to participate in the anti-communist chain. Here, too, the Mackinder hypothesis seemed to have been confirmed by the military activities which subsequently took place along the Sino-Indian border in 1962—the first (and so far the last) example of direct military invasion of a non-communist state by either of the Communist super-powers during the post-war balance of terror. Peripheral states outside the anti-communist defence ring seemed ready prey for the expansionist Heartland.

As far as one can tell, British politicians during the 1950s were content to support and follow the American-led strategy of containing communism, and there are late echoes of such compliance in the British Prime Minister's view in the mid-1960s that Britain's frontier lay on the Himalaya. Nevertheless, few geographers interested themselves in problems of military strategy at this time, and those who did attempt to evaluate the respective strengths of the contending power blocs seemed to prefer the evaluation of "hard" data, such as statistics of iron-ore output or petroleum, to any examination of the geostrategic preceptions of the leaders of each bloc.

Towards the end of the 1950s, however, the relatively stable pattern of the post-war world began to fragment rapidly. The sin-virtue polarity beloved of both Joseph Stalin and John Foster Dulles was increasingly blurred by the rifts which emerged in both the communist and the self-styled Free World. The former monolith split across the heart of Asia, while Europe's rapid decolonisation produced still further centrifugal pressures in the struggling states of what came to be termed the Third World.

The emergence of a heretical Chinese challenge to Moscow within the Heartland, reinforcing the earlier but much smaller challenge of 1948 from Yugoslavia, seemed to undermine the simplistic scenario for which Mackinder had long been reproached by his academic critics. The so-called Heartland, it was concluded, was bi-polar rather than monolithic, and time would reveal continued ideological divergence (polycentrism) rather than

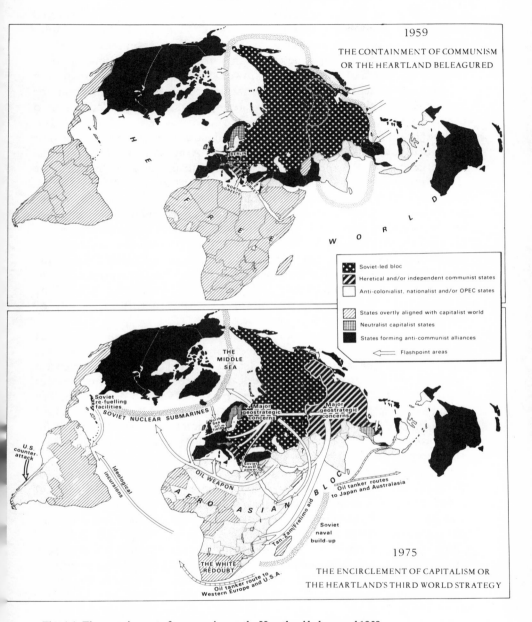

Fig. 4.1. The containment of communism or the Heartland beleaguered 1959

Fig. 4.2. The encirclement of capitalism or the Heartland's Third World strategy 1965

convergence. In particular, a growing rift could confidently be expected between two communist superpowers of such markedly dissimilar economies, cultures, population pressures and military resources.

Meanwhile, on the perimeter of this fractured monolith, the once tightly-knit system of alliances also showed signs of unravelling. Revolution in Iraq in 1958 was an early portent of the new turbulent impulses within the Middle Eastern girdle set up by the western powers. The Baghdad Pact had hastily to be re-drawn (and re-designated) and was replaced by CENTO. Although still lingering on to this day, it can hardly be regarded as a firm or trustworthy system—given the tensions of the Arab/Israeli conflict and the Organisation of Petroleum Exporting Countries—and it has become effectively moribund (G. Hadley, 1971). Pakistan, deeply angered by American policy during the Indian sub-continent's wars of the early 1970s, has furthermore disintegrated into two states, both of which have ceased to be part of the already weak anti-communist ring across southern Asia. In Vietnam the American humiliation and withdrawal exposed to irresistible communist pressures the neighbouring states of Cambodia and Laos, while Thailand adopted an increasingly neutral posture. The communist observer looking southwards from either "pole" within the Heartland might well be persuaded that politically and militarily Asia had a soft underbelly of doubtful resistance to digestive processes.

But the fissile pressures of nationalism and anti-imperialism quite apart from communism itself, can be felt much more widely still, right across the south-western flanks of the World Island and beyond to the somewhat tender as well as sensitive Latin American underbelly of the United States itself. In short, the ring of alliances set up in the 1940s to defend the Free World against communism has virtually disintegrated. Moreover, the Third World beyond this old boundary fence has increasingly shown that it no longer wishes to be defended by former imperialist powers whose motives are still deeply distrusted.

This is not to say that the nationalist regimes of the Afro-Asian bloc (which itself is a distinctly euphemistic term in its implication of concerted activity) intend to be pro-communist, either domestically or in foreign policy. Yet the strategy of the communist powers—and here we can legitimately refer without distinction to both the Soviet Union and the People's Republic of China—is based upon a model of historical development which sees nationalism and anti-imperialism as steps on the road to socialist revolution. What we see in the Third World may well include the neo-colonialism which is constantly alleged against the former imperialist powers; but we should also identify a far from unsuccessful process which might be termed salami communism, in which the Marxists within the post-colonial states seek to form broad "anti-imperialist" alliances designed to undermine the strength of the metropolitan capitalist world by slicing to pieces the trading alliances on which that world rests.

The analogy here is with the Chinese even more than with the Bolshevik Revolution. Mao's Revolution was based upon building such a broad alliance within the predominantly rural areas, whence the consolidated power of the masses (led by the dedicated and far-seeing communists) would emerge and encircle and pick off successively the isolated strongholds of the class enemy. It is a strategy which is both patient and flexible, yet it has a precisely defined ultimate objective. It has some affinity, in fact, with Lenin's justification for the Bolshevik Revolution in 1917 on the argument that monopoly capitalism could be locally defeated, and thereby weakened overall, by putting pressure on its weakest sector. The weakest sector in 1917 happened to be Czarist Russia, whereas the weakest link today (again as seen from Moscow and Pekin alike) is the underdeveloped, overpopulated, and certainly politically and socially excitable region which we call the Third World.

This strategy has recently gained much greater persuasiveness by the striking evidence that the metropolitan stronghold is critically dependent upon the supplies, and the terms of trade, which were inherited from the commercial relationships of the former imperialist period. Thus, in encouraging such trade and price policies as those pursued by the OPEC states, the Soviet Union and China have deliberately sought to weaken the economic basis on which the politics of liberal democracy grew and flourished. Far from the communist powers today seeing themselves as being encircled by imperialism, they see their position as one of growing strength vis-à-vis an encircled and beleaguered imperialist world. In the map of 1975 an attempt has been made to delineate in deliberately broad strokes this communist perception of geostrategic balance of the mid-decade (Fig. 4.2). Perceived in this way, not only is southern Asia ripe for the plucking but the whole of the Third World can be visualised as the soft, heaving underbelly of the surviving capitalist trinity of Anglo-America, Western Europe and Japan.

This thesis may seem deeply pessimistic and alien to the great ideals of brotherhood and peace which have spawned the United Nations, UNESCO and similar world institutions during the post-war years. Yet inspection of the map of the world with the eyes of both a politician and a geographer makes for a disconcertingly stereoscopic image of the potential for conflict during the next quarter-century. The appropriate political response to such a sombre forecast, even among those who agree with its broad outlines, will obviously depend upon many variables, such as whether one claims the moral right to kill or be called up in the defence of one's country. But whatever our personal pre-occupations, we should not be misled into thinking that other people necessarily see the world as we do. Those who claim a "scientific" communist perception of history, and of historical inevitability, may well see it as their responsibility to exploit the potential for revolutionary change, not least by probing and emphasising the geostrategic weaknesses of the enemy. Military commanders down the ages have been familiar with this subversive form of hostilities, and it was well understood by the United Kingdom during the Malayan Emergency. The democratic public, however, soon grows weary of such *realpolitik,* perhaps finding it somewhat offensive, and the democratic politician is usually ready to indulge his constituency.

CODA

In this brief selection of policy issues where at least one geographer developed strong views as a politician, examples have been deliberately chosen where platitude rather than polemic dominated the 12 years the author spent in both the local and the parliamentary arenas. Perhaps this experience was untypical, but Richard Crossman's posthumous confirmation of the Departmental secrecy and innate conservatism of Whitehall suggests that a more stringent scrutiny of the great issues of prosperity and peace would not come amiss at this time of national crisis.

REFERENCES

Brooks, E. (1974) "The Brazilian road to ethnicide", *Contemporary Review,* **224,** 232-8.
Hadley, G. (1971) "CENTO, the forgotten alliance", Institute for the study of International Organisations Monographs, 4, University of Sussex.
Halsey, A. H. (ed.) (1972) *Educational Priority* (see esp. Ch. 4, "Definition of E.P.A."), H.M.S.O., London.
House, J. W. (ed.) (1973) *The UK Space,* Weidenfeld and Nicolson, London.
Mackinder, H. J. (1904) "The geographical pivot of history", *Geog. J.,* **23,** 421-37.
Mackinder, H. J. (1919) *Democratic Ideals and Reality,* Constable, London.
Manners, G., D. Keeble, B. Rodgers and K. Warren (1972) *Regional Development in Britain,* Wiley, London.
Manser, W. A. P. (1974) "Economic crisis 1974", *National Westminster Bank Review,* November, pp. 28-39.
Metcalf, D. and R. Richardson (1972) "The nature and measurement of unemployment in the U.K.", *The Three Banks Review,* **93,** 30-45.
National Youth Employment Council (1974) *Unqualified, Untrained and Unemployed,* H.M.S.O., London.
Salt, J. (1967) "The impact of the Ford and Vauxhall plants on the unemployed situation of Merseyside, 1962-1965", *Tijdschrift voor Economische en Sociale Geografie,* **58,** 255-64.
Sweezy, P. M. (1942) *The Theory of Capitalist Development,* Oxford University Press, New York.
Walters, R. E. (1974) *The Nuclear Trap,* Penguin Books, London.

CHAPTER 5

ACADEMICS AND GOVERNMENT

M. D. I. CHISHOLM

University of Bristol

The first few pages of D. Cohn-Bendit's *Obsolete Communism* convey a vivid impression of life on the revolutionary barricades of Paris, 1968. Everything on the move, activity, excitement and above all the conviction that the whole political edifice was about to crumble into dust from which a new one, phoenix-like, would arise—this was the heady stuff of life. Yet it was the barricades that collapsed, not the government of the day. Arguably, future historians will regard the 1974 Presidential victory of Giscard d'Estaing as the real break-point for social and political reform in France. Be that as it may, Cohn-Bendit's account of events in the streets of Paris leaves a vivid impression that can be adequately conveyed only by an analogy, an analogy that provides the central theme around which this essay develops.

The surf-board rider must have great skill to use the forces of the wave on whose crest he rides. Acutely aware of the power which he appears to control, he is exhilarated by his own rapid progress among the surging seas. For a few giddy moments, nothing can stand in his way. And yet the wave's impetus abates, the waters retreat and the shore remains proudly unperturbed. Our surf rider must now return seawards to await a suitable wave, pick his moment and regain his position on—or rather, just in front of—the crest.

To use Cohn-Bendit as the text for a sermon may seem passing strange, yet herein lies a lesson that some geographers in particular, and academics more generally, apparently ignore. Since 1971, the journal *Area* has carried an important discussion on the "relevance" of geographical work, a discussion echoed in other geographical journals. One contributor expressed a fairly widely-held view when he averred that: "To be effective we, as geographers, must be . . . able to take decisions. . . . What is now needed is the formulation of policies and the power to implement them" (A. T. Blowers, 1974, pp. 34, 36). This is an outrageously naive position that ignores two crucial issues. If perchance the policies prove to be "wrong" or inadequate, then those who are too closely identified with them may be discredited, even on other issues where they were right. The doubts expressed early in September 1974 by Sir Keith Joseph, and shared by a former chairman of the Bank of England, concerning the premises of economic policy followed by successive British governments in the realms of employment/prices/money supply reflect disenchantment at the manifest failure of the best economic brains to find an answer that simultaneously curbs inflation, maintains full employment and provides for rising standards of living. However, the fear of being wrong should not be the main reason for caution; there is an altogether more important reason.

How far is the decision-maker, with the power to put his policies into practice, really altering the course of events? Or is he the surf-board rider, whose field of decision is to select the right wave and the moment to mount it but who cannot command the wave to change direction, nor create one where none exists? With waves, the real power lies with the storms that whip up the oceans; also the configuration of the coasts is a determinant of the precise direction of wave approach and the conversion of the oscillations into surging breakers.

By now the initial proposition will have become clear: all that glisters is not gold. There is nothing new in this observation. From the time that history was first written, men have asked whether Kings and Emperors made history or were prisoners of their destiny. The fact that we now have Ministers and "decision-makers" does not make this problem go away.

It is not the intention of this chapter to propound a modern version of historical determinism. On the other hand, the latter-day exponents of the decision-makers' Free Will miss the mark just as disastrously. It is self-evident that any decision-maker must work within the constraints of his time and place. In some circumstances, the constraints are tight and unrelenting; in others, a great leader may have a very free hand. Given this basic premise, it then becomes useful to examine the ways in which specific policies may be affected—in varying degree according to the circumstances of the occasion.

The four ages of policy

In a parliamentary democracy, there are four stages through which major policies go, from the germination of an idea to their implementation:
1. The process by which "problems" are identified and impinge on the awareness of either the public at large, or government, or both.
2. The process whereby these problems are formulated, i.e. the causal chains identified and the points of legal leverage thereby recognised.
3. The translation of this formulation into an Act of Parliament, the text of which embodies the operational version of the intentions of the Commons and the Lords.
4. The actual implementation of the Act. In some cases, an Act is virtually

a dead letter the day it receives the Royal Assent (e.g. the Litter Act of 1958); in others, the actual implementation may in practice produce results contrary to those intended (e.g. the Industrial Relations Act of 1971).

Not every administrative action of government requires the prior assent of Parliament; Ministers are authorised to exercise discretion, often within very loosely defined limits. Thus, in place of the Parliamentary process (stage 3), there is the analogous stage of policy formulation that goes on within the Civil Service, resulting in the issue of a circular to local authorities to lay down guidelines for action (especially common in the fields of Education and Planning), or in a specific Ministerial/Cabinet decision, such as the abandonment of the Maplin airport scheme in 1974.

Academics contribute to all four stages in the process outlined above. The real question at issue is the relative importance of the four stages and the role of geographers, along with other academics, in each. For this essay, the thesis to be developed is as follows. At the first stage, there is an infinite array of problems which might be noticed and brought to public attention, and each problem might itself be approached in numerous different ways. At the second stage, as the causal chains are unravelled, however imperfectly, the range of feasible solutions begins to narrow and is further reduced in the Parliamentary process, which introduces all manner of "political" considerations that limit the practicable courses of action. By the time policy is ready for implementation, it may be radically different from that which started on the obstacle race. Thus, at stage 4 there may be little scope for initiative on the part of the individual "decision-maker".

To return to the analogy of the surf rider. Stage 4 in the process outlined above is the time of doing, the action phase. On the other hand, stage 1 is the time when the oceans are perturbed by storms that are out of sight and out of mind. In terms of this crude analogy it is implicit that the first stage is more important than the last; such an implication is not intended. However, it is with this possibility in mind that the way in which local government in England came to be reformed will be examined.

LOCAL GOVERNMENT REFORM IN ENGLAND

The problem crystallises

Over the past century and longer, attitudes to and the functions of local government have changed dramatically. From the time of the earliest recorded city charter (Barnstaple, A.D. 930), and for many centuries thereafter, the conferment of civic dignities upon a town constituted a bargain struck with the Crown. For a specified sum of money or other contribution to the royal coffers, a town could purchase a limited measure of

Spatial Dimensions of Public Policy

freedom from the arbitrary power of the sovereign, an important part of the checks and balances necessary to the maintenance of any form of liberty and especially before the days of parliamentary democracy. Alongside the boroughs, there were the parishes, responsible for such matters as roads and the care of the poor and destitute. As the centuries slipped away, these two kinds of authority became less and less suited to the needs of the time; turnpike roads and the Poor Law were two responses signifying that the old order was inadequate. Consequently, as the nineteenth century wore on, the nation came to accept that a radical reorganisation was essential. An Act of 1888 established the counties in a form comparable to that which exists today (V. D. Lipman, 1949). Six years later, the lower tier authorities within the provincial counties were rationalised—as County Boroughs, Municipal Boroughs, Urban Districts and Rural Districts—and then in 1899 the Metropolitan boroughs were established in London. Apart from the creation of the Greater London Council, which became fully operational in 1965, the system that had been created in the last decades of the nineteenth century remained in being until an entirely new system came into operation in England and Wales on 1 April 1974, following the Local Government Act of 1972. Notwithstanding the long endurance of the system created in the late nineteenth century, the pattern then established was criticised almost from the time of its inception (B. Smith, 1965), but the critics went largely unheeded until more recent decades.

As Table 5.1 shows, the reform implemented in 1974 involved a drastic reduction in the number of local authorities in England and Wales. In the

TABLE 5.1. *The number of authorities in England and Wales 1888-1974*

Year	County Councils	County Boroughs	Municipal Boroughs	Urban Districts	Rural Districts	London Metropolitan Boroughs and the City of London	Total	Parishes
1888	61	61	—	—	—	—	—	—
1901	62	67	249	805	664	29	1876	14,900
1911	62	75	250	812	657	29	1885	14,614
1921	62	82	274	798	663	29	1908	14,483
1931	62	83	285	780	645	29	1884	14,209
1945	62	83	309	572	476	29	1531	11,100
1951	62	83	309	572	477	29	1532	11,175
1961	62	83	317	564	474	29	1529	10,890
1971	58	83	259	522	468	33	1423	—
1974	53	←————— 369 —————→				33	455	—

Sources: J. Stanyer, 1967, p. 106; Department of the Environment and Welsh Office, 1971; L.G.B.C., 1972; *Local Government Act 1972,* H.M.S.O.
N.B. The Greater London Council became fully established in 1965.

years preceding this reform, generally accepted ideas on local government had crystallised on the idea that there were too many authorities that were too small to be effective. There had also been related developments of some import for local government. In the following paragraphs, some of these converging trains of thought are examined in turn: the order in which they are treated carries no implications regarding either the chronology of events or the relative importance of the contributory factors.

Perhaps the first point to note is the practical experience gained in trying to make the system created in the nineteenth century work. One of the major premises of the nineteenth-century reforms was that urban and rural areas should be kept separate, and this separation

> came to be seen as local government's major weakness. . . . it became more and more difficult to keep the boundaries of urban authorities in line with the physical edge of a town. The growth of suburbs made boundary extensions logically necessary, but county councils became increasingly unhappy at losing territory and resources to county boroughs, as did rural districts to boroughs and urban districts. Proposals for boundary extensions to county boroughs were therefore almost always strongly contested by counties and districts. Governments were reluctant to seek a radical solution to this problem, and local-authority boundaries in many areas became more and more obviously out of date. A cold war between authorities (particularly between counties and county boroughs) continued to develop until it could be checked only by the creation of a new structure of local government. (Lord Redcliffe-Maud and B. Wood, 1974, p. 3).

Quite apart from the "cold war" situation, the multiplicity of local authorities created very real problems of coordination and cooperation even when goodwill prevailed. Some years ago, for example, it was reported that inspection of the county development plans revealed that collectively the amount of *new* shopping space intended to be provided exceeded the aggregate existing floor area: development plans had to be adjusted. Underlying practical problems of this kind was the fact of increasing spatial interdependence, such that a town or rural area simply could not be administered as if it were an isolated nation-state beholden to no one.

One manifestation of this interdependence became less and less easy to shrug off. The share of the national income spent by the government was rising during the nineteenth century and continued its upward course in the twentieth (A. T. Peacock and J. Wiseman, 1967). Local government shares with central government responsibility for this trend. At least as significant, however, has been the shift in sources of income for local authorities. Locally levied rates were becoming less and less able to support local expenditure, with the result that, in one way or another, subventions from the Exchequer have increased in absolute and relative importance. So far has this process gone that at the General Election in October 1974 the Conservative Party proposed the abolition of all rate levies, at least for householders, thereby going even further than the Labour administration, which had previously put in hand a thorough review of the situation. This shift in the source of funds for local government carries an obvious implication: the nation at large has a proper and *increasing* interest in the efficiency with which resources are being used and the factors that might govern variations in efficiency.

Parliament has its own machinery for checking how well public funds are spent, in the form of Expenditure Committees of the House of Commons. Though there has not recently been such a Committee on local government, the same kind of question has attracted the attention of academics, notably B. Davies (1968). Though less conclusive than one would wish, his attempts to measure the level of "need" and the extent to which it was being met for various forms of social service reflect the combination of social compassion and economic rationality that has become increasingly prevalent. Another study, less strictly economic in outlook but nevertheless concerned with variations in efficiency, is J. Packman's (1968) analysis of children in care (of local authorities and charitable organisations); her work was taken further by Davies and others (1972) in a more rigorous statistical examination.

Enquiries of this kind lead naturally to the question: if local authorities share certain characteristics (shall we say of costs of providing a given service such as education) do they also share characteristics that could be regarded as *causing* the observed phenomenon? Various approaches to this question might be adopted, including that used by C. A. Moser and W. Scott in their study *British Towns* (1961), though this particular study was essentially classificatory in character. Much more important in the present context has been the interest shown by numerous workers in the effects of scale, or city size, on unit costs.

One of the pioneering studies concerned with the effect of size upon the performance of local authorities in providing services was published by K. S. Lomax in 1943. His data, relating to the period 1930-1/1936-7, were for rate fund expenditures on specified services and in aggregate, in the 83 county boroughs of England and Wales. The average total expenditure per person was at a minimum (£7.91) for county boroughs in the population range 100-150,000; for boroughs of 75,000 and less, the figure was £8.16 and at 300,000 and over £9.84. After carefully examining the evidence available, Lomax concluded that these differences genuinely reflected variations in efficiency and not quality of service provided. Other workers have disagreed with Lomax's findings. In the European context, several studies indicate that the net social cost curve is much flatter than is suggested by the data Lomax used, so that urban centres as small as 10,000 or 20,000 inhabitants may be as "efficient" as much larger ones: the net conclusion arrived at by P. B. M. James *et al.* (1968, p. 95) was that "the average net social cost curve is fairly flat over a considerable range. . . . We suggest that this would be between populations of about 30,000 and 250,000". Under Australian conditions, it appears that private firms gain an advantage by locating in cities with populations between 200,000 and one million, but social disadvantages begin to be manifest above about 500,000 (G. M. Neutze, 1965). On the other hand, W. Alonso (1971) concluded that, at least for the United States, the economies of urban scale are not exhausted even when an urban agglomeration reaches New York's 9 million residents.

Sceptics who questioned whether urban scale economies could usefully be measured (H. W. Richardson, 1973) were not able to stem the growing conviction that, however the arithmetic might be done, too many local authorities in England were too small to be economically efficient (see Table 5.2). Consequently, some degree of amalgamation came to be seen as absolutely essential, a matter with which no one would disagree. "Perhaps

TABLE 5.2. *Size distribution of authorities in non-metropolitan counties of England*

Population range, 1971	Number of authorities	
	Pre-1974 reform	Post-1974 reform
under 20,000	526	0
20,000- 40,000	240	14
40,000- 65,000	107	52
65,000- 75,000	28	45
75,000-100,000	21	104
100,000-120,000	6	40
over 120,000	21	41
	949	296

Source: L.G.B.C. 1972.

the most frequently voiced criticism of the present structure is that many local authorities, whether county, county borough or county district councils, are too small in terms of area, population and resources" (Royal Commission, 1969, vol. 1, p. 28). Not surprisingly, therefore, the Royal Commission, charged with examining the structure of local government, sought evidence regarding the main duties. The evidence they were able to obtain was largely the collation of informed opinions and did not amount to a rigorous scientific analysis. The best judgment they were able to make was that "the minimum size for all main services is, desirably, a population of some 250,000" (Royal Commission, 1969, vol. 1, p. 28).

Towards a solution

By the mid-1960s, there was virtual unanimity that the number of local authorities must be substantially reduced. The main points at issue had become:

1. How great should the reduction be?
2. On what principle or principles should the new authorities be defined?
3. What powers should be exercised by the new local authorities?
4. Should a single system be applied to the whole country outside London, or should the conurbations be treated differently from the rest of the country?

There is not space in this essay to examine all of these questions and attention will be concentrated on the second. The fundamental point at issue is the following. However great may be the perceived need for reform, it is unlikely that anything will be done unless there is available some rational, or at least plausible, principle that can be called in aid. It is in this context that geographers have been particularly prominent.

For many years, geographers and others have been concerned to devise efficient systems of regional sub-division. In the nineteenth century, this interest focussed on the identification of "natural" regions that would be an appropriate framework within which to synthesise a large mass of information. Early in the present century, C. B. Fawcett (1919) adapted this approach to the practical problem of delimiting *provinces* in England and Wales. The principles that he adopted were, in his own words, as follows:

1. The provincial boundaries should be so chosen as to interfere as little as possible with the ordinary movements and activities of the people.
2. There should be in each province a definite capital, which should be the real focus of its regional life. This implies further that the area and communications of the province should be such that the capital is easily accessible from every part of it.
3. The least of the provinces should contain a population sufficiently numerous to justify self-government.
4. No one province should be so populous as to be able to dominate the federation.
5. The provincial boundaries should be drawn near watersheds rather than across valleys, and very rarely along streams.
6. The grouping of areas must pay regard to local patriotism and to tradition.

The above list amounts to the amalgamation of two functional principles; river basins and the pattern of human organisation. The latter had been foreshadowed by H. G. Wells in 1902 (see Smith, 1965, p. 7) but was not really formalised as a concept until W. Christaller (1933) produced his hierarchy of central places. Even then, only with the publication of R. E. Dickinson's book *City, Region and Regionalism* in 1947 did the city/region as an organisational principle gain widespread recognition in the English-speaking world. Nevertheless, by the time of the 1969 Royal Commission, the ground had been well prepared for the city-region concept to be forcefully advocated by numerous witnesses, including the Ministry of

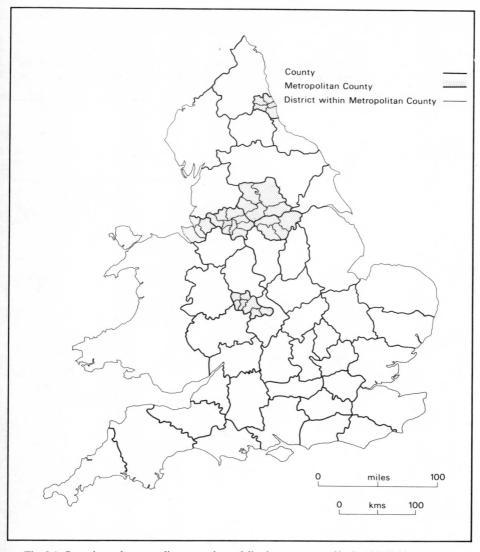

County ——————
Metropolitan County ▓▓▓▓▓
District within Metropolitan County ———

Fig. 5.1. Counties and metropolitan counties and districts as proposed in the 1971 White Paper

Public discussion of these proposals was vigorous. Although the principles for reform adopted by the Government were criticised, attention focused on the details of the proposed county structure. As a result, when in November 1971 the Local Government Bill was published, the map of proposed county boundaries, and of some districts in the metropolitan counties, differed significantly from the one published 9 months previously (Fig. 5.2). Inevitably, the Bill was amended, and in some cases counter-amended, in its passage through Parliament, with the result that the geographical pattern of authorities actually brought into being under the 1972 Local Government Act differed in some important respects from the pattern initially proposed

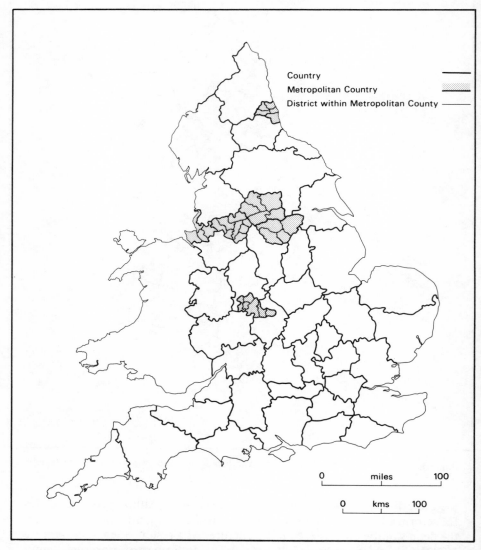

Country
Metropolitan Country
District within Metropolitan County

0   miles   100

0   kms   100

Fig. 5.2. Counties and metropolitan counties and districts as proposed in the 1971 Local Government Bill

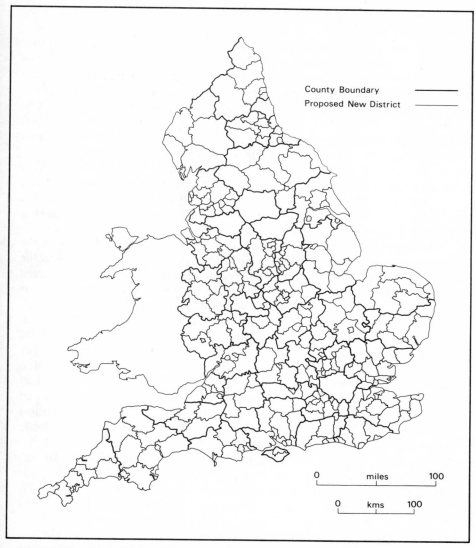

Fig. 5.3. Counties and metropolitan counties and districts as authorised by the 1972 Local Government Act

for Parliament's consideration (Fig. 5.3). The changes made during the passage of the Bill stemmed at least as much from political and emotional considerations as from any regard for disinterested principles of rational organisation. Nevertheless, a workable framework passed into law in December 1972.

Making the 1972 Act work: the Local Government Boundary Commission

A necessary condition for the operation of the 1972 Act, though clearly not a sufficient condition, was the definition of the second tier authorities within the non-metropolitan counties. The Act provided for the establishment of a Local Government Boundary Commission, whose first, but by no means only, task was to prepare proposals for defining the new districts. These proposals were to be laid before the Secretary of State for the Environment, who would then lay an Order in the House of Commons for their implementation, either unmodified or with modifications. Though technically not the decision-makers, the Boundary Commission's proposals were in fact accepted and implemented in their entirety and without modification. Thus, the way in which the Commission went about their task of defining the non-metropolitan districts throws some light on the decision-making processes of government and the role that an academic can play therein.

The timetable for reform imposed constraints on what could or could not be done. The Bill was published in November 1971, with 1 April 1974 as the date for the new authorities to take over. Shadow councils were to be elected in early summer 1973 to provide for an orderly transition. For these elections to be feasible, it was necessary that the new districts (and indeed counties) be defined several months previously, so that electoral lists could be compiled, polling arrangements made and so on. Yet the Bill became an Act, with the full force of law, only in November 1972! With this impossible situation in mind, the Commission was appointed in November 1971 as a Commission *Designate*. Not to put too fine a point on it, the Commission *Designate* had no legal status but had to depend on the willingness of local authorities and others to cooperate in the *expectation* that its activities would in due course be legitimised. This cooperation was in fact forthcoming in a wholly admirable fashion. Between November 1971 and November 1972 the Commission *Designate* completed the task of drawing up proposals for the second-tier districts in the non-metropolitan counties, notwithstanding the fact that the county boundaries were amended during the passage of the Bill. The Secretary of State for the Environment received the first report of the Local Government Boundary Commission for England, proposing a pattern of new districts, within 24 hours of the Commission being legitimised (L.G.B.C., 1972). There was then just time for the requisite 40 days from the laying of the Order to give effect to the proposals to elapse before Parliament rose for the Christmas recess. By the slenderest of margins, the new districts had been defined in time for the 1973 "shadow" elections.

For its work between November 1971 and November 1972, the Commission *Designate* was charged with the following terms of reference:

Population, the county patterns of districts and the identity of towns:
1. The Boundary Commission should recommend a pattern of districts for the non-

metropolitan counties ranging upwards in population from 40,000. Only very exceptionally should a district be proposed with a population under 40,000.

2. Except in sparsely populated areas the aim should be to define districts with current populations generally within the range of about 75,000-100,000. These figures are in no sense absolute limits: some districts will be larger or smaller, according to local circumstances; but regard should be had to the desirability of producing in each county a pattern of districts which are broadly comparable in population and conducive to effective and convenient local government throughout the county as a whole.

3. The identity of large towns should be maintained. The whole designated area of a new town, or the whole of an area defined for town development, should ordinarily fall within one new district.

4. Normally it will be necessary to take only current population levels into account in considering the size of district to be proposed. Account should be taken of a town's engagement in an approved programme of rapid expansion, e.g. under the New Towns Act or Town Development Act, but even in these cases regard must also be had to the population level needed to sustain efficient services in the meantime.

Definition of new districts

5. Wherever reasonably practicable a new district should comprise the whole of one or more existing county boroughs or county districts. Where this is not practicable, the new district should comprise whole parishes or wards. Because of the need to concentrate on the main pattern of the new districts, new boundaries which do not follow the boundary of an existing local government unit or electoral area should be proposed only in special circumstances. Once the new authorities have taken over, the Commission will be invited to carry out a thorough review of proposals for detailed adjustment of boundaries, including those of the counties and metropolitan districts.

General considerations

6. In formulating their recommendations the Commission should weigh all relevant considerations in the light of the general objectives of local government reorganisation as set out in the Government's White Paper, Cmnd 4584. Among other things they should have particular regard to the wishes of the local inhabitants, the pattern of community life, and the effective operation of local government services.

7. The Commission will also wish to take note of the pattern of Parliamentary constituencies in each county.

Consultations

8. The Commission should consider suggestions and proposals put to them by local authorities and other persons and bodies for the pattern of districts in each county, and should then make draft proposals. These should be published as a basis for the fullest practicable consultation with the existing authorities and so that, when formulating their final recommendations, the Commission can also have regard to any further representations and to representations from members of the public.

Timetable

9. The Commission's recommendations should be submitted to the Secretary of State for the Environment in time for them to be debated in Parliament in the autumn of 1972 and for the boundaries of the new districts to be established by order before the end of that year.

The Commission therefore invited proposals for the districting of the non-metropolitan counties, considered the various and at time conflicting suggestions for each county, formulated draft proposals which were published in April 1972 (L.G.B.C. *Designate*, 1972), received representations thereon, conducted some local enquiries on especially difficult cases and reached conclusions, all within 12 months. Altogether, representations were received from most of the then existing local authorities (nearly 1000 in total) and from 2500 organisations and members of the public. Members of the Commission *Designate,* as distinct from the staff of the Secretariat, did all this on a part-time basis, meeting regularly once every week.

It will be immediately clear that a timetable of this kind, based on the maximum feasible participation of the public and the existing local authorities, precluded an approach based on careful independent research (other than on special cases) and forced the Commission *Designate* to act more in the role of arbiter—hopefully, a wise arbiter—between conflicting proposals. This is the first, and perhaps crucial, point to be made.

Several other points deserve notice. That the second-tier authorities should be substantially larger than those that then existed was made clear in the guidelines quoted above, the preferred population being 75-100,000 persons. That this preferred population range is lower than many of the figures previously cited need occasion no surprise, as the districts are not all-purpose (or "main function") authorities. Perhaps equally significant were the two following requirements. First, *within* each county, the pattern of districts should be "broadly comparable in population", so that they should have as nearly as possible the same degree of influence in the county. Second, the new districts should be formed from "the whole of one or more existing county boroughs or county districts". If this were impracticable, then the smallest unit of sub-division was to be the parish or ward. This provision might seem odd. However, using existing authorities as the building blocks meant that complicated legal issues regarding the disposition of assets could be avoided, as well as the administrative problems of allocating existing staff to the two or more successor authorities among which an existing district might be split. The provision that, where a district must be split, the parishes or wards would be the smallest units served to reduce, but not eliminate, the problems of organising the elections for the new districts. To take the liberty of putting numerous new boundaries through existing districts, as did Senior in his Memorandum of Dissent to the 1969 Royal Commission, would have entailed a substantially longer period of transition and/or a good deal of otherwise avoidable confusion.

Overall, therefore, the Commission *Designate* had to work within the following constraints, plus others specified in the guidelines:

1. The county boundaries were inviolate.

2. The basic building-blocks were to be whole existing districts.

3. By clear implication, though not explicitly, the new districts must have no detached parts.

4. Within any one county, the new districts were to be as nearly as possible equal in population.

5. The preferred population range was to be 75-100,000; districts should only have less than 40,000 in very exceptional circumstances.

In preparing the draft proposals, the Commission *Designate* not only acted as an adjudicator on the one or more district schemes submitted for each county but also took the initiative on several occasions by suggesting in the draft proposals ideas different from any that had been received. When the draft proposals were reviewed in the light of the representations received and, in relevant cases, the evidence elicited by local enquiries, some substantial changes were made prior to making the final recommendations. And then, at the end of the day, there was the tangible achievement of an entirely new map of local authorities; at the district level, each segment of boundary represents a "decision", positively in its favour and negatively against one or more other possibilities. Of course, given the constraints under which the boundaries were drawn, a decision regarding one segment of boundary had repercussive effects throughout the whole or part of the county in question. In practice, therefore, it was common for there to be only one or two basic patterns that could be accepted for each county; in most of the remaining counties, the real problem lay in choosing between several possibilities for only one part of the county.

In sum, therefore, the Commission *Designate* did indeed take a very large number of decisions, with a direct effect upon large numbers of people. On the other hand, these decisions cannot be said to have affected the fundamental nature of the reform that was implemented, since they were concerned with details and not with the broad principles. In terms of the surf-riding analogy, the ground-swell was represented by the Bill (which became the 1972 Act) and the guidelines given to the Commission *Designate*, and the function of the Commission was to choose which particular waves to mount from among the large number that presented themselves.

The general thrust of this essay will by now be clear. For the year from November 1971, the Boundary Commission *Designate* was exceedingly busy taking very large numbers of "decisions" that were in fact implemented. At the end of this period, there was a very real sense of achievement and the resulting pattern of new districts formed an essential part of the edifice of reformed local government. Yet all of the decisions were taken in highly constrained circumstances and in many cases the nature of these constraints meant that the effective range of choice was limited. At the end of the day, it is also manifestly true that decisions taken by the Commission *Designate* did not affect the broad principles on which the reform was based but merely served to interpret them in the context of each county. In this respect, the activities of the Commission *Designate* were probably of much less real significance than the build-up of public consensus about certain features requisite in a reformed system.

Some reflections

The author's own personal experience has not taken him far into the corridors of Whitehall. Clearly, the nearer a person is to the ear of Ministers and of the Prime Minister himself, the greater is his power to contribute *directly* to decisions of importance. However, any decision must be taken in the context of prior events and also with a view to the degree of support it will receive. For those of us who are only on the edge of the Whitehall maze, or yet further from the seat of government, there is an indispensable role to play in helping to create the groundswell of opinion. It is that groundswell which constrains government, directing its attentions one way rather than another, affecting the range of effective choice available.

We may therefore ask ourselves the following question. How can a university don most effectively alter the nature of the groundswell? By being an active "decision-maker" himself, or by other means? Or perhaps by some combination of the two? Furthermore, it is obvious that innumerable academics have had a major impact on the reform of local government without being "decision-makers" in this context. From the abstract thinking of Christaller, through the empirical work of many geographers, economists and others, to the apostolic work of publicists, all have contributed; and without the one, the work of the others might have been in vain.

Thus, it is idle to dream of the day when geographers, or the practitioners of any other discipline for that matter, sit on the throne of "power", making "decisions" on behalf of their fellow men. Even supposing that the geographer knows best, others in government and the populace at large must be persuaded of this fact. More important, though, however good the solution that is offered—whether for reform of local government or the planning of a city—the academic is contributing both expertise and opinion to what is essentially a political process. Therefore, to take the view expressed by Blowers (1974), that geographers now need the power to implement policies they have devised, is to imply the end of consultative democracy and the ushering in of dictatorship by technocrats. The author is content with a much less ambitious view of what academics can hope to achieve, being of the opinion that most fundamental reforms take a long time to mature. In most cases, he who begot the idea is not the same person as gains the passing glory of implementation.

REFERENCES

Alonso, W. (1971) "The economics of urban size", *Papers,* Regional Science Association, **26,** 67-83.
Blowers, A. T. (1974) "Relevance, research and the political process", *Area,* **6,** 32-6.

Christaller, W. (1933) *Central Places in Southern Germany,* first published in German and translated into English by C. W. Baskin, 1966, Prentice-Hall, Englewood Cliffs.

Cohn-Bendit, D. and G. Cohn-Bendit (1968) *Obsolete Communism. The Left-wing Alternative,* Deutsch, London.

Davies, B. (1968) *Social Needs and Resources in Local Services,* Michael Joseph, London.

Davies, B., A. Barton and I. McMillan (1972) *Variations in Children's Services among British Urban Authorities. A Causal analysis,* Occasional Papers on Social Administration, Bell, London.

Department of the Environment and Welsh Office (1971) *Rates and Rateable Values in England and Wales 1971-72,* H.M.S.O., London.

Dickinson, R. E. (1947) *City, Region and Regionalism: a Geographical Contribution to Human Ecology,* Kegan Paul, London.

Fawcett, C. B. (1919) *Provinces of England. A Study of Some Geographical Aspects of Devolution,* revised edition 1960, Hutchinson, London.

James, P. B. M. *et al.* (1968) *Regional Policy in EFTA. An Examination of the Centre Idea,* Oliver and Boyd, Edinburgh and London.

Lipman, V. D. (1949) *Local Government Areas, 1834-1945,* Blackwell, Oxford.

Local Government Boundary Commission for England (1972) *Report No. 1,* Cmnd. 5148, H.M.S.O., London.

Local Government Boundary Commission for England *Designate* (1972) *Memorandum on Draft Proposals for New Districts in the English non-Metropolitan Counties Proposed in the Local Government Bill,* H.M.S.O., London.

Lomax, K. S. (1943) "The relationship between expenditure per head and size of population of county boroughs in England and Wales", *Journal of the Royal Statistical Society,* **106,** 51-9.

Moser, C. A. and W. Scott (1961) *British Towns: a Statistical Study of Their Social and Economic Differences,* Oliver and Boyd, Edinburgh and London.

Neutze, G. M. (1965). *Economic Policy and the Size of Cities,* Australian National University Press, Canberra.

Packman, J. (1968) *Child Care: needs and numbers,* Allen and Unwin, London.

Peacock, A. T. and J. Wiseman (1967) *The Growth of Public Expenditure in the United Kingdom,* revised edition, Allen and Unwin, London.

Redcliffe-Maud, Lord and B. Wood (1974) *English Local Government Reformed,* O.U.P., Oxford.

Richardson, H. W. (1973) *The Economics of Urban Size,* Saxon House, Farnborough.

Royal Commission on Local Government in England 1966-1969, (1969) *Report,* Cmnd. 4040, H.M.S.O., London.

Secretary of State for the Environment (1971) *Local Government in England. Government proposals for reorganisation,* Cmnd. 4584, H.M.S.O., London.

Secretary of State for Local Government and Regional Planning (1970) *Reform of Local Government in England,* Cmnd. 4276, H.M.S.O., London.

Smith, B. (1965) *Regionalism in England,* vol. 2, *Its Nature and Purpose 1905-1965,* Acton Society Trust, London.

Stanyer, J. (1967) *County Government in England and Wales,* Routledge and Keegan Paul, London.

CHAPTER 6

THE GEOGRAPHER AND POLICY-MAKING IN MARGINAL RURAL AREAS: THE NORTHERN PENNINES RURAL DEVELOPMENT BOARD

J. W. HOUSE
University of Oxford

PLANNING AND THE RURAL PROBLEM

In Western urban and industrial societies there has usually been scant and belated attention to rural problems, in spite of the fact that the polarisation of life to the cities has had serious, persistent and growing adverse effects upon the remoter and poorer areas of the countryside (J. Ashton and W. H. Long, 1972). The problems of such rural margins concern both land and people (J. W. House, 1966, 1970). In the national context it is issues relating to the most effective use, or coordination of uses, of abundant though low-grade land that predominate. Locally, the well-being of the rural community is the paramount consideration, in terms of income, employment opportunity, social provision and general quality of life. In national terms the need for food and timber from the hills is matched, even more and more dominated, by increasing demands by urban man for access to, and recreational use of, rural resources. More parochially, these issues are interpreted in their impact upon farm and forest households or the small central places in the countryside. This chapter is concerned with one attempted solution to these problems at the regional and local scales, the short-lived Rural Development Boards, and with the contribution of a geographer to that solution.

The planning and management of rural resources in Great Britain has traditionally been weakly-formulated, inadequately coordinated and lacking in overall coherence and concern for common goals (M. C. Whitby *et al.*, 1974). A major reason for this lies in the marked division of views as to the seriousness of rural problems and the extent to which public intervention is either possible, or even desirable. One line of argument runs that the decline in rural population is an inevitable market trend, the product both of attraction to the towns and of push factors, the poorer social and economic

86

conditions of the countryside. Furthermore, it is seen as but the latest manifestation of a trend that began a century ago and that could be stabilised or reversed only at an unacceptably high national cost. Indeed, the more extreme views assert that such rural run-down may even be desirable, locally as well as in the national interest. The man-land ratio is said to have been improved in many areas as a result and, in any case, only in the towns can adequate living standards, earnings and variety of jobs be assured. By this thinking, even if rural life could be seen to have unique qualities, the nation could not afford to subsidise them. It is further reasoned that it is urban demands upon the countryside that will control its future, with the farmer acting as the custodian or caretaker of a national landscape estate. Recreational use will require ever more rural space and farming will be permitted only the pattern and structure that its sales can justify.

The counter-argument sees positive merit in sustaining a rural way of life within an urban industrial society, and underlines that countryside resources are presently in a critically vulnerable state and may degenerate rapidly if not carefully planned and managed. The strategic argument for sustaining an adequate food supply from the hills is today buttressed by the need to conserve scarce foreign exchange and use home resources of land and labour to the full. In practice, given the conflicting priorities and political constraints of the democratic process, a middle course of limited sectoral rather than deliberately spatial public intervention has usually been followed. The outcome has not infrequently been piecemeal and uncoordinated, and in total has proved consistently insufficient to arrest or to stabilise continuing decline, much less to contribute to creative revitalisation. As a result there has been a general but slow deterioration in economic and social conditions in most remote rural areas, with the emergence of acute conditions in certain localities, valleys or sub-regions.

RURAL PLANNING AND DEVELOPMENT ORGANISATIONS: CONTEXT FOR THE RURAL DEVELOPMENT BOARD

There is no single organisation with the remit and the powers to implement comprehensive rural planning. On the contrary there is such a multiplicity of bodies with sectoral or spatial responsibilities as to make coordination and harmonisation a major issue, to say nothing of wasteful duplication and overlap at times.

The direct responsibility for the rural economic base is the concern of the Ministry of Agriculture, Fisheries and Food and the Department of Agriculture and Fisheries for Scotland, in respect of land structure and management, pricing and support policies for farm products (prior to British entry into the European Economic Community). The Forestry Commission has a specific remit concerned with developing and managing a national reserve of mainly softwood timber and has increasing regard for the recreational implications of forest land (Forestry Commission, 1972). Though the Ministry of Agriculture has regional representation, it is still right to think of its interventions as primarily sectoral rather than overtly spatial and it is not concerned directly with regional or sub-regional strategies for the management of rural resources. Under the 1967 Agriculture Act, however, the setting up of Rural Development Boards (RDBs) was envisaged. This chapter is concerned with a geographical contribution to the work of the only Rural Development Board to function operationally, that for the Northern Pennines (1969-71). The Board proposed for Mid-Wales never came into being.

In physical planning the responsibility for rural areas falls to the county (and, in Scotland, regional) authorities, but there seems to be general agreement among planners that rural planning had scarcely begun seriously before the mid-1960s (A. S. Travis, 1972), that it tended to be town-planning "writ small", and that development decisions in rural areas have usually been the product of land ownership rather than of statutory planning, since planning has had so few powers over either agriculture or forestry. Economic planning for rural areas has been the responsibility of Economic Planning Councils (EPCs), and the first-stage strategy documents for each region have usually had a sectoral statement on rural conditions, priorities, and prospects. The Northern Economic Planning Council (1969) had a rural spatial component, in part a geographical contribution, in its second-stage settlement strategy.

The National Parks Commission, later (1968) the Countryside Commission, and the Countryside Commission for Scotland (1967) have been concerned with "the provision and improvement of facilities for general enjoyment, beauty and amenity, and access for the public". The Development Commission, on the other hand, was established as far back as 1909 to administer the government-financed Development Fund for the economic and social benefit of rural areas. Since 1960 the Commission has concentrated on reducing rural depopulation and has both financed small advance factories in rural parts of the Development (Assisted) Areas, and also defined "trigger areas' in Mid-Wales and the Eastern Scottish Borders in which coordinated economic and social aid has been provided for the first time. Aid was also granted to Rural Community Councils, Councils of Social Service and Women's Institutes, to strengthen social life in rural areas.

Among the multiplicity of other statutory bodies with rural responsibilities, but often with different spatial jurisdictions, must be included the infra-structural Ministries such as the Department of Health and Social Security, and the Department of Employment, the Department of the Environment and the Scottish Development Department (both of which have an overall strategic view of planning), the nationalised industries concerned with rail transport and the provision of electricity and the Regional Water Authorities and Tourist Boards. It is little wonder that, with this lack of clear rural goals and given the extremely varied terms of reference of so many organisations, the state of the more remote rural areas did not prosper, in spite of many pockets of piecemeal public investment.

The Development Board Concept

The prototype Development Board was that for the Scottish Highlands and Islands (1965), with a statutory area (Fig. 6.1) and powers to "initiate, promote and assist economic and social enterprises". Many disseminated investments have been made in fisheries, tourism, manufacturing or land development, but there have also been large-scale proposals to create major coastal growth areas. In rural planning, however, the Highlands and Islands Development Board had to work within the framework of statutory local authorities, and it had fewer direct powers concerned with the economic base activities of farming and forestry than the Rural Development Boards authorised under the Agriculture Act 1967, though that Act did confer on the Secretary of State for Scotland power to designate all or part of the Highland Board's area as a Rural Development Board.

THE NORTHERN PENNINES RURAL DEVELOPMENT BOARD (NPRDB), 1969-71

Objectives and Powers

Though the principle was first envisaged in the White Paper of 1965 the legislation to set up Rural Development Boards (RDBs) was enacted in the Agriculture Act 1967. The concept of these boards differed from that of the Highlands and Islands Development Board in that, for the first time, priority was to be given to reinforcing and making coherent public intervention and support at the level of the farm or forest holding. Under preceding Agriculture Acts such support had been related primarily to stimulating or subsidising farm production, improving the quality of the land, and aiding approved investment projects on individual farms. Additionally, the Payment to Outgoers Scheme had made a very limited but useful contribution to the overriding need for restructuring farms. In forestry the Forestry Commission (which had been founded in 1919) had become a major entrepreneur in post-war years, directly in major schemes of afforestation in upland Britain (House, 1956), and indirectly in the aid given to estate owners for private plantings under the Dedication of Woodlands Scheme.

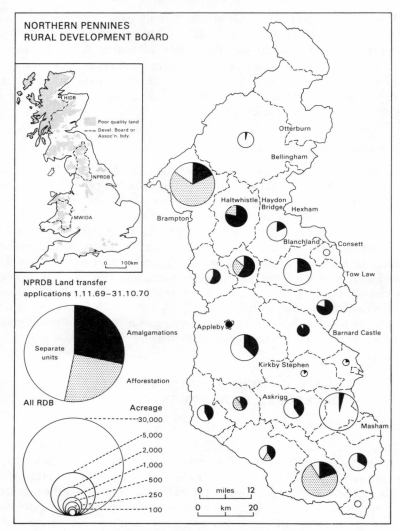

Fig. 6.1. Northern Pennines Rural Development Board

The RDB proposals were intended to reinforce such existing powers, which had hitherto applied to all farms and forest holdings throughout the land, by directing attention to key rural problem areas in the hill country, and by widening the range and increasing the intensity of direct public involvement under the 1967 Agriculture Act. The overall purpose of the NPRDB was defined as dealing with the special problems and special needs of a two million acre (800,000 ha) tract of the Northern Pennines, stretching from the Cheviot Hills southwards through the Border Fells, the Alston Block and the Yorkshire Dales to Ilkley Moor (Fig. 6.1). To achieve this purpose there should be the promotion of balance between the whole potential of the land and the number of human beings who depend upon it for a livelihood, surely an essentially geographical task. This potential came, as it had traditionally long done, from the extensive pastoral economy, mainly for sheep but also for hill cattle, supplemented by commercial forestry in some areas, and here and there by sporadic income derived from tourism.

Basically four inter-related problems were posed in formulating a management strategy for the NPRDB area. First and foremost was the difficult matter of fostering the creation, by farm re-structuring and amalgamations, of viable commercial farm units in the hills. Solutions to this central problem had hitherto proved to be very elusive, and the 1967 Agriculture Act for the first time introduced the highly-controversial powers of land acquisition to facilitate the process of change. Secondly, and in the event almost equally controversially, the working out and initiation of a satisfactory set of balances between farming, forestry and amenity were to be explored. This, too, was a pressing and highly-charged issue in respect of which existing statutory powers of physical planning had proved, and still prove, to be altogether inadequate.

Thirdly, and this was a wide-ranging objective which almost defied expression in a set of explicit goals, the interests of the countryman were to be reconciled with those of the townsman, given the latter's wish for access for the enjoyment of the countryside. The NPRDB had only limited powers to further this objective, through a micro-strategy of investment in provision for tourists such as parking space, and supplementation of existing provisions for amenity. Fourthly, the social provision and public services of the Northern Pennines were to be conserved and, at a later stage, developed in a harmonious way. Given the small scale of potential investment by the NPRDB, this objective could be promoted only by supplementing, in a small but often very significant way, the efforts by other planning bodies, for example, in respect of public transport subsidies, by the improvement of rural roads or the widening and strengthening of bridges to carry milk-tankers.

Taken together, the objectives for the NPRDB were as comprehensive a set of rural development aims as had yet been formulated. Translation of these objectives into an operational programme, for the short- as well as the longer-term, faced formidable difficulties. The Board consisted of a chairman and eleven members, individually appointed by the Minister of Agriculture; most were farmers or landowners, but there was also a rural technologist and one geographer (J. W. House). The technical staff of the Board comprised land-agents and administrators. The boundaries of the

NPRDB area were defined by 1969 (Fig. 6.1), after some litigation, and the Board had to become fully operational only a few months later.

At the outset there was thus a two-fold need, first to formulate an inter-related framework of decision-taking to implement the Board's objectives in a coherent and progressive manner; secondly, as from the operational date, to adjudicate, in an objective way within the provisions of the 1967 Act, upon every application to transfer a farm or plant a unit of more than 10 acres (4 ha) of trees. At the same time the more general rural social purposes of the Board's activities had to be codified in such a manner that the Treasury would sanction the objective and the appropriate expenditure of public money. In this sense both a comprehensive and an individual decision-taking model had to be designed and implemented concurrently. Not only had the multiple objectives of the Board to be harmonised as well as promoted, they had also to be related to the programmes of countless other organisations with statutory responsibilities, or even of those merely interested in or jealously guarding some aspects of the countryside.

No existing resource-allocation models (K. G. Willis, 1973) were directly relevant to this intensely practical task, nor could they have been deployed in the limited time available; above all, there was no initial way of incorporating a discriminatory spatial variable to take account of the geographical diversity of the Board's area and the undoubted range of severity in the mix of rural problems in particular dales or sub-districts. Areal differentiation was to be defined later, and the important spatial variations over the Northern Pennines were increasingly taken into account, thereby introducing some flexibility into the operational programme. Both the rates of change to be accommodated and the extent to which any discriminatory stimulus should be applied in particular areas varied; furthermore, the intricate spatial variety in rural problems set boundary conditions to the implementation of the broad objectives in specific localities and sub-regions.

From a geographical point of view the excellent series of maps prepared by the Ministry of Agriculture for the Board's area, on a scale of 1:250,000, provided the basis for a sub-regionalisation of composite rural problems and a spatial framework for the testing of the impact and the multiplier effects of individual decisions taken. Among other topics, these maps showed farm size and labour intensity (measured in Standard Man Days, SMDs, of annual labour inputs); population trends, including the all-important criteria of volume, rates and time-incidence of rural out-migration; forest cover; and rural social provision and transport facilities. A map of administrative units of local government in the Board's area immediately focussed attention on its fragmentation into parts of seven counties, three economic planning regions, and a multiplicity of second-tier (rural district) and third-tier (parish) units. Few of the larger units were wholly within the NPRDB designated area. When the different mixes of rural policies pursued by different authorities were added to the territorial balkanisation of the Northern Pennines, one of the major liaison problems facing the NPRDB was dramatically highlighted.

The operational programme

In essence the Board had to respond to the initiative of farm- or forest-based entrepreneurs wishing to change the structure of land-holdings or, in the case of forestry, significantly to extend the acreage under trees. Likewise in investment for the provision of tourist facilities, amenity, or infrastructure the Board had limited powers to initiate action, at least in the earlier phases of its life. Had time permitted there would later have been implemented a more coherent strategy for the stimulus and coordination of investment, including both publicity and direct and personal encouragement by the Board's agents. Certainly throughout most of its short life the Board perforce had to play a passive rôle, once the range of opportunities for aid had been established and fully publicised to all likely beneficiaries.

The Board established four operational groups, each concerned with policy, preliminary decisions and monitoring of change, viz.: land transfer, restructuring and amalgamations; the farming-forestry balance; tourism and amenity; and administration. The work of the first three groups will now be reviewed.

Land transfer and farm amalgamations

At the heart of the rural problem in the more remote or poorer marginal hill country lay the unsatisfactory size and structure of farm-holdings, and the sheer unprofitability of farming in the uplands in the early 1970s. Even allowing for the desirability of the life-style which some hill-farmers would add to the benefit side of the cost-benefit equation, or the greater probability that many were prisoners of a low living standard, it was soon abundantly clear that on many family farms the net income was little greater than the sum of the subsidies. Moreover, the mosaic of farm sizes and fluctuating profitability varied almost from valley to valley in the Northern Pennines, and in some localities very severe deprivation was being experienced.

With certain exceptions concerning family transfers, inheritance or mortgage foreclosures, the Board had powers to refuse consent to the transfer of land (Section 49 of the 1967 Agriculture Act), if the outcome would result in or perpetuate an uneconomic holding. Furthermore, if the Board were to refuse consent for transfer it might be required to purchase the land and hold it in a "land bank" against eventual restructuring. With virtually no exceptions these powers to refuse consent were witheld and the patient and slow work of restructuring farm units was carried on voluntarily, with the Board acting as a positive catalyst for change, through the widespread and appreciated individual advice tendered by its land-agents.

In principle, the rules for the game of restructuring farms into units of viable commercial size seemed simple (Section 48). To the Ministry of Agriculture a yardstick of 600 SMDs characterised a commercial farm unit, involving notionally family labour and one hired man; 275 SMDs was a family farm, and anything less than that level of labour inputs was an economically unviable farm. The theoretical objective was thus to move towards the creation of units of at least 600 SMDs at the earliest opportunity, but this foundered on the twin difficulties of complex existing geographical realities and the realisation that even the 600-SMD unit itself was often not viable, and was indeed increasingly threatened by the shortage and expensive nature of hired labour in the hills (J. R. Raeburn, 1972).

Surveys showed that only one-third of the 6246 farms in the Board's area were of 600 SMDs or above, a further third were between 275 and 599 SMDs, whilst the remaining third were clearly non-viable, at least by the economic criterion of labour inputs. But they did exist and many had done so for some considerable time. Moreover, there was a complex intermingling of units of different size in any one valley and only limited units of land were transferred in any one year and these in an irregular and piecemeal fashion. Restructuring would thus be a slow process in any event and a longer-term programme had to be formulated from the case law of countless individual decisions en route. This has been the experience also of the only comparable organisations, the SAFER in France (Sociétés d'Aménagement Foncier et d'Établissement Rural). More intricate amalgamation schemes for lands around a particular settlement, similar to the French policies of "remembrement", were possible under Section 51, with the consent of a sufficient number of farmers, but time did not allow for this more creative work by the Board. Fragmentation nevertheless remains as an intractable problem around some villages in the Pennine limestone dales.

The Board recognised early that the inter-relationships between the farmer, the local economy and the community were complex, and that unilateral action taken on farmland alone should not ignore these wider implications for society. In the event the Board decided to move to the 275 SMD unit as a first priority, without prejudice to a longer-term objective of 600 SMD units when economic conditions improved. Such relaxation of a primary objective was intended to safeguard even the intricate patterns of part-time farmers, augmenting their incomes outside agriculture, where these could be seen to be an integral part of the pattern of rural society. It also soon became clear that types of farm production and efficiency in management were variables causing significant differences between holdings which might be classified as uniform by the single factor of labour inputs.

During the Board's lifetime 37,000 acres (14,970 ha) of farmland were transferred, or just under 2 per cent of the total North Pennine area, and of this about one-third was for farm amalgamations (Fig. 6.1). The pastoral economy of the hills was decidedly unstable at this time: gross farming incomes were low and usually insufficient to provide a capital surplus for the improvement of the holding; borrowed capital was uniquely expensive and farm assets often proved insufficient security for loans; the benefits of economies of scale in farming were very uncertain; and the demand from the lowlands for store lambs and draft ewes was declining. For these and other reasons the Board had to adopt a primarily defensive strategy in the short-term, to counter a deteriorating economic and social situation on farmsteads and forest holdings. No action was taken which might have precipitated further rural depopulation, the conservation of smaller farm units was seen as an essential first step for many on to the "farming ladder", and the integral part of the part-time farmer in the rural community was respected. Within these voluntarily imposed constraints, the Board promoted sensible farm restructuring. In practice, this amounted to the same as any vendor's aim, which was to get the best price from the market. There was no inherent conflict and the Board could and frequently did influence helpfully the way in which farms were presented for sale.

Farming-forestry balance

Under Section 52 of the 1967 Act the Board had powers to license or to refuse authority for the planting of trees in units of more than ten acres (4 ha) in any one year. To use these powers in the furtherance of a "proper" balance between farming and forestry in the Northern Pennines, with the interests of the local people primarily in mind but with least disturbance to the views of the many other interested parties, proved to be both difficult and increasingly controversial. Because the use of land for agriculture or forestry had not been regarded as "development" under the Town and County Planning Act of 1947 statutory planning authorities had never been able to control, even scarcely to influence, one of the major rural land-use changes in the post-war period, that of increasing afforestation. This is not to say that planning bodies did not hold strong views on amenity aspects of afforestation, but they were largely powerless to intervene. The most that had been accomplished were the so-called Voluntary Agreements, as in Northumberland, to limit afforestation in certain areas of high landscape quality.

Some 10 per cent of the Board's area was under forest, including the massive state plantations of conifers in the Border Forest Park (Kielder, Wark). Elsewhere forestry was very patchy, but in some areas, notably the

Yorkshire Dales National Park, afforestation was a very sensitive issue indeed. Most of the Northern Pennines are ecologically suited to commercial timber-growing on marginal land and, during the Board's life, the pressures to purchase farm land for afforestation were both strong and growing. Equitable adjudication between forestry and hill-farming for the use of the same marginal hill country is notoriously difficult. Direct economic comparisons based on bid-rent price between the two uses showed that over much of the Northern Pennines in the early 1970s private forestry interests could out-bid the hill farmers in the ratio of two or three to one, at the point of a proposed sale of farmland. It must, however, be admitted that beneficial provisions under the tax and estate duty introduced an artificial element into the bids to purchase land for afforestation. It will be interesting to see if the constraints introduced by the Finance Act of 1974 will restore competition between farming and forestry to a more equitable level.

Calculations based upon sustained wealth yield per unit area for forestry and for farming produced results which varied according to the assumptions built in, the length of the period considered, and the assessment of the national interest in alternative uses for the marginal hill land. In fact, the calculations appeared at times to show unprofitability, at least in the short-term, on all counts. Calculations of employment in terms of manpower per unit area under sustained yield management, favoured forestry in most parts of Great Britain. In the Scottish Highlands farming employed 26, and forestry 65 men per 10,000 acres; in Wales the figures were respectively 58 and 80 (N.P.R.D.B. staff). In rural management policies with a strongly social orientation, to reduce rural depopulation and stabilise communities, these figures strengthened the case for afforestation, at least when it was done on a sufficiently large scale, though it is only fair to add that there is some dispute nationally about the manpower requirements for forestry (J. N. R. Jeffers, 1966; P. Wardle, 1966; and M. S. Philip, 1966).

Apart from these arguments based upon returns in capital or in revenue from local use of the hills there were powerful external forces which did not enter into any costings and could deprive a farmer of his right to sell land for afforestation without any compensation from public funds. The Board never unreasonably withheld the granting of forestry licences and attempted to give precedence to the rights of local people, whether farmers or foresters. Without the right to sell land for tree-planting, or to plant it themselves, local people ran the risk of injustice in that they were required to forgo development rights without compensation, in the interests of some principle of assumed public environmental conservation often sponsored by those living in remote towns and cities. The case of the small farmer on the Craven lowland who was denied the right to sell his farm for afforestation on the grounds that it contained glacial drumlins of special scientific interests was perhaps the most notorious case of all. The embittered controversy over the sanctioning by the Board of limited proposals to afforest a fairly inconspicuous part of lower Langstrothdale in the Yorkshire Dales National Park emphasised both the conflicts of interest involved and the extent to which town-based pressures could enforce solutions contrary to local interests, without any of the concomitant financial responsibilities being accepted. Settlement of this kind of issue is the more urgent in that those directly affected in rural areas already have for the most part low living standards and limited economic prospects.

Tourism

Apart from a section of the Yorkshire Dales National Park and the country along the Roman Wall, most of the Board's area was upland of second grade landscape quality. Nevertheless, with the saturation of the Lake District in the summer tourist season and through improved access by motorway along the flanks of the uplands, the tourist potential of the Northern Pennines should not be underestimated. It was clear at the outset that without regarding tourism as a panacea of all rural ills it could provide a valuable seasonal supplementation of earnings on those farms or forest holdings whose owners chose to participate. Such a programme could spread the effects of tourism and would not conflict with public aid to rural hotels, which was already available.

Under Section 47 of the 1967 Act the Board was empowered to grant aid in the provision of tourist accommodation, both residential and in caravans, on farm and forest holdings. A detailed policy for assessing individual claims was agreed by the Treasury, but its operation proved to be intricate to administer and monitor. Grant aid of up to 50 per cent of capital outlay was initiated for a wide variety of projects. The sporadic claims which came in response to publicity about such aid could not be fitted into any optimising strategy for supplementing incomes in those localities with the more serious problems. Nevertheless, there developed a clash of policy in respect of caravan sites between the Board, which preferred to support the more impoverished, remote farmers and thus favoured a programme of dispersing aid, and local planning authorities which favoured the grouping of caravans on fewer and larger inconspicuous sites in the lower parts of the dales. Once again, no compensation was available to those who were denied the right to develop and in this instance the view of planning authorities was decisive, since all development proposals had to be submitted for planning approval.

Other aid

The topping-up of public transport subsidies beyond the 50 per cent of revenue generally allowed was a valuable means of preserving bus services in the more remote rural areas. In each case a cost-benefit study, supplemented by a simple form of network analysis for costing the routes, established the priorities and helped to determine the level of support. This procedure was in effect counteracting the adverse effects of the marginal pricing of unremunerative services, with a view to stabilising population and at the same time having a multiplier effect by reducing the cost of overheads to the rural household. Similar action concerned capital supplementation for the maintenance or improvement of certain rural roads, which may have had a low priority in county programmes, but had a high priority in terms of access to and from more remote settlements and farms. Specific instances concerned the enlargement of bridges to take the large milk-tankers which could not otherwise service some of the less accessible farmsteads. Grants for meeting the exceptional costs of installing telephone links to isolated farms provided a further example of support for the most marginal households of the rural community.

AN ASSESSMENT

The Board had a short-lived existence and thus any summing-up on its merits or shortcomings can only be indicative and not conclusive. It is appropriate to look first at its impact on the rural problem as faced by the primary units of the economic base, the farmer and the forester, and then to review the wider context of the Board's achievements within the work of other organisations responsible for the total rural community; at both levels the significance of a geographical perspective will be assessed.

The central problem, of an adequate real income to the farm or forest household in marginal hill country, long pre-dated the Board's establishment and has moreover outlived its existence. Indeed, the differentials in living standards between countrymen and townsmen have increased further, to the detriment of the former. Entry to the European Economic Community is likely, in the short-term at least, to aggravate an already disturbing differential. Though some comfort may be derived from the positive policies of support to depressed marginal agricultural areas under the FEOGA funds (Fonds Européens d'Orientation et de Garantie Agricole), the longer-term implications of the Common Agricultural Policy (CAP) or the Mansholt Plan seem likely to be a worsening rather than an improvement of the lot of the hill-farmer.

Previous research (House, 1956,1965,1966) had shown that problems in the rural margins of the Northern Pennines were endemic and had been developing over a long period. Furthermore, the balance between man and land, the level of living standards, the range of options and the quality of life had all been deteriorating and in many localities had already reached critical thresholds at which the stability of the remaining primary farm-based populations was threatened; for any further reduction in numbers risked setting in train a scarcely controllable downward spiral, which might result in the abandonment of land already being farmed in an increasingly extensive manner. There was a built-in unprofitability in hill-farming for either beef cattle or sheep, scarcely redeemed by price support policies or subsidies. There was no indication that such problems were self-rectifying or that they could be substantially ameliorated with existing policies. The need for the RDB experiment was thus well established.

Criticism of the Board focussed particularly on its controversial powers over land transfer, certain of its decisions in favour of afforestation in sensitive areas and the slow rate of change it was promoting. On land transfer powers it must be said that these were of last rather than first resort and that in practice the Board acted as a valuable catalyst in facilitating restructuring and amalgamation of farms at the point of sale. In any case, it became abundantly clear that the restructuring of farmland must be seen as a long-term development in the prevailing uncertain economic climate and the general low levels of profitability and capital generation in the hill country. To rely upon market forces would be to risk the disintegration of rural life in the poorer, more remote areas and thus indirectly an inefficient management of resources.

The geographical input to this primary problem related to its spatial manifestations and interactions (House, 1972). The Northern Pennines were seen to be spatially differentiated in a complex manner. As policies were formulated and implemented by the Board the spatial dimension was seen to be of recurring and growing importance. Secondly, and equally geographically, the total environmental context of almost every case and issue was clearly significant, offering scope for the study of the inter-relationships between man and milieu. The parameters of the rural problem and both the constraints and opportunities offered through the Board's terms of reference, were incapable of resolution within any single spatial decision-taking model. Furthermore, constraints upon the types of project on which public money might be spent and the lack of powers for the Board to discriminate among worthy applicants, with a view to helping those in the most distressed localities first, were allied with the sporadic manner in which requests for aid came in. There was no sense in which a spatial diffusion model explained the patterning of requests or the flows of information and the subsequent investments.

Undoubtedly, however, the use made of spatial interpretation in the difficult task of bridging the gap between case study and general precept or statutory enactment was an effective application of traditional techniques and perspectives in geography. A full understanding of areal differentiation of the Northern Pennines contributed to more sensitive policy-making and implementation. But clearly the geographer's perspective was but one of several. The Board developed its own research and intelligence section and was moving to support research schemes by academics from sociology, planning, geography and social administration at the time of its dissolution. Furthermore, Board decisions were taken by farmers and landowners who were the great majority on the Board. They brought to the task an immense practical knowledge of the use of land resources and of understanding and furthering the interests of the rural community. Technical decisions on particular cases were the responsibility of experienced land agents and farm surveyors.

The wider issues of rural development

This chapter began by questioning the nature and achievements of British rural planning in managing resources, in the light of regional and national policies. Particular attention was drawn to the ill-coordinated, overlapping nature of the responsibilities of the multifarious organisations concerned with the countryside. The effects of this unsatisfactory state of affairs upon the work of the NPRDB were two-fold: first, it was difficult to put the rôle of the Board into a coherent context of wider rural development and planning, since this was either piecemeal or non-existent; and secondly, there was the risk of constant friction as organisations contended for the determining rôle in issues which were thought to be under their jurisdiction.

The Board was in a somewhat difficult position. Its powers were clearly defined and related to the statutorily demarcated area of the Northern Pennines. Outside these boundaries the Board had neither powers, nor frequently any effective flow of information. On the other hand, other organisations were responsible for only parts of the Board's area, and these parts were frequently the more remote, less important areas in terms of resources or priorities and thus had received less attention by other bodies. Moreover, all organisations other than the second- and third-tier units of local government were based outside the Northern Pennines, so that externalities were often predominant in policy attitudes to the Board's area and its activities.

Liaison, interchange of information, publicity and public relations thus became a vital element in establishing the work of the Board. In geographical terms the wider spatial context of the Board's area provided an increasingly important frame of reference for decisions taken within the Northern Pennines. A North Pennines Forum was pioneered by the Board to bring together representatives of all organisations with a common concern for particular rural problems and policies, with a view to harmonising attitudes and promoting cooperation. Nevertheless, clashes of interest continued, instanced by those over tree-planting licences in the National Park, the denial of the right of the hill-farmer to sell land to forestry interests without any means of public compensation for this loss, or the conflicting policies on siting caravans in upper rather than lower dales.

The disappearance of the Northern Pennines RDB has left many of these wider issues unresolved and has, at the same time, deprived farmers and foresters of the coordinated aid which the Board's powers were permitting it to generate with rising momentum. At a broad strategic level the Northern Economic Planning Council is responsible for formulating economic and social policies, within which the structure plans of the new local government planning authorities are to be fitted. The Outline Strategy published by the Northern EPC in 1969 had a rural component (Fig. 6.2), which was based on a pattern of "anchor-point" settlements, whose function was to help arrest the decline in the population of surrounding rural hinterlands. This was part of a geographically-derived spatial framework, intended for the inter-related management of the entire regional settlement hierarchy (House, 1974). Growth was intended to occur at the larger nodally-situated towns and cities which would be inter-linked by improved communications. Such polarisation of economic growth was seen as likely to cause a further decline in a peripheral sparsely-settled rural hinterland. The beneficial "spread" effects by the diffusion of growth from the major centres were expected to be more than counteracted by the adverse "backwash" effects, which would drain the marginal rural areas even more of their scarce resources of manpower and skills and thus weaken the community in the process (G. Myrdal, 1957).

At the present time a third, tripartite regional strategy is in course of preparation for the Northern Region and, contemporaneously, structure plans are being formulated by the local planning authorities. Rural planning is now recognised to be a distinctive and integral counterpart to town planning. Yet planning powers over farmland or afforested areas continue to be minimal and thus the central questions of a proper balance between farming and forestry in the hills and of a reconciliation of the interests of the countrymen with those of the townsmen are as difficult as ever to resolve. Rural decisions on development are still mainly the product of land ownership rather than deriving from planners, and there are large tracts of marginal hill country which are under the management or supervision of bodies with substantially non-economic objectives (notably the Countryside Commission, the Ministry of Defence, the National Trust and the Nature Conservancy Council). Planning for the Northern Pennines is thus a delicate and difficult task of inter-relationships, with minimal powers to affect considerable change. Self-generating solutions are made more difficult by the general marginality of conditions and the widespread non-viable nature of many activities, such as hill-farming, public transport, and social provision for small, scattered populations.

At the heart of effective rural planning lies improvement of the economic

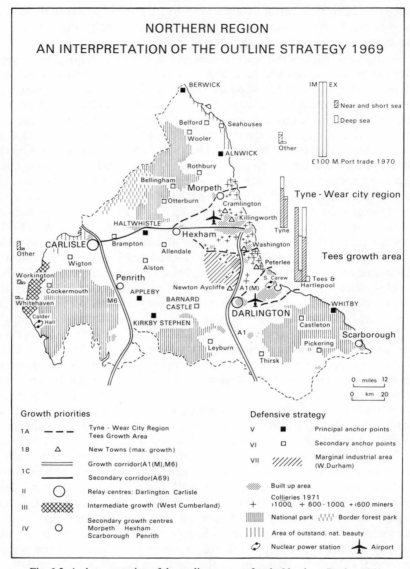

Fig. 6.2. An interpretation of the outline strategy for the Northern Region 1969

base activities of farming and forestry, from which the export potential of
the hill country is generated. The concept of the Rural Development Board
was intended to reform, reinforce and promote this export base and at the

same time to contribute to the needs of the wider rural community. In the continuing absence of any effective substitute the prospects for coherent, constructive rural planning in the Northern Pennines surely become more problematical.

REFERENCES

Ashton, J. and W. H. Long (eds.) (1972) *The Remoter Rural Areas of Britain,* Oliver and Boyd, Edinburgh.

Department of Education and Science (1966) *Report of the Land Use Study Group, Forestry, Agriculture, and the Multiple Use of Rural Land,* H.M.S.O., London.

Forestry Commission (1972) *Forest Policy,* H.M.S.O., London.

House, J. W. (1956) "Afforestation in Britain: the case of the Anglo-Scottish Borderlands", *Tijdschrift voor Economische en Sociale Geografie,* **47,** 265-76.

House, J. W. (1956) *Northumbrian Tweedside,* Rural Community Council, Newcastle-upon-Tyne.

House, J. W. (1965) "Rural North East England, 1951-61", *Papers on Migration and Mobility* 1, University of Newcastle-upon-Tyne, 49 pp.

House, J. W. (1966) "Margins in regional geography. An illustration from North-East England", in J. W. House (ed.) *Northern Geographical Essays in Honour of G. H. J. Dayoh,* Dept. of Geography, University of Newcastle-upon-Tyne, pp. 139-56.

House, J. W. (1970) "Depopulation in the uplands", Ch. 8 in *The Changing Uplands,* Country Landowners Association, pp. 43-7.

House, J. W. (1972a) "Geographers, decision-takers and policy-makers", Ch. 8 in M. Chisholm and B. Rodgers (eds.) *Studies in Human Geography,* Heinemann, London, pp. 272-305.

House, J. W. (1972b) "Northern Pennines Rural Development Board", in Select Committee on Scottish Affairs, *Land Resource Use in Scotland,* H C 511-v (1971-2), H.M.S.O., London, Appendix A34, pp. 164-9.

House, J. W. (1974) "Regions and the system", in J. W. House (ed.) *The UK Space,* Weidenfeld and Nicolson, London, pp. 1-74.

Jeffers, J. N. R. (1966) "Relationship between staff and work-load in individual forest units", in Forestry Commission, *Report on Forest Research for 1965,* H.M.S.O., London.

Myrdal, G. (1957) *Economic Theory and Underdeveloped Regions,* Methuen, London.

Northern Economic Planning Council (1969) *An Outline Strategy for the North,* Newcastle-upon-Tyne.

Philip, M. S. *et al.* (1966) *The Economic Use of Private Forestry,* University of Aberdeen, Department of Forestry.

Raeburn, J. R. (1972) "The economics of upland farming", Ch. 1 in J. Ashton and W. H. Long (eds.) *The Remoter Rural Areas of Britain,* Oliver and Boyd, Edinburgh, pp. 186-201.

Travis, A. S. (1972) "Policy formulation and the planner", Ch. 10, *Ibid.,* pp. 186-201.

Wardle, P. (1966) "Land use policy", *Timber Grower,* **19,** 18-25.

Whitby, M. C., D. L. J. Robins, A. W. Tansey and K. G. Willis (1974) *Rural Resource Development,* Methuen, London.

Willis, K. G. (1973) *Economic Policy Determination and Evaluation in the Northern Pennines,* Agricultural Adjustment Unit, M 3, University of Newcastle.

CHAPTER 7

RESEARCH AND POLICY IN OUTDOOR RECREATION: THE CONTRIBUTION OF THE TOURISM AND RECREATION RESEARCH UNIT

J. T. COPPOCK

University of Edinburgh

Involvement by academics in research related to public policy is, in the United Kingdom at least, a very haphazard matter. Clearly the discipline must be thought to have something to contribute and individuals or organisations must be identified in whom official agencies can feel confidence; at the same time there must be a perceived need for work to be done. In an ideal world, needs would be perceived well in advance, a research programme would be formulated to provide the necessary answers and work would be commissioned and undertaken. In practice, government departments and agencies do not work in this way and tend to react to, rather than to anticipate, pressures upon them; long-term strategies are vague and priorities likely to be altered in response to such pressures. An additional problem from the viewpoint of universities, as one of the potential sources of expertise, is they are generally ill-equipped to undertake contract research which must be completed in a prescribed period; for their priorities are inevitably dictated by their responsibilities for teaching. Research, whatever the lip-service paid to it, is consequently often a residual legatee. Furthermore, the distinction between pure and applied research is often difficult to draw, particularly in an emerging field where basic research has not yet been undertaken and methodologies rest on insecure foundations; any enquiry to serve the needs of public policy thus involves some "pure" research to make the applied research possible. Only rarely can the client say exactly what he wants done or the contractor state precisely how he proposes to do it.

The undertaking of applied research is particularly difficult in a field such as recreation which has been expanding rapidly over the past two decades; for public policy towards recreation is still in its infancy, at least in the United Kingdom, while funding for research is on a very modest scale and was virtually non-existent before the 1960s. The same is true, to greater or lesser degree, of other parts of the world. Tourism, especially in so far as it is a source of foreign exchange, has been a subject of public concern for rather longer, but here too, expenditure on research, especially of a fundamental kind, has been very small. The distinction between tourism and recreation is often difficult to make, for the tourist is often a recreationist, and the main difference seems to rest on whether the recreationist travels to a recreational site from his home or from a temporary residence; for spatial links between dwelling and place of recreation are as important a feature of home-based recreation as they are of recreation by visitors. This spatial dimension is one in which geographers have a close interest and, partly for this reason and because of their concern for the environment, geographers have in fact played a leading role in research in these fields in Great Britain. This chapter is concerned with the experience of one research team, the Tourism and Recreation Research Unit in the University of Edinburgh, a multi-disciplinary team led by geographers.

Policy and Research in Tourism and Recreation

While some components of recreation and tourist policy have long antecedents—powers to provide urban parks, for example, dating from the nineteenth century—the recentness of what Michael Dower (1965) has called "The Fourth Wave" has produced a situation in which most public bodies with responsibilities in this field are still feeling their way towards policies and the factual and research bases for such policies are often lacking. The public provision of all facilities is generally a local government responsibility and is supported from rate revenue (local taxes), though increasingly with some contribution (often substantial) from central government. In the past, the powers of local authorities were mainly discretionary and much variation existed between authorities; but the great increase in personal mobility provided by the rapid growth in car-ownership has made local authority boundaries less appropriate, particularly in a rural context where recreationists are often urban-based and local authorities poor.

By their nature, recreation and tourism embrace a very broad range of activities and responsibility is widely diffused among government departments, notably Trade and Industry, Education and Science and the Environment (and their Scottish equivalents in the Scottish Economic Planning Department, the Scottish Education Department and the Scottish Development Department). However, much of the responsibility for advice and policy in these fields has been given to autonomous or semi-autonomous agencies, notably the Countryside Commissions, the Sports Councils and the Tourist Boards. Additionally, there are several agencies with responsibility for other sectors of the economy, but with subordinate interests in recreation, such as the Forestry Commission and the Regional Water Authorities, and one regional authority with both grant-giving and executive powers, the Highlands and Islands Development Board. There is no body like the Bureau of Outdoor Recreation in the United States with responsibility for taking an overall view of recreation. Responsibility for supporting fundamental research is also diffused, though the Natural Environment Research Council and the Social Science Research Council have interests in this field.

Much of this diversity emerged in the 1960s when the increasing scale of participation in recreation and tourism became apparent. Before 1965, the Department of Scientific and Industrial Research was the only body capable of supporting fundamental scientific research and the National Parks Commission was the only statutory agency with responsibilities in these fields (though there were several non-statutory agencies). The research programme of the Tourism and Recreation Research Unit was thus undertaken in a changing environment for a number of agencies, most of which were feeling their way towards the formulation of policy. A good example of such an evolutionary approach to policy is provided by the evidence of the Countryside Commission for Scotland to the Select Committee on Scottish Affairs (1972, Vols. 3 and 5), particularly that relating to a park system for Scotland (Countryside Commission for Scotland, 1975).

The Origins of the Tourism and Recreation Research Unit

Although the Tourism and Recreation Research Unit (TRRU) has primarily been concerned with contract research for official agencies, the origins of the Unit are to be found in a project funded by a research council. In 1966, the Natural Environment Research Council awarded a grant for £9200 to permit a reconnaissance investigation of the impact of outdoor recreation on the countryside of central Scotland. This project was undertaken with primarily scientific aims in mind and, although by the standards then prevailing in the United Kingdom (though not in North America) the grant was a large one, it permitted the appointment of only one full-time researcher. The original programme of work had included a period of extensive enquiry in the field and among clubs, agencies, the police, associations of landowners and the like, to establish the broad parameters of recreational land use in central Scotland; it had then been intended to identify representative sites and to monitor their use in detail. During the course of the preliminary enquiries, it became clear that the local authorities, who had been charged by the Secretary of State for Scotland with preparing plans for tourism and for landscape conservation, were also interested in investigations into outdoor recreation, and it seemed likely that it would be mutually beneficial if the respective interests were co-ordinated, the university team contributing professional expertise and the local authorities providing the additional resources for the team to undertake much more thorough field enquiries than would otherwise have been possible. As a result of these discussions, Lanarkshire County Council commissioned an evaluation of outdoor recreation in that county (Fig. 7.1).

Members of the research team felt that it would be helpful for the development of sound policies for outdoor recreation in central Scotland if

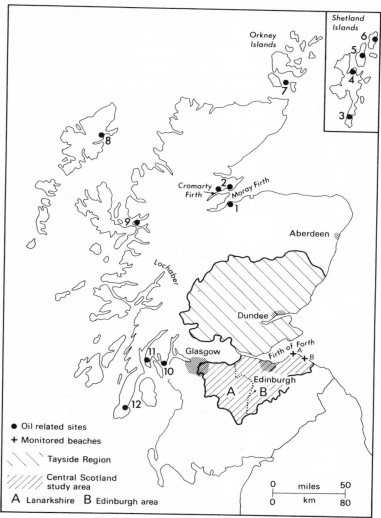

Fig. 7.1. Recreational research in Scotland
(see p. 117 for oil related sites; 5 is Yell and 6 Unst)

such enquiries could be conducted in three types of areas. The first should be an area where pressures were heavy and demand greatly exceeded supply, as in Lanarkshire (which lies on the edge of the Glasgow conurbation and has limited resources for outdoor recreation). The second area should be one in which demand and supply were roughly in balance, while the third should be rich in recreational resources but not yet under pressure from primarily urban-based recreationists. In the event, no local authority in the last category could be persuaded to participate, perhaps because they failed to perceive the nature of the potential threat to their established way of life or because they considered that, by making no provision for future recreationists, they could in some way be prevented from coming in increasing numbers. An example of the second category was provided by Greater Edinburgh, and Edinburgh City Corporation and the County Councils for East, Mid- and West Lothian and Peeblesshire agreed, with the support of the Countryside Commission for Scotland, to finance a similar study of Edinburgh and its hinterland, or more strictly, that part of it south of the Firth of Forth which lay within these four counties. The total budget for these two projects (Lanarkshire and Greater Edinburgh) was £6000.

These two investigations were conducted on identical lines, using the same methodology so that the results are strictly comparable; indeed, the reports even share one common component, a study of the impact upon, and attitudes of, those who own or otherwise control land in the two study areas (B. S. Duffield and M. L. Owen, 1970 and 1971a). These reports were not intended to be plans, but rather analyses of the demand for and supply of recreational facilities in this part of central Scotland; they did, however, include recommendations and those for Lanarkshire were accepted by the local authority and incorporated into the county's recreational plans. In evidence to the Select Committee on Scottish Affairs (1972, Vol. 3, p. 4), the Countryside Commission for Scotland recognised the scarcity of recreational planning at a regional level and identified these two studies as models of the kind of work which should be undertaken.

The Unit's existence was formally recognised in 1972 by the University and a varied and increasing programme of work was undertaken. The permanent staff was increased to eight, including two geographers (one with a training in statistics and the other in physical education), a systems analyst and programmer. Additional full-time staff recruited for particular projects have included an ecologist, an economist, a mathematician, a planner, a sociologist and a statistician, as well as other geographers, and the Unit has made extensive use of consultants from the same disciplines and from architecture. Temporary staff were also needed and as many as 200 have been employed as interviewers, office staff, field co-ordinators and the like at peak periods. The Unit's budget for work in hand to be completed in 1975-6 had risen to £75,000 in 1975 and the total of grants and contracts obtained by mid-1975 exceeded £250,000. The Unit has received increasing national and international recognition, acting as host to the annual conference of the Countryside Recreational Research Advisory Group in 1974 and receiving a steadily growing number of visitors from abroad.

The Research Programme: Comprehensive Surveys

The programme of work undertaken by the Unit falls broadly into four categories: the demand for (or, more strictly, participation in) outdoor recreation; the supply of recreational resources; recreational travel, at varying scales and of varying kinds; the impact of outdoor recreation. In three investigations, the studies of Lanarkshire and Greater Edinburgh and the Scottish Tourism and Recreational Survey, several of these elements were present; in most of the remainder a single aspect has been tackled. Nearly all have been undertaken with the support and generally at the request of one or more public bodies.

The studies of Lanarkshire and Greater Edinburgh represented attempts to take a comprehensive view of outdoor recreation. The underlying concept was a simple demand-supply model, the former being determined mainly by an interview survey of a random sample of households in the area, as derived from the rating (local taxation) lists, the latter by an inventory of resources known to be used on the one hand and an evaluation of recreational potential on the other. The household survey was a straightforward undertaking, with questions designed to obtain information on participation in a large number of outdoor pursuits as well as a range of socio-economic variables such as education, occupation and ownership of, or access to, a motor vehicle. A total of 2367 interviews was completed, compared with 324 for Scotland in the Pilot National Recreation Survey and a total of 3167 interviews for the whole of Great Britain in that survey (British Travel Association—University of Keele, 1967). Indeed, at that time the sample represented the largest regional enquiry undertaken for any comparable area of the United Kingdom.

Even so, because levels of participation in many kinds of active recreation are very low, results even from as large a sample as this may be liable to relatively large sampling errors. Accordingly, additional qualitative information was sought in a special survey made of all clubs and associations in the area to determine their membership and catchment area. This survey, which was conducted by post, also collected information on the areas used by members of these clubs and associations. Additional information on the resources used was collected by enquiries from the police, the Automobile Association and other bodies knowledgeable about the area, and by interviews at recreational sites, which were visited from time to time by teams of interviewers who questioned those at each site about the purpose and frequency of their visits. Additionally, a technique of rural traverses was devised to cope with the large but unknown number of recreationists visiting the country at large, using a team which toured rural areas at intervals to interview those recreationists who were parked at other than recognised sites (Duffield and Owen, 1970).

The main emphasis in respect of the supply of recreation was, however, on potential supply (Coppock and Duffield, 1975). The limited resources available to the research team could not support an extensive field survey, and reliance had to be placed primarily on evidence from maps and air photographs, with field checks of the accuracy of such information and to clarify obscurities. The objective was to identify at a regional scale "recreation environments", areas which were capable of supporting and sustaining similar levels of recreational use. Four components were identified (capability for land-based recreation; capability for water-based recreation; scenic quality; and ecological significance) and a value for each component was computed for each square of a grid, scoring being on the basis of one point for each occurrence. The criteria for assessing capability to support land- and water-based recreation were determined empirically by obtaining best estimates from authorities in the different kinds of recreation, for no adequate research base existed for deriving these objectively; the classification of scenery was adapted from a method developed by D. L. Linton (1968), involving the grading and synthesis of land-use and land-form landscapes, and the measurement of ecological significance was based on an approach devised by D. R. Helliwell (1969) in which habitats were graded according to their biological richness. In synthesising these components to produce recreation environments, it was decided that no weighting should be applied because too little was known about the relative importance of the components, though the method used made it very simply to employ weights at a later stage if these were shown to be valid.

The third component of these surveys was a study of the recreational journeys linking the areas of demand (mainly in the cities) to the sites used, the so-called "journey to play". Some complementary evidence on this movement was available from the surveys already discussed; for the household interview survey and the surveys of clubs and associations provided some indications of the areas used, though this information was largely qualitative, and the site surveys also yielded data on the origins of visitors to those sites. In view of the deficiencies of these data, it was decided to undertake a cordon traffic survey.

The main obstacle to this approach was its cost. The method adopted was to establish a cordon around each of the main sources of recreationists, viz., the Glasgow conurbation and the city of Edinburgh, a team of interviewers being located on each of the major routes out of these cities (24 for N.W.

Lanarkshire and 12 for Edinburgh). Resources were sufficient for a survey on only one day in each area and even these undertakings required one-eighth of the total budget available; however, it was felt that, in view of the lack of data, even this limited information would be valuable. Interviewing bays were set up on two fine Sundays in August and, with the cooperation of the police, random samples of motorists were questioned on the purpose of their journey and, if this was recreational, their origin and destination, time of departure and estimated time of return. In all, 15,366 recreationists were interviewed and, while the results must be treated with caution because they refer to only 2 days, the pattern on each route is sufficiently consistent to allow some confidence to be placed upon them, a view which is supported by the evidence of two other surveys in Great Britain (R. T. Colenutt, 1969; G. Wall, 1972). The Scottish surveys revealed that, contrary to the usual assumptions of traffic modelling, the volume of recreational traffic did not decline with distance but rose to a secondary peak at distances between about 20 and 40 miles (32-64 km), a fact which has significance both for theory and for planning, the former because it showed that the gravity model was inappropriate for such informal journeys and the latter for the guidance it offered on where to locate recreational facilities.

The last component of the Lanarkshire and Greater Edinburgh surveys was a study of the impact of outdoor recreation upon other land users. Again the method of study was dictated by the resources available, which were sufficient only for a postal enquiry. The cooperation of the Scottish Land Owners Federation, the National Farmers Union of Scotland and the Scottish Woodland Owners Association was sought and obtained, and questionnaires were sent to all the members of the Federation and of the Association and to one in four of those of the National Farmers Union. A response rate of 31 per cent was achieved, a not untypical value for a postal survey of this kind; furthermore, many of the non-respondents were owners or occupiers of only small acreages. Information was sought from landholders on the recreational and other use of the land they controlled, their plans (if any) for recreational developments and their reactions to recreation and to the public generally. This, too, is a unique set of data in a field in which there is little firm information.

While the resources for these surveys were, in hindsight, quite inadequate for the work to be done, without them no comprehensive surveys of any kind would have been possible. Funding for the third project, commissioned in 1972 by a consortium of the Countryside Commission for Scotland, the Forestry Commission, the Highlands and Islands Development Board and the Scottish Tourist Board and with a budget of £65,000, was at a much more appropriate level in relation to the work to be done. This was a survey of recreational demand and use throughout Scotland, and was intended to provide the sponsors with a basis for their national policies for Scotland. The project required a stratified random sample of some 7000 Scottish households as well as 13,000 interviews with visitors to Scotland as they left the country at the conclusion of their holiday. The Scottish sample could easily be drawn from the valuation (local taxation) rolls, but the only effective way of drawing the sample of visitors was by means of cordon surveys which sampled all visitors whatever their mode of travel and point of exit. Most of these visitors would probably be travelling by car, and these could be interviewed by establishing a cordon of census points on roads crossing the Scottish border; for other forms of travel, it was found to be more efficient to place interviewers on coaches, trains and ferries than at the point of embarkation, though the latter approach had to be adopted for those travelling by air, since interviewing on aircraft was not permitted. Where only a short interview was possible, respondents were given a self-administered questionnaire to complete and return; possibly owing to the introduction of an incentive scheme (inclusion in a draw for hampers of Scottish foodstuffs) a response rate of 78 per cent was achieved. For this survey it was decided to collect nearly all the information by questionnaire and respondents were asked to indicate the route they followed on road maps of Scotland or of the appropriate regions; they appeared to enjoy doing so and to have little difficulty in completing the maps. These data have been subject to preliminary analysis and seven reports (two general and five specific to the interests of individual sponsors) have been compiled. Much more extensive analysis is possible and the survey data have also provided valuable inputs to other investigations, particularly a series of regional studies which the sponsors are undertaking, and the studies of the economic impact of tourism and the effects of the oil-related industries which are discussed below.

The Research Programme: Recreational Travel

A major theme in the research programme has been the study of recreational journeys. The Lanarkshire and Greater Edinburgh studies had already thrown considerable light on the nature of recreational travel and this was also investigated with the support of a grant from the Social Science Research Council (Duffield, 1973). The Scottish Tourism and Recreation Study will provide a further opportunity for greatly improving understanding of recreational travel when the data on these recreational journeys are fully analysed. In addition, the Unit has undertaken several other investigations into recreational movement, at scales ranging from the individual site to Scotland as a whole. Some of these surveys have had, and others are likely to have, a considerable impact on the policies of the agencies and all are of considerable methodological interest.

As an extension of the reconnaissance study of the impact of outdoor recreation on the countryside of Central Scotland, it was decided to measure the effects of recreational use of two coastal areas, White Sands and Yellow Craigs, owned and managed by the East Lothian County Council and used for informal recreation (Fig. 7.1). As part of this investigation, a record was kept of pedestrian movements within these areas, both of them covered by dunes and traversed by a network of footpaths (Coppock, 1973, p. 493). Counts were kept of numbers of people moving along each link of the network under different weather conditions and varying levels of visitor pressure and attempts are being made to model these movements, as an aid to estimating likely recreational pressures. A second local survey of recreational traffic was undertaken for the Countryside Commission in the Pentland Hills south of Edinburgh. This area was being studied by a technical team from the local authority and the Countryside Commission with a view to designating part of the area as a Regional Park. Information was required on the volume and pattern of recreational traffic entering the area and a modified cordon technique was adopted similar to that used in the Lanarkshire and Greater Edinburgh studies, traffic counters being placed on all roads giving access to the area and a sample of drivers stopped for questioning (Duffield and Owen, 1971b).

At the other end of the scale, as a guide to policy for touring caravans (or trailers in North American terms), a comprehensive analysis was undertaken for the Scottish Tourist Board of movements of caravans throughout Scotland and of the relationship between the capacity of sites available in each region and the number of caravans visiting that region. The method used was itself innovative and was partly dictated by the limited resources available for the study. A continuous count of vehicles throughout the holiday season was provided by traffic counters (read at intervals) which were linked to single-shot ciné cameras mounted at strategic location and adjusted to photograph every tenth vehicle recorded by the counters. The resulting photographs were then analysed to obtain the proportions of caravans and these were then applied to the traffic counts to provide estimates of the total number of caravans. While the method has a number of weaknesses, these counts, together with interview and questionnaire surveys, have provided the basis for a revised official policy towards touring caravans in Scotland (Owen and Duffield, 1971). A related survey was undertaken in the same year when the Unit was asked to report on Summer Holiday Traffic in Scotland (Duffield and Owen, 1972). This survey similarly involved monitoring traffic moving along the main routes into Scotland and northwards from central Scotland into the Highlands; but since such traffic could not be identified by observation, a more conventional approach had to be adopted, with a cordon of survey points being established on the main routes and a sample of drivers stopped for questioning about the purpose of their journeys. The method of sampling (as on all the surveys in which roadside interviews were used) was for the police officer controlling traffic to stop the next vehicle to pass once an interview with a driver had been completed.

While all these investigations have involved analyses of the resulting data, the main emphasis has been on field survey and data collection. Two other investigations of a more fundamental kind, one major, the other minor, have also been undertaken. The first was the construction of a traffic mix model for recreational traffic for the Transport and Road Research Laboratory, using harmonic analysis and records for fifty roads in Great Britain. This model is required to permit predictions, with a high degree of accuracy from a small number of sample observations, of recreational traffic, both in total and at different seasons of the year.

The smaller study is a pilot investigation undertaken for the Countryside Commission for Scotland into the reactions of drivers and their passengers to different kinds of roads, traffic conditions and scenery as an input to the design of rural roads, and adopted a similar approach to that used by Kevin Lynch (1964). The surveys were conducted on five roads in the Scottish Highlands and a sample of drivers was requested to allow an interviewer armed with a tape recorder to travel with the driver on part of his route and to question him and his passengers about their reactions to such features as road surface, speed, other traffic and the scenic quality of the route; little difficulty was experienced in securing such cooperation. Transcripts of the conversation were assessed independently and the results subjected to factor analysis; the results confirmed the need to define a typology of roads which recognises the varying functions of different holiday routes.

It is clear that, while much useful information has been collected, new techniques devised and valuable analyses undertaken, all of them contributing in some way to policy formation, there is a great need for more fundamental work on recreational traffic. The assumption used in the empirical investigations have not always been very firmly based on theory and doubts have been cast on some of the assumptions underlying earlier attempts at modelling recreational traffic, especially those using a gravity-type model. The Social Science Research Council has agreed to support a preliminary investigation of the merits of gravity and systems models of recreational travel, and subsequent policy-oriented work cannot fail to benefit from these developments.

Recreational Programme: Impact Studies

The third major area of investigation has been the impact of recreation, one of the most important from the viewpoint of public policy. Impact can be considered in several ways, viz., the effect on the physical environment, especially vegetation; the impact on other users of the countryside; the impact on the local economy through the money injected by visitors to an area; and the impact on the non-land owning population of the area. Aspects of each of these have been investigated by the Unit.

The physical impact of recreation was a major concern in the first investigation, sponsored by the Natural Environmental Research Council, the objective being scientific rather than policy-oriented (though the results would have obvious implication for policy). However, it soon became clear that the complexity of factors affecting the natural environment was such that the first task had to be the establishment of base lines from which subsequent changes could be monitored. Accordingly, a detailed topographic survey was undertaken of the two areas already mentioned, White Sands and Yellow Craigs, and the vegetation and soil in quadrats at each intersection of a 100-metre grid were studied by a team of ecologists, the base line of the grid being recorded by permanent markers so that the survey could be repeated. A detailed vegetation map of the area was also compiled at a scale of 1/500 by balloon photography, using a camera, worked by a clockwork motor activated from the ground and suspended from a tethered balloon (Duffield and J. Forsyth, 1973). Each of the sites is accessible only from a car park controlled by the local authority, whose staff recorded the daily numbers of visitors to the site; in conjunction with the modelling of recreational movements of visitors on the site, discussed earlier, this information will make it possible to estimate the degree of visitor pressure and its effect on vegetational change.

In interpreting the impact of outdoor recreation on other land uses, it must be remembered that outdoor recreation in Great Britain is normally a junior partner in various systems of multiple land use, particularly with woodland and with rough grazings; even in areas of more intensive agriculture, especially around towns, informal recreation (often without permission) is an important consideration in farmers' and landowners' decisions. The survey of landholders which formed part of the Lanarkshire and Greater Edinburgh survey has already been discussed, and remains one of the few examples of specific information in a field in which rumour and prejudice abound. It shows that most landholders do not object to well-behaved recreationists and suggests that education is one of the most effective ways of minimising friction (Duffield and Owen, 1970).

The third type of impact, the economic impact of visitors to an area, has been the subject of an investigation of the Tayside Region of Scotland commissioned by the Scottish Tourist Board (Fig. 7.1). Although tourism (which, in a Scottish context, largely overlaps outdoor recreation) has been advocated as a major prop for the economies of impoverished rural areas, there has been considerable dispute about the benefit which tourism brings, and opponents have claimed that much is quickly lost to the area through payments to outside bodies for goods and services provided. Objective assessment of the true contribution of tourism depends on the use of the economic concept of the multiplier, and although this has been employed to assess the impact of tourism on the economy of a country as a whole, it has been used at a sub-national scale only in a pioneer study of Anglesey (B. H. Archer, 1973). Such information will be required for the series of regional appraisals of recreation and tourism in Scotland which the Scottish Tourist Board and other public bodies with responsibilities for recreation intend to promote, and the Board therefore commissioned this study both to develop an appropriate methodology and to provide specific information about the Tayside Region.

It was intended to devise multipliers not only for the region as a whole, but also for each of five different types of communities within it, viz. nodal town, Highland centre, coastal resort, rural area and special activity centre. Two main kinds of data were required: on numbers of visitors to the region, their length of stay and pattern of spending, and on business with tourists, of firms catering directly or indirectly for the tourist trade, their sources of supply and the like. Collecting the first kind of data required the construction of a cordon of survey points around Tayside to sample visitors leaving the region by all forms of transport. Data of the latter kind required the cooperation of a sample of firms engaged in a wide variety of economic activities in each of the five types of community identified. In all, over 2000 visitors were interviewed and 286 firms provided information, and while the latter sample was too small to give statistically reliable estimates at the community level, it was sufficient to indicate the efficiency of the methodology. Both income and employment multipliers were calculated, and these showed that most of the benefits were generated at the community level, the income multiplier at this level being 0·26 per £ of expenditure and that for the region as a whole 0·32 (Tourism and Recreation Research Unit, 1975a).

As part of the Tayside study, the Unit was also asked to undertake a pilot study of the social impact of visitors to the region, by holding a series of interviews with representative groups in each community and recording and analysing the resulting discussions. This experience provided valuable insights into the fourth kind of impact, which is the subject of the most recent major investigation that the Unit has been commissioned to undertake for the Highlands and Islands Development Board and the European Economic Community. This is a study of the effect of the industrial developments associated with the exploitation of North Sea oil on provision for recreation and leisure in the small communities of the Highlands and Islands of Scotland. Six areas are involved, each of them sparsely populated and most of them handicapped by poor natural resources, by long-continued emigration and by unbalanced age structures, with marked deficiencies in the middle-age groups and high proportions of elderly people. The six areas are

(Fig. 7.1): the Cromarty (2) and Moray Firths (1), the initial focus of development where steel platforms are being built; Shetland, particularly the oil-supply base as Sumburgh (3) and the oil landing and storage points at Sullum Voe (4); Orkney, in particular the oil landing and storage points in Flotta (7); Stornoway (8) in the Outer Hebrides, where construction sites are being established; Loch Carron (9) where concrete oil platforms are being built; and Ardyne Point (10), Portavadie (11), and Campbelltown (12) in south Argyll which are also sites for concrete platforms. The sponsors' remit requires the Unit to investigate the present use of resources for recreation and leisure and the likely effects of both the temporary construction force and the smaller permanent labour force on the existing facilities, and to make recommendations for improving the situation; additionally, an established industrial area, Lochaber, is being investigated to determine whether this earlier development provides any lessons for the oil-related sites. The remit also requires the Unit's team, which comprises geographers and sociologists, advised by a consultant architect specialising in recreational provision, an economist and a planner, to have regard for the wishes of the local inhabitants. The remit presents challenging problems, not only because of the scattered nature of the communities, which makes the organisation of services difficult, and their small population, which affects the size of sample required, but also because little work has yet been done in this field. On the other hand, this investigation, perhaps more than any other, is likely to provide a considerable input to public policy.

Tourism and Recreation Information Package (TRIP)

One further activity of the Unit bears on all the survey and analytic work described in preceding paragraphs, the construction of a computer-based information system for tourism and recreation in Scotland. In 1972, the Countryside Commission for Scotland and the Scottish Tourist Board commissioned the Unit to construct such an information system and they were later joined as sponsors by the Forestry Commission, the Scottish Sports Council and the Scottish Arts Council. The objective was to devise a system which could be made to work in the short run with the data which were then available and which was capable of assisting the sponsors in undertaking their statutory responsibilities. Initially, data sets were limited for those which the sponsors could readily provide or which the Unit could easily obtain from maps or other sources; but it was intended that all data from subsequent surveys commissioned by the sponsors would be added to the data bank, and the analysis of the data from the Scottish Tourism and Recreation Survey has been deliberately designed with this information system in mind.

Initially the basic unit of the information system was the 5 km grid square of the National Grid, of which there are 3416 covering Scotland and which was sufficiently small a unit to provide a satisfactory overview of Scotland and its major regions (Tourism and Recreation Research Unit, 1974 and 1976). Data were recorded for points, lines and areas, and the basic unit was later modified to a 1 km square, of which there are some 85,000 in Scotland, so that more detailed local analyses can be undertaken. The system can provide listings of data in the bank and analyses of any selected data; if appropriate, output can be in the form of tables or maps (the latter being produced on a specially modified line printer). The analyses can also be linked to a variety of statistical procedures, and a particularly useful facility is the ability to search adjacent cells of the grid within any prescribed radius, an approach which has been used in estimates of potential population pressure on recreational resources. A variety of analyses has already been undertaken using the system. The Scottish Tourist Board, for example, has used TRIP in investigations of the development and marketing of sports facilities and of the Scandinavian market for visits to Scotland. In the former investigation, it was first necessary to identify those areas where facilities for, say, fishing were adequate to meet the needs of the resident population; estimates were made of average provision in Scotland; these were then related to the actual resources available to identify areas with an unused capability for fishing; and, finally, hotels with spare capacity and within easy travelling distance of unused resources were located, to provide an indication of those areas where development might profitably take place.

A similar investigation was undertaken for the Countryside Commission for Scotland, though the objective of this analysis was less to produce definitive answers than to aid the formulation of policy and to show the consequences of adopting different policies. The Countryside Commission for Scotland (1974) has been considering the nature of a park system for Scotland and the initial objective in using TRIP was to test the use of various criteria for the selection of areas which might be designated as part of such a park system (Duffield and Coppock, 1975). The approach was to identify those physical and human resources which would have to be considered in any evaluation of areas for a Scottish Park System and to construct from these a series of resource surfaces (analogous with the ''potential surfaces'' used by planners) which were then combined in various ways to identify potential areas. Both the values for individual squares and also those within prescribed radii were used in this analysis, the latter in order to identify areas of potential pressure and to smooth data so that only those features of regional significance were displayed.

The range of application is extending and the system is now available to sponsors and to others as a routine service. Both the capabilities of the system and the range of data in it will be enlarged and its usefulness increased, not only to the sponsors but also to other public authorities in Scotland, particularly the new regional authorities which took up their duties in May 1975. It has, of course, a number of imperfections, but it has two advantages which distinguish it from many of the sophisticated systems which have been developed or partly developed elsewhere; it is already operational and, since it has been commissioned by users and designed with their needs in mind, it can be, and is being, used for practical purposes. It can confidently be predicted that this use will grow as the nature of the system becomes more familiar.

Evaluation of the Research Programme

This research undertaken by the Tourism and Recreation Research Unit has been commissioned by a number of agencies and hence has not been devised as an integrated programme, though success in particular areas has understandably encouraged new or existing sponsors to commission projects which take advantage of the skills and experience which have been developed by the Unit. While the emphasis has been on survey, every field survey presents a challenge and nearly all result in the acquisition of data suitable for further research in a field in which good, reliable data are hard to obtain. Surveys have frequently presented challenges to devise new methods and approaches and have pointed to serious gaps in knowledge and theory. This is not surprising in a field of research which is so young, and the data collected and the insights into the nature of outdoor recreation which are gained by observation in the field and by contact with recreationists provide a sound basis on which hypotheses can be formulated and fundamental research undertaken. Some support for fundamental research has, of course, been provided, though such funding by research councils represents only about one-tenth of the total income of the Unit. There is, however, clearly a need for a coherent programme of long-term basic research in this field, whatever the source of funds, to provide a proper basis for policy-oriented investigations.

The programme of work undertaken for sponsors, all of which have been public agencies, whether of central or local government, has not always had a specific policy objective in view, although new policies have sometimes resulted, as with the Lanarkshire study and the survey of touring caravans in Scotland; for the output of many of these investigations has been a necessary factual input to policy at a later stage. So far, despite an enquiry by a Select Committee of the House of Lords into Sport and Leisure (1973), governments have not held recreation high in their priorities, particularly in respect of its spatial aspects which have been a central theme of this programme of research; but the Department of the Environment's white paper on Sport and Recreation (1975) suggests that these topics are likely to be given greater attention from government than they have hitherto received, at least when the economic state of the United Kingdom improves.

The Unit's experience also demonstrates that field work to acquire the necessary data on outdoor recreation and tourism is expensive, in part because of the diversity of activities and their wide distribution in space. A very large share of the funds received by the Unit has been spent on travel, payments of interviewers and other aspects of field work, so that the total sums received for research are misleading. It is to be hoped that, in future, official agencies can be persuaded to collect data on recreation as a routine matter, just as statistics on agriculture, employment, manufacturing and the like are collected by government. More effort can then be devoted to basic research; for this is urgently required to underpin the even larger volume of applied research which is needed by the growing number of bodies in local, regional and national government with responsibilities in the field of recreation, sport and tourism (all of which are relevant, because the dividing line between them is not easy to draw).

The experience of the Tourism and Recreation Research Unit also demonstrates that both applied contract research and multi-disciplinary research can be undertaken within a university environment. As has been noted already, this environment is by no means ideal for contract research, particularly by teaching staff who cannot guarantee to devote the necessary time to it owing to their prior commitment to teaching duties, while full-time research staff suffer because of lack of tenure and of a proper career structure. Whether there is a critical mass in respect of such teams of research workers is worth further investigation; but at the least, the Unit's experience suggests there must be a core of several permanent staff if such a team is to succeed in the longer term.

As far as is known, the Tourism and Recreation Research Unit represents the first such unit in a British university to be established under geographical auspices and to depend almost entirely on contract research for its survival. Yet, while the direction of research has been geographical, and spatial and environmental aspects have always held a prominent place, the research programme has been essentially multi-disciplinary, including ecology, economics, planning, sociology and statistics as major components. While this variety reflects the nature of recreation research, it also demonstrates that multi-disciplinary work is possible within a university. The record of collaboration betweeen disciplines in British universities is generally not good, perhaps because the departmental structure makes scholars in different disciplines competitors for funds and offers only a single disciplinary avenue of promotion. In a research unit or in a research team, however, where departmentally-based power and resources are not involved, such collaboration is effective, and members of the team work together to solve the common problems which they face.

Conclusion

This account of research undertaken in the Department of Geography at Edinburgh University is not exhaustive; many lesser projects have been undertaken for public agencies. Increasing numbers of post-graduate students are pursuing research in this field and such studies cannot fail to be mutually beneficial, both to the research students, who gain from the expertise and other resources of the Unit, and to the Unit in respect of the flow of new ideas and of investigations which will increasingly stem from the work of the Unit itself. Unfortunately, all this work rests on a balance which is precarious at all times and is particularly so in a period of rapid inflation when research budgets are the first to be cut. While the Unit's reputation and experience should enable it to weather the present storm, it seems highly unlikely that, however desirable the work it has undertaken, such an enterprise could have been started in the harsh climates of the mid-1970s. The Government has accepted the Rothschild recommendations on contract research (Lord Privy Seal, 1972) and in many fields this can be conveniently undertaken in existing laboratories in universities and with existing staff; but in the field of recreation research such expertise does not generally exist either in the universities or in government, and can be guaranteed only if resources are committed in the long term to a coherent programme of research.

The research outlined in this chapter has been undertaken during a period in which policies for recreation and tourism have been emerging, many for the first time, and in which new organisations have been gaining experience. Several initiatives aimed at closer collaboration are beginning to bear fruit. For example, those organisations concerned with recreation in rural areas have come together in the Countryside Recreation Research Advisory Group in an attempt to coordinate research. A dialogue has also been established between this Group and the Social Science Research Council, as a result of which working parties have been established to investigate needs in particular areas of research. The reorganisation of local government in England and Wales in 1974 and that in Scotland in 1975 have led to the emergence of Departments of Leisure and Recreation, though their diversity in staffing and organisation is considerable. In 1974, the Government appointed a Minister for Sport and Recreation in the Department of the Environment and its views have now been published in the white paper (1975). All these developments will require a considerable input both of data collection (to provide the basis of new policies and to monitor existing policies) and research if consistent and soundly-based policies, capable of attaining the goals sought, are to emerge.

REFERENCES

Archer, B. H. (1973) *The Impact of Domestic Tourism,* Bangor Occasional Papers in Economics, No. 2, University of Wales Press, Bangor.

British Travel Association—University of Keele (1967) *Pilot National Recreation Survey,* Report No. 1, University of Keele, London.

Colenutt, R. J. (1969) "Modelling travel patterns of day visitors to the countryside", *Area,* No. 2, pp. 43-7.

Coppock, J. T. (1973) In discussion on Symposium on Recreation and Resources, *Geographical Journal,* **139,** 492-4.

Coppock, J. T. and B. S. Duffield (1975) *Recreation in the Countryside,* Macmillan, London.

Countryside Commission for Scotland (1974) *A Park System for Scotland,* Countryside Commission, Perth.

Department of the Environment (1975) *Sport and Recreation,* Cmnd. 6200, H.M.S.O., London.

Dower, M. (1965) "The fourth wave", *Architects Journal,* **141,** 123-90.

Duffield, B. S. (1973) *Outdoor Recreational Traffic Patterns in the Edinburgh Area,* TRRU Research Report No. 10, Tourism and Recreation Research Unit, University of Edinburgh.

Duffield, B. S. and J. T. Coppock (1975) "The delineation of rural landscapes: the role of a computer-based information system", *Transactions of the Institute of British Geographers,* 66, 141-8.

Duffield, B. S. and J. Forsyth (1973) "Assessing the impact of recreational use on coastal sites in East Lothian", in Countryside Commission, *The Use of Aerial Photographs in Countryside Research,* Report of a Conference, London.

Duffield, B. S. and M. L. Owen (1970) *Leisure + Countryside = : a Geographical Appraisal of Countryside Recreation in Lanarkshire,* edited by J. T. Coppock, Tourism and Recreation Research Unit, University of Edinburgh.

Duffield, B. S. and M. L. Owen (1971a) *Leisure + Countryside = : a Geographical Appraisal of Countryside Recreation in the Edinburgh Area,* edited by J. T. Coppock, Tourism and Recreation Research Unit, University of Edinburgh.

Duffield, B. S. and M. L. Owen (1971b) *The Pentland Hills: a Research Study,* Tourism and Recreation Research Unit, University of Edinburgh.

Duffield, B. S. and M. L. Owen (1972) *Summer Holiday Traffic,* Tourism and Recreation Research Unit, University of Edinburgh.

Helliwell, D. R. (1969) *Survey of Severnside: a method of Evaluating the Conservation Value of Large Areas,* Internal leaflet produced by the Land Use Section, Nature Conservancy, Shrewsbury.

Linton, D. L. (1968) "The assessment of scenery as a natural resource", *Scottish Geographical Magazine,* **84,** 219-38.

Lord Privy Seal (1972) *A Framework for Government Research and Development,* Cmnd. 5046, H.M.S.O., London.

Lynch, K. (1964) *The View from the Road,* M.I.T. Press, Cambridge, Mass.

Owen, M. L. and B. S. Duffield (1971) *The Touring Caravan in Scotland,* edited by J. T. Coppock, Scottish Tourist Board, Edinburgh.

Select Committee of the House of Lords on Sport and Leisure (1973) *2nd Report, Minutes of Evidence and Appendices,* House of Lords Paper 193, H.M.S.O., London.

Select Committee on Scottish Affairs (1972) *Land Resource Use in Scotland,* Report, Minutes of Evidence and Appendices, House of Commons Paper 511, H.M.S.O., London.

Tourism and Recreation Research Unit (1974) *TRIP Series: No. 1 System Description,* TRRU Research Report No. 11, Tourism and Recreation Research Unit, University of Edinburgh.

Tourism and Recreation Research Unit (1975a) *The Economic Impact of Tourism: a Case Study in Greater Tayside,* TRRU Research Report No. 13, Tourism and Recreation Research Unit, University of Edinburgh.

Tourism and Recreation Research Unit (1976) *TRIP Series: No. 2 Introductory Users Guide,* TRRU Research Report No. 12, University of Edinburgh.

Wall, G. (1972) "Socio-economic variations in pleasure trip patterns: the case of Hull car-owners", *Transactions of the Institute of British Geographers,* **57**, 45-58.

CHAPTER 8

CONTACT STUDIES AND DECENTRALISATION OF OFFICES FROM LONDON AND STOCKHOLM

J. B. GODDARD

University of Newcastle-upon-Tyne

INTRODUCTION

One of the aims of this chapter is to set some recent research on office location in the context of a rapidly developing concern on the part of public policy makers with issues relating to office location. Research has contributed to the public discussion of office location by highlighting the increasing significance of office jobs to the economic development of cities and regions. It has progressed from basic descriptions of the distribution of office employment to a broader understanding of the role of these activities in steering urban and regional development (J. B. Goddard, 1975).

The policies that have emerged from such discussions have been principally concerned with promoting the decentralisation of offices from capital cities. These policies have in turn influenced the nature of further research. Particular attention has been focussed on the nature of the constraints that appear to tie office jobs to the city centre and also on the social and economic consequences of office decentralisation. Research has therefore begun to move from description to prescription in attempting to evaluate the possible consequences of alternative policies. But while thus contributing to the possible revision of reformulation of policy some studies have also given new theoretical insights into the location processes that underpin this aspect of urban and regional development. Studies of office location clearly illustrate the dialogue between theoretical work and public policy that is necessary if research is to make a meaningful contribution to the solution of urban and regional problems.

With established policies being an important factor shaping research on office location it is not surprising that the most extensive contributions can be found in the United Kingdom and Sweden, two countries which have active policies of decentralisation of economic activity from their capital cities. The remainder of this chapter will be concerned with reviewing office location policy and research in these two countries: attention is focussed especially on studies that have aimed at identifying offices for decentralisation from London and Stockholm and estimating the likely consequences of relocation on the functioning of the activities concerned. The particular investigations reviewed in detail are similar in that they are primarily concerned with the communication factor in office location and use similar research methods; they are different in that the London studies are concerned with firms in aggregate while the Stockholm study is concerned with one large organisation, namely the Swedish Civil Service.

OFFICE LOCATION POLICY AND RESEARCH IN THE UNITED KINGDOM: ASSESSING OFFICE LOCATION PRIORITIES IN CENTRAL LONDON

The 1950s in the United Kingdom was characterised by a remarkable 40 per cent growth in office occupations and a great deal of this growth was concentrated in London. Indeed by 1966 one out of every seven office workers in the United Kingdom were to be found in the 10 square miles (26 sq km) of Central London. It was in this context that a ban on office building was first introduced in London in 1964; would-be developers had to obtain an Office Development Permit from the central government as well as normal planning permission from the local authority. In applying for a permit, the developer had to argue that the occupier of the proposed office space was tied to London and could not operate elsewhere. The criteria laid down by the Government explicitly acknowledged the importance of linkages in assessing the need for a London location, but in the absence of any hard evidence the ministry concerned found it hard to distinguish between those activities that needed a central location and those that did not. Similarly the Greater London Development Plan of 1970 declared as key objectivities that "the activities that need to be in Central London . . . should be given more opportunity to develop" (Greater London Council, 1970, p. 39), but while recognising the need for a selective approach towards planning the economic structure of the city centre, the Council had little evidence as to what activities should be encouraged and by what criteria appropriateness for the centre was to be assessed (Goddard, 1970).

Controls on office development were coupled with the establishment of the Location of Offices Bureau whose purely advisory role was to promulgate the cause of office decentralisation from Central London, to help firms seeking a non-central location for their offices and to research into factors influencing the location of office activities. In the period 1963-74 the Location of Offices Bureau advised 3500 firms, 1615 of whom decentralised some or all of their work from Central London, involving a total of 133,248 jobs. Forty-two per cent of the moves were to other locations within Greater London and 85 per cent were confined to the prosperous South-East region (L.O.B., 1974). In spite of the need for office jobs in the Development Areas only 7 per cent of all jobs were moved this far from London.

Two important points emerge from these figures: the large number of firms who consider but reject relocation (i.e. who approach the Location of Offices Bureau but then decide not to move) and secondly the dominance of relatively short-distance moves. A survey of firms falling into the first category (non-movers) commissioned by the Location of Offices Bureau revealed a belief that vital personal contact with clients, suppliers, advisers and the like—in fact the pool of information that was readily available in Central London—would be lost if they moved too far away. This was by far the most important reason for rejecting decentralisation (L.O.B., 1968).

In the light of these considerations two major surveys have been undertaken: one for the Department of the Environment which issues Office Development Permits and the other for the Location of Offices Bureau. The primary aim of the first study was to identify those types of offices at present located in Central London which appear to have the strongest communication ties to the city centre (Goddard, 1973). The aim of the second study was to investigate the possible impact of relocation on the offices that had already moved different distances from London by comparing their communications behaviour with that of the city centre firms previously investigated (Goddard and D. M. Morris, 1975). Since offices that decentralise could be a distinctive subset of Central London firms the second study also included a comparison of the communications behaviour of firms about to decentralise (the movers) and others who had rejected decentralisation specifically on communications grounds (the non-movers). In this way it was hoped to identify objectively the communications factor in decisions on office location.

The data for all of the studies were obtained using a contact diary based on a model first used by B. Thorngren in studies of information flows in Swedish industry (Thorngren, 1970) but subsequently adopted in the study of the Swedish Civil Service referred to later in this chapter. In the Central London study the diaries were distributed to a selection of 700 executives in a sample of 70 London offices, a sample which had been stratified according to business sector. The survey of decentralised offices consisted of a sample of firms stratified by distance moved from Central London while the sample of Central London "movers" identified firms who had made a definite decision to relocate but had not yet moved. The Central London "non-movers" were identified from Location of Offices Bureau records as firms who had approached the Bureau but had subsequently rejected decentralisation primarily on communications grounds.

OFFICE LOCATION POLICY AND RESEARCH IN SWEDEN: SELECTING GOVERNMENT AGENCIES FOR DISPERSAL FROM STOCKHOLM

The most comprehensive descriptions of location trends for office activities have been conducted in Sweden (G. Törnqvist, 1970). Here the perspective has clearly been one of regional concentration in the three largest cities rather than local decentralisation from the capital. Unique occupational data indicate that employment in higher level office jobs during the 1960s increased by around 63 per cent in Stockholm, Gothenburg and Malmö compared with 43 per cent for the 43 smallest city regions (M. G. Engström and B. Sahlberg, 1974). Pioneering research by Swedish geographers suggested that contact need was the prime motive force for this pattern. A survey of persons travelling on Swedish domestic airline flights for purposes of business contact provided data which, when compared with data on the distribution of different office occupations, revealed a marked relationship between contact intensity and employment concentration in the capital city (B. Sahlberg, 1970). It was in the public sector especially that top office jobs were most heavily concentrated in Stockholm—58 per cent of all such jobs compared with only 29 per cent of all white collar workers in this sector.

The policy response has involved, on the one hand, a procedure for consultation whereby firms wanting to expand their offices in the Stockholm area are required to take advice from a government board as to possible alternative locations and on the other hand relocation of central government agencies from Stockholm (EFTA, 1973; Friedly, 1974). As it has not been backed up by mandatory controls, the process of consultation has resulted in little redistribution of commercial office employment. On the other hand, 11,000 central government civil service jobs (about 25 per cent of the total) are in the process of being relocated from Stockholm to urban centres principally in the less developed regions of Sweden.

As one guide to selecting government agencies for decentralisation a survey of inter-agency communications was undertaken, using contact diaries and analytical methods broadly similar to those adopted for studying commercial linkages in Central London. The principal difference was that all 18,500 employees in 34 agencies under review completed contact diaries for two separate 3-day periods. (It should be emphasised that there are differences in the administrative structure of Swedish and British central government. In Sweden executive functions are allocated to a large number of autonomous public agencies while policy making is confined to small ministries directly serving the Government of the day. The agencies vary considerably in size and many, especially the largest, have substantial staffs at the regional (county) and local (commune) levels.) The survey of Swedish public agencies was not a sample survey so it was possible to produce objective measures of contact levels which could be directly used in the decision-making process. So while the London investigation could be used only as a background to public policy, the Swedish investigation was a direct input to specific decision making (Thorngren, 1971).

VOLUME OF CONTACT AND DECENTRALISATION

The most basic measure that can be used to differentiate between offices in terms of their need for a central location is the volume of contact—in the London study with other firms and in the Stockholm study with other agencies and outside bodies. To facilitate comparisons between offices of different size standardised contact figures can be derived by dividing the number of contacts by either the total number employed, including those with no contacts, or only by the total number of individuals recording contacts (the contact actors).

The survey of firms about to decentralise from London compared with those rejecting decentralisation reveals that volume of contact is indeed a significant factor in location decisions. Contact actors in the non-moving firms have on average 58 per cent fewer external telephone contacts and 55 per cent fewer meetings than individuals in non-moving firms (an average of 6·2 calls and 1·3 meetings a week as against 19·2 calls and 3·0 meetings for the non-movers). Comparison of these figures with the average for Central London suggests that offices that have made a conscious decision to remain in the city centre have significantly more contacts than the average while those selected for dispersal have a below-average contact level.

It is therefore not surprising to find that the average pattern for Central London conceals considerable variation in contact intensity between business sectors (Table 8.1). Not unexpectedly, sectors concerned with finance have a higher contact intensity than the average for all manufacturing sectors but within this latter group there are again significant variations ranging from 5·3 contacts in a 3-day period for the engineering sector to 11·3 for the construction sector. Similarly, within the service sector, business service firms record an average of 12·5 contacts compared with only 7·4 for professional service firms.

If these sample figures are grossed up to take account of variations between sectors in levels of office employment many manufacturing sectors reveal higher contact levels per employee than apply in the financial sectors. This is possibly because manufacturing firms tend to locate only a limited number of key office workers in the city centre, these being selected on the basis of their need for contacts. In contrast, many financial organisations with the bulk of their employment in the City of London maintain a substantial support staff many of whom have little or no external contact work.

TABLE 8.1. *External contact intensity by sector: Central London*

Sector	Telephone		Face-to-face	
	A	B	A	B
Manufacturing (all)	*6·5*	*1·7*	*1·9*	*0·5*
Chemicals	(7·3)	(2·9)	(2·3)	(0·9)
Engineering	(3·9)	(0·9)	(1·4)	(0·3)
Paper, printing and publishing	(4·2)	(0·9)	(1·0)	(0·1)
Construction	*9·3*	*1·4*	*2·0*	*0·3*
Finance	*7·9*	*1·0*	*2·5*	*0·3*
Insurance	(5·3)	(0·3)	(2·7)	(0·2)
Banking	(6·2)	(1·0)	(2·9)	(0·5)
Other Finance	(9·9)	(1·6)	(1·4)	(0·2)
Business Services	*9·2*	*0·9*	*3·3*	*0·3*
Professional Services	*5·9*	*0·3*	*1·5*	*0·1*
All sectors	*7·4*	*0·8*	*2·6*	*0·3*

Notes

A = Number of contacts per actor.

B = Number of contacts per office employee in the sector as a whole.

Source: Goddard, 1973a.

Discrepancies in contacts per actor and per employee are also recorded in the Swedish data. Here the differences are more meaningful since all employees were given diaries but many recorded no contacts. Of 16,775 respondents only about 6000 recorded face-to-face meetings with other

TABLE 8.2. *Face-to-face contact intensity for selected central government agencies: Stockholm*

Agency	Contacts per actor	Contacts per employee
High contact intensity		
Bank Inspection Board	4·2	2·7
Swedish Agency for Administrative Development (Investigation Unit)	5·0	3·7
National Institute for Radiation Protection	6·6	2·8
Board for Technical Development	4·1	2·1
National Board of Education (Central divisions)	6·0	3·8
Low contact intensity		
State Power Board	2·6	0·9
National Telecommunications Administration (Central division)	2·7	0·8
Patent Office (Corporate division)	2·4	0·4
National Tax Board (Tax division)	2·3	0·7
National Bacteriological Laboratory (Chemical, Technical and Economic division)	4·6	0·9
All agencies	*3·3*	*1·1*

Source: Thorngren, 1971.

government agencies and outsiders. Average contact time for all employees for face-to-face meetings accounted for 6 per cent of working time; if individuals with no contacts are excluded this figure rises to 18 per cent of working time (23 per cent if travel time is added). In general external contact work accounts for more than a fifth of working time for about a third of all employees while the remainder have little or no external contact.

Table 8.2 reveals considerable variations in contact levels for a selection of Swedish public agencies. Again a financial agency, the Bank Inspection Board, comes high on the list in terms of face-to-face contact events per actor with 4·2 meetings in a 3-day period. In the main it is the large agencies with a substantial executive component in their activities (such as the State Power Board) which have low contact levels. At the agency level high or low contact intensity for individual actors tends to be repeated throughout the agency: only in a few specialised agencies, such as the National Bacteriological Laboratory, are large volumes of contact confined to a few individuals.

THE GEOGRAPHICAL DISTRIBUTION OF CONTACTS AND DECENTRALISATION

Another possible indicator of communication ties is the proportion of contacts with other organisations in the capital as opposed to locations elsewhere in the country. A firm or government unit with a large volume of its contacts with a specific locality outside the capital would be an obvious candidate for decentralisation. It is therefore not surprising that individuals in firms that have rejected relocation from Central London have 63 per cent of their external telephone contacts and 79 per cent of their external meetings with other firms in the centre as opposed to 42 per cent and 50 per cent respectively for firms about to decentralise.

Amongst Central London firms as a whole there are again considerable variations in the relative importance of city centre contacts. Because such a large proportion of the nation's financial employment is concentrated in the City of London, it is not surprising to find the external contacts of individuals in this sector principally with other people working in Central London whereas individuals in manufacturing sectors have a more geographically dispersed contact network (Table 8.3). Business service firms tend to meet the needs of the Central London community and therefore have proportionately more local contacts than professional firms serving a regional and national market.

OFFICE CLUSTERS AND JOINT RELOCATION

There are equally wide variations between Swedish public agencies in the relative importance of Stockholm as a source for face-to-face contacts—from

TABLE 8.3. *Geographical distribution of contacts of Central London by region*

	Manufacturing	Finance	Business services	Professional services
Telephone	%	%	%	%
Central London	47	74	71	37
Greater London	22	12	17	20
S.E. Region	11	4	4	11
Rest of U.K.	16	7	7	27
Overseas	4	3	1	5
Total (= 100%)	2096	1797	764	
Meetings	%	%	%	%
Central London	53	76	83	37
Greater London	20	8	9	20
S.E. Region	7	3	2	11
Rest of U.K.	10	6	5	27
Overseas	10	7	0	5
Total (= 100%)	1045	855	366	

Source: Goddard, 1973a.

100 per cent for the Transport Commission to 32 per cent for the Civil Defence Board. Variations in the spatial distribution of contacts in both the Swedish and London studies are partly a function of the allocation of contact needs between different parts of central and local government and different business sectors. Some Swedish agencies have a larger volume of contact with the private sector than others, and most higher level commercial offices are to be found in Stockholm; other agencies have the bulk of their contact with their own regional branches and local authorities outside Stockholm.

It is possible to derive a matrix of inter-sectoral and inter-agency contacts from the diary data which indicates the overall pattern of information connectivity. Analysis of such matrices for telephone calls and meeting contacts reveals that information flows are far from random. In the commercial sector in particular functional differences between offices mean that the activities of one type of office are frequently complementary to those of another. Given the specific nature of these inter-office complementarities, in which the "outputs" of one unit are the "inputs" of another, certain groups of office are likely to be more closely linked to one another and have far weaker connections with offices falling into other groupings. The network of contact linkages between offices in the city centre may therefore be defined as a system containing a number of inter-related sub-systems or office complexes analogous in many respects to individual complexes.

Factor analysis of the inter-sectoral contact matrices for Central London identifies six such functional complexes (Fig. 8.1); banking and finance; civil engineering; commodity trading; publishing and business services; official

Telephone Contacts
Salient Transactions

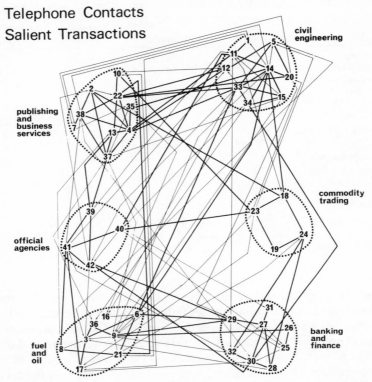

Fig. 8.1. Telephone contacts in Central London: salient transactions between business sectors

agencies; and fuel and oil (L. L. M. Baker and Goddard, 1972). The civil engineering complex includes architects, consulting engineers and brick and cement manufacturers. The group focusses on general construction companies from which most contacts originate. It is well known that many aspects of a civil engineering project are contracted out to different types of firms; inevitably this procedure will lead to a substantial amount of contact between the various contractors.

Figure 8.1 reveals that while distinctive complexes of inter-related office activities can be identified there are equally important links between different spheres of business activity which are indicative of the diverse functions performed by many individual office sectors. Indirect linkages in which one activity knits together otherwise independent sub-groupings may be particularly significant.

In view of this very complicated pattern of linkages, policies of controlling development and dispersal obviously need to be managed with considerable care. If employment that was central to a particular complex was to decline through planning intervention, the external economies the complex offers to its members could be undermined (Thorngren, 1967,1968). On the other hand increases in employment in sectors that are weakly connected could have undesired side effects by adding unnecessarily to the costs of congestion in the city centre in terms of higher prices for land, labour and other economic factors.

Analysis of inter-sectoral contacts can provide a number of important policy indicators. These include measures of the extent to which a sector is involved in one or more functional complexes, measures of indirect connection to other sectors and the extent to which contacts are concentrated to one or two other sectors. In addition such data can be used to suggest how complexes of related office activities can be established in office centres outside the capital through the relocation of groups of interlinked functions and the local encouragement of specific activities needed to complete a particular complex. Although such complexes characterise capital cities (cf. M. Bannon's (1972) study of Dublin) these are notably absent in provincial cities (cf. N. Croft's (1969) study of Leeds).

Similar analytic methods were applied to the Swedish contact data with the aim of identifying groups of closely interlinked agencies which could be relocated together. However, in the majority of cases the contact data revealed that external linkages with other organisations inside and outside Stockholm were far more important than links with other central agencies in the capital. The grouping therefore had to take account of these external links, including their geographical location, with the aim of identifying "open clusters". Three types of clusters were suggested (Fig. 8.2).

1. Closed clusters where internal links predominate.
2. Open clusters with *direct* connection to a common external contact source.
3. Open clusters with *indirect* connections to a common external contact source.

The final analysis produced nine groups of agencies defined in terms of their pattern of connection with the internal *and* external environment of the

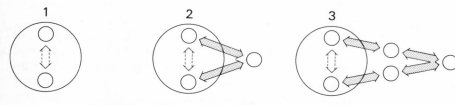

Fig. 8.2. Types of clusters for Swedish central government agencies

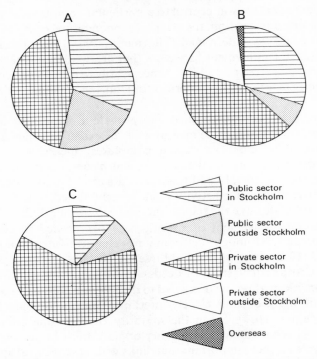

Fig. 8.3. Distribution of contracts for three basic clusters of central government agencies in Stockholm

Civil Service. The clustering was made on the basis of one type of contact—"planning contacts"—identified through a multivariate classification, which is discussed later in the essay (Fig. 8.3). The first three groups (A, B and C) were principally of types one and two and composed of a number of relatively small agencies with common patterns of external links. In the first group links in Stockholm with other central agencies and with ministries were balanced by equally significant links with societies and associations and private consultants. In the second group research organisation accounted for 30 per cent of the Stockholm contacts and 56 per cent of the contacts with the rest of Sweden. For the third group, the private sector in Stockholm, especially consultants and computer firms was the dominant contact source. The remaining six groups had the common characteristics that regional and local parts of their own and other agencies dominated the contact patterns, principally because the agencies concerned were large central units in an extensive regional structure. Six separate groups were defined primarily because a single reception area would be able to accommodate only one large agency.

THE IMPACT OF RELOCATION ON CONTACT NETWORKS

The clusters of Swedish central government agencies on the basis of existing contact patterns could be directly used in informing the decision as to which groups of agencies should be moved to which towns. On the other hand the findings on contact networks in Central London are expressed only at the level of the business sector since under present arrangements public policy guidelines can be drawn up only at this aggregate level. However, within a sector there may be considerable variations between firms in contact patterns, depending especially on the range of departments operating from a particular office, the functions these departments are expected to perform and the status levels of the staff employed. Table 8.4 indicates that in aggregate there are greater variations in contact intensity between different types of departments in different firms than were revealed between business sectors. In view of such problems the contact data are probably of greatest value to the managers of individual firms in assessing their own location requirements. As in the Swedish study the data may be used to indicate which departments have weak linkages with the city centre and are therefore likely candidates for decentralisation.

However, even with this type of information on contact volumes and decentralisation it is still extremely difficult to predict exactly what will happen if a particular office relocates. A great deal of uncertainty will still surround such questions as:

1. What proportion of existing contacts will no longer take place if the office decentralises?

TABLE 8.4. *External contact intensity for selected types of department: Central London*

	Telephone calls per actor	Meetings per actor
High contact intensity		
Buying	17·8	4·5
Public relations	11·3	2·7
Finance	10·3	3·2
Export/distribution	13·5	1·6
Advertising	8·1	4·5
Low contact intensity		
Computer services	2·3	1·4
Organisation and Methods	4·4	0·8
Typing/despatch	2·5	2·6
Accounts	5·8	0·7
Research and Development	5·5	1·4
All departments	*7·4*	*2·6*

Source: Goddard, 1973a.

2. Will this proportion be affected by the distance moved?
3. If some links at present maintained through face-to-face meetings cannot be stretched over space through longer travel can they be:
   (a) substituted by telecommunication
   (b) substituted by new links in the decentralised location?

Some of these questions were of particular concern to the researchers attempting to estimate the consequences for communication of dispersing certain parts of governmental head office work from London (Goddard, 1971; United Kingdom, 1973). By using individual's estimates of the amount and significance of contacts between individual blocks of government work at present located in London and by assuming that existing meetings would either be abandoned, one or more of the participants would travel or telecommunications would be substituted for travel, an attempt was made to estimate the monetary cost or "communication damage" to existing links for alternative patterns of dispersal. Similar approaches have been adopted in examining the travel cost consequences of alternative strategies of relocation from Stockholm for the Swedish civil service (Persson, 1974).

However, a number of difficulties arise with the "communications damage" approach, especially in any consideration of links with the external environment (Goddard, 1973b). In concentrating solely on the *volume* of existing links there is a danger of overlooking organisational processes to which communications are related. The possibility of dispersal is not simply a matter of the cost of stretching existing links because contact patterns in any location reflect a complex relationship between the organisation and its environment. The nature and significance of contacts is determined by the joint characteristics of the office in question and of the other offices with which it has connections. By changing the location of an office new patterns of access to the environment will be established and consequently new patterns of communication will emerge. In the short run some old contacts will be maintained but in the long run the nature of the office activity itself will change as it adapts to the opportunities and constraints presented by the new situation and the local environment itself also adapts to the injection of additional office employment.

The importance of the immediate locality in determining the nature of this process of adaptation cannot be over-emphasised. Because of fundamental time-geographic considerations it is inevitable that individuals have the bulk of their personal contacts with other persons from their immediate environment. In Central London 78 per cent of all journeys for the purpose of business contacts last less than 30 minutes. Almost identical figures have been recorded by Thorngren (1970) in four Swedish cities (Stockholm, Gothenburg, Sundsvall and Umea) and for a random sample of offices throughout the United Kingdom in a study conducted for the Post Office by S. Connell (1974). But while a 30-minute radius from the centre of a metropolitan city will reach out to a potentially very large number of high-level contacts, in another location the same length of journey is likely to encompass fewer and less rich contact sources.

So whether it is planned or not it is highly likely that decentralisation will in the long run imply some change in the way an office functions. While such changes may not be formally recognised in the structure of the organisation they will be reflected in the actual pattern of internal and external contacts. In particular, as work contacts are far from uniform in their characteristics and purposes it is highly likely that various types of contact will be differentially effected by relocation.

Conclusive evidence about the impact of relocation on patterns of office communications can come only from studies conducted before and after a move. The results of only one such study have been published (Thorngren, 1973). This was of the relocation in 1966 of the head office of the Swedish Defence Industry Procurement Board from Stockholm to Eskiltuna some 120 km (75 miles) away. A contact survey was conducted 3 months before and 8 months after the move. Contacts were classified into three groups: internal contacts between the head office and other units, one of which had been located in Eskiltuna for some time; external contacts directly related to buying and selling (i.e. "economically controllable" contacts where contacts were paralleled by monetary transactions): and "economically uncontrollable" contacts with Government, research institutes and associations (Fig. 8.4).

After relocation the number of external commercial contacts with Eskiltuna increased from nil to 36 per cent. The number of internal meeting contacts with Eskiltuna also increased both absolutely and relatively (from 11 to 63, or 9 per cent to 63 per cent). In contrast external non-commercial contacts were relatively unaffected principally because most of these contact sources were unique to Stockholm and no local alternatives were available. Not surprisingly the relative distribution of telephone contacts of each type was less affected by the relocation than the corresponding meetings.

If the adaptive view of organisation that these results imply is accepted, then many of the so-called communication *costs* of relocation associated with the non-adaptive view (i.e. the need to maintain *all* existing contacts with old locations) many turn out to be *benefits* for *certain* types of relationships an organisation has with its environment. In an interview study of decentralised offices J. Rhodes and A. Kan (1971) found that many managers quoted benefits arising from a change in communication behaviour: for example regular planned discussion often proved more productive than informal and endless chats which took place when the individuals were close together in the City. Decentralisation could release time for important internal matters which might be neglected in the contact rich environment of the city centre. Equally a local service firm (e.g. accountants) could replace an overloaded city centre firm and provide a more personal service.

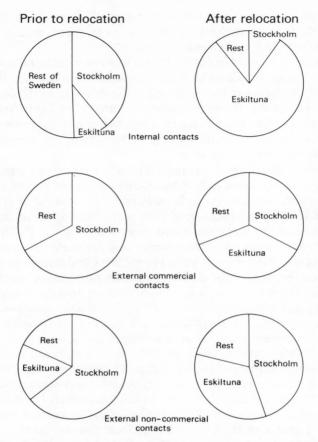

Fig. 8.4. Distribution of face-to-face contacts of public agency before and after decentralisation from Stockholm to Eskiltuna

Further evidence of the possible transfer of contacts to the decentralised location can be inferred from a comparison of the spatial patterns of contacts of firms that have decentralised from London with those remaining in the centre. Figure 8.5 reveals that the proportion of external contacts which decentralised offices maintain with Central London decreases with distance moved most dramatically for moves of over 60 miles (96 km). On average individuals in Central London have 58 per cent of their external telephone calls with other people in the centre compared with 38 per cent for those moving over 60 miles. Conversely the number of contacts with places outside the South East increases with distance moved. Although it has been noted that firms about to decentralise have more contacts than average with places outside Central London, some of the contacts recorded here must be "new" contacts established subsequent to the move.

The sharp decline of contacts with Central London for moves of over 60 miles can be related to the geography of contact opportunities and the pattern of decentralisation. In spite of the large amount of office employment in the South East Region outside London, much of this is extremely dispersed; consequently the possibilities of establishing local contacts with the immediate

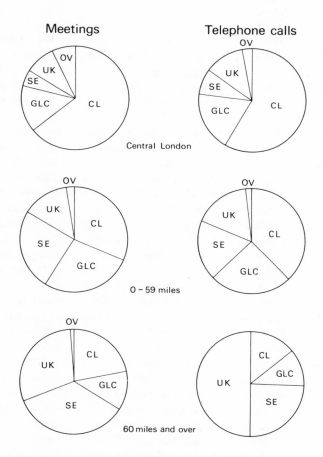

Distribution of external contacts : central London and decentralized offices (from Goddard and Morris, 1975)

CL – Central London, GLC – Greater London, SE – South East Region, UK – Elsewhere in UK, OV – Overseas

Fig. 8.5. Distribution of external contacts: Central London and decentralised offices

environment are limited. London therefore exerts a strong shadow effect. However, over 60 miles from London, larger office centres can be found which can provide realistic alternative contacts to London.

Differences in the geographical distribution of contacts for short- and long-distance movers are reflected in average journey times to meetings; firms moving a long way from London have on average *shorter* journeys to business meetings than firms moving less far. For example, 33 per cent of business journeys of firms moving over 80 miles (108 km) last less than 30 minutes, compared with an average of 10 per cent for firms moving between 20 (32 km) and 80 miles. Nevertheless, the amount of time spent on business travel by those in decentralised offices is obviously much greater than that spent by those in offices in Central London or in long-established offices elsewhere, reflecting the fact that many of these firms have not yet completely adjusted to the contact opportunities of their local environment and also possibly a mistaken choice of isolated suburban rather than city-centre sites in the new locations.

The Swedish findings suggest that only certain types of contact will be involved in this transfer process. The characteristics of the contacts themselves, measured in terms of features such as mode (telephone or face-to-face), length, frequency and subject matter discussed, can provide one of the best indicators of the likely impact of relocation on communication processes. Thorngren (1970) has argued that different types of contact have different organisational significance in terms of the information that passes through them. He distinguishes three types of processes and related contacts. Orientation processes, which involve long-term and wide-ranging scanning of the organisation's knowledge and values environment, are essentially characterised by a *broad and diverging* contact network: large meetings bringing together new combinations of people for wide-ranging discussions are often the medium through which orientation processes operate. Planning processes, in contrast, involve a more directed development of previously identified alternatives and more *intensive* contact relations between limited sets of familiar individuals who can sometimes use the telephone instead of a face-to-face meeting. Finally, programmed processes involve the day-to-day management of existing resources and therefore concern essentially a *large volume* of routine contacts; individuals are either in contact on a regular basis or come together usually by telephone for one-off and specific enquiries.

The locational significance of this classification is that certain spatial environments may be more appropriate for one type of communication process than another; contacts of each type are therefore likely to be differentially affected by relocation depending on the nature of the activity involved and the characteristics of the receiving locations. Only the metropolitan city offers the breadth of potential contacts with government, researchers, financial institutions and organisations, which is essential for the conduct of orientation processes. Unlike orientation, planning work is less dependent on random contact: indeed the great variety of information thrown up in the large metropolis may conflict with the development of a specific project and therefore lead to "communication overload". Being familiar with one another, individuals involved in planning contacts can use telecommunications, provided there are opportunities for regular meetings. These conditions suggest that planning activities are suitable candidates for decentralisation; however, as individual contacts frequently form a chain of related events considerable advantage could accrue to a large organisation by relocating clusters of planning activities. Finally, the routine nature of programmed relations means that these are most likely to be substitutable by new contacts in the decentralised location. The extensive use of telecommunications also favours decentralisation although the large volume of contact could create technical problems in the short run especially in a poorly served remote location.

It is on these sorts of grounds that the characteristics as much as the volume of existing contacts were selected as being the most useful basis on which to rate public agencies in terms of their need for a Stockholm location. In particular, the classification into orientation, planning and programmed contact provides a fundamental dimension along which the likely impact of relocation on communication can be measured.

Thorngren has pioneered the use of a technique of multivariate classification, latent profile analysis, as a tool for classifying contacts on the basis of their observed characteristics (cf. W. A. Gibson, 1959; P. P. Lazerfeld and M. W. Henry, 1968). One such classification—of contacts recorded in Central London—is shown in Figure 8.6. The three classes can be loosely related to the conceptual classification into orientation, planning and programmed

TABLE 8.5. *Classification of contacts*

Location	Orientation	Planning	Programmed
	%	%	%
Central London			
External	14·5	4·2	81·2
Decentralised			
Locations			
Internal	7·3	17·7	74·9
External	10·3	1·1	88·6
Movers			
Internal	6·5	17·7	75·8
External	14·8	3·5	81·7
Non-Movers			
Internal	6·9	32·2	60·9
External	24·1	8·5	67·4
Stockholm Agencies	9·0	31·0	60·0

Source: Goddard and Morris, 1975.

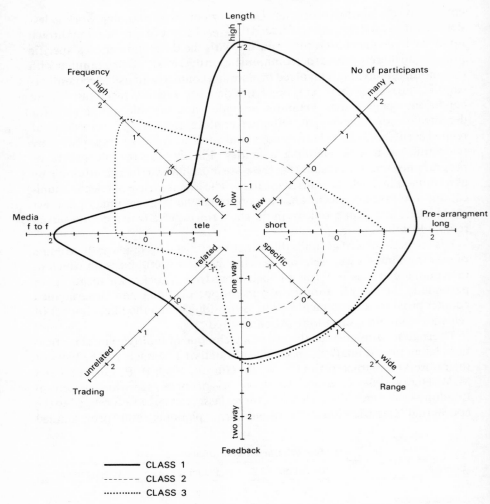

Fig. 8.6. Multivariate classification of external contacts of offices in Central London

contacts. Class 1 corresponds to orientation contacts, Class 3 to programmed contacts and Class 2 to planning contacts.

Although all three types of contact can be identified in most organisational and locational situations, their relative importance varies considerably according to the position of the unit in the organisation and the particular segments of the environment with which it has contact. Table 8.5 indicates that orientation contacts are less important in decentralised locations than in Central London, a reflection of the fact that fewer contacts are with the information rich environment of the city centre. The division of contacts into those that are internal and external to the organisation suggests that the planning function is essentially an internal one. The table also suggests that the characteristics of contact networks also have an important bearing on location decisions. Firms that have rejected decentralisation from Central London (the non-movers) have significantly more external orientation contacts than firms about to decentralise (24 per cent compared to 15 per cent) and also significantly more internal planning contacts (32 per cent compared with 18 per cent). These differences can again be largely attributed to the fact already noted that non-movers have significantly more contacts with other firms in the city centre.

These differences in contact characteristics obviously have a bearing on contact volumes in different locations but it is the characteristics of the contact themselves that are most significant. Thus decentralised offices have 5 per cent fewer external calls and 25 per cent fewer meetings than other firms in Central London prior to moving, suggesting a possible loss of some contacts. (Internal meetings, on the other hand, are 50 per cent more numerous in decentralised offices, suggesting that more time is devoted to internal matters.) These differences largely stem from the fact that external contacts occur less frequently in decentralised and non-moving offices. For example, 22 per cent of the telephone calls of non-movers occur on a daily basis, compared with only 6 per cent for movers and 8 per cent for decentralised offices. Because of their close connection with contact frequency, a wide range of other differences follow from this basic distinction. Frequent contacts tend to be shorter, unarranged or arranged only the day before, and to involve a limited number of familiar people in rather specific discussions. A short contact is therefore likely to involve simply the giving or receiving of information rather than wide-ranging exchange. Frequent short contacts therefore tend to fulfil a different function than long pre-planned meetings.

CONCLUSION: COMMUNICATIONS RESEARCH AND THE REFORMULATION OF OFFICE LOCATION POLICY

The traditional concern of office location policy in the United Kingdom especially has been the dispersal of office employment from the Metropolis with little attention being paid to where this employment is relocated. The outstanding conclusions of much of the research that has been reviewed is that this office dispersal needs to be concentrated into a limited number of major office centres with an adequate contact infrastructure. Since this public policy can only be effected through the locational decisions of individual organisations, how can research be used to inform such decisions?

Before deciding on a relocation an individual organisation clearly needs to take account of its existing and future communications requirements. A communications survey of existing internal (inter-departmental) and external (inter-firm) contacts can suggest a strategy of relocation which supports management objectives. The findings that individuals communicate in different ways in different places suggests that relocation can be used as a positive tool in management; for example it can be used to bring together departments which need to communicate more with each other and perhaps less with other firms; to improve linkages with other firms that are located elsewhere, perhaps in newly emerging spheres of interest for the organisations; to encourage the devolution of some functions to lower levels in the organisation thereby creating space and time in a city centre office for decision-making activities.

The important point is that some strategies of relocation may be more appropriate than others for achieving particular management objectives. For example, short-distance relocation to a small office centre will not encourage the establishment of new local linkages which might be an essential component of a strategy of administrative decentralisation. It is therefore necessary to distinguish between the *dispersal* of offices—which is a purely geographical concept—and *decentralisation* which is also a functional concept which geographical separation may encourage. If, however, there is a need to release time for essential internal matters then movement to a minor office centre not far from the capital may be a good alternative for planning or research and development functions.

The success or otherwise of the relocation will need to be monitored by regular communications surveys or "audits". These data may suggest additional changes in the formal organisational structure or new telecommunications devices that are needed in order to derive the maximum benefits from the new location. In addition to evaluating the relocation as such, the audits may indicate potential future problems that may have to be dealt with by further organisational/locational adjustments. For example, the audits may indicate "blind spots" in external contact networks (e.g. sectors of the environment not covered by any part of the organisation) or a failure to link up external and internal networks so that outside information is not channelled to the appropriate parts of the organisation.

Here as elsewhere in this chapter emphasis is placed upon the role of information flows in the development of organisations. Little attention has been paid to the direct costs of communications. The ease with which contact networks can adjust to new organisational and locational situations means that attempts formally to determine the communications costs and benefits of particular location strategies are of limited validity. Because of the large area of uncertainty and the speed with which changes can occur in environmental conditions, a process of monitoring a selected strategy coupled with appropriate adjustments in that strategy is probably more appropriate than a "one shot" cost-benefit analysis. Decentralisation should therefore be seen not solely as a short run economic decision with respect to such factors as rents, labour costs and telephone bills, but as part of a process by which organisations can adapt to changing environmental conditions. So although a relatively short distance move to a small office centre may suit present-day contact requirements and also be the most economical solution on a number of other cost grounds, only a large office centre can offer the number and variety of local contact opportunities that can sustain an office organisation when external conditions change.

So a public policy of *concentrated decentralisation* may also bring long-run benefits to individual firms. For example, within such centres there will be possibilities of using relatively cheap group audio telecommunications for more expensive conference video intra-urban contact: telecommunications in public studios would then be used for inter-city contact. It is unlikely that a large number of dispersed locations will be equipped with such facilities, at least in the short run. The public benefits of such a pattern are numerous. On the economic side there is the possibility of the development of complexes of inter-related office functions which can provide external economies for the constituent activities but also act as a stimulus for growth and change in the surrounding region. So although the growth centre based on a propulsive industry may not be particularly useful in terms of material linkages such a centre could have very real meaning in terms of office location and associated information flows. On the social side there are the benefits to be gained by individuals from a labour market with a diversified occupational structure and possibilities for the use of public transport.

Unless present-day policies are modified and decisions about the relocation of individual offices coordinated, an opportunity for creating such centres may be lost. Concentrated decentralisation clearly needs some new instruments to bring about the detailed steering of economic activities that this policy implies. The existing system of blanket controls on physical development and financial incentives applied over equally wide areas of the country provides very blunt policy instruments. The subtle ways in which firms can adapt to environmental change through administrative reorganisation which may include alterations in the division of office functions between locations suggest that the location process as such is extremely difficult to control from the point of view of regional policy.

Because the process of environmental adaption is heavily constrained by information channelled through established networks, contact patterns are a key element in the process of change *and* also control. Firms frequently make sub-optimal decisions based on a failure to appreciate fully the constraints on information flows imposed by their own organisational structure. Communications audits administered by a public body could be a very powerful tool in regional policy by highlighting for firms the opportunities of alternative locational/organisational arrangements, especially the advantages to be gained through different but complementary offices locating in similar areas. Communications surveys could also reveal the possibility of linking up complementary functions in different offices in nearby regions perhaps in order to complete an office complex. In addition to encouraging the relocation of specific office functions to specific places policy would also need to recognise the importance of new office activities that are indigenous to the area in question.

This approach implies a much greater involvement of government in a collaborative way in the long-run strategic planning decisions of commercial office organisations rather than a crude carrot and stick approach applied to the geographical environment and not to the decision-making units the policy is aimed at. Nevertheless this is not to deny the need for spatial policies which designate office growth centres and thereby provide a basis for linking urban and regional policy and coordinating these policies with investment in passenger transport and telecommunications. Unless far-reaching changes in government policy which take account of the influence of contact possibilities on regional development are implemented, the existing spiral of over-concentration will continue. Indeed investment in communications infrastructure such as conference video facilities and advanced passenger trains that are uncoordinated with location policy is only likely to increase regional differentials in contact opportunities and ultimately in economic and social development.

REFERENCES

Baker, L. L. N. and J. B. Goddard (1972) "Inter-sectoral contact flows and office location", in A. G. Wilson (ed.) *London Studies in Regional Science,*

Bannon, N. (1972) *Office Location in Ireland: the Role of Central Dublin,* An Foras Forbartha, Dublin.

Connell, S. (1974) *The 1973 Office Communications Survey,* Communications Studies Group, London (mimeo).

Croft, N. (1969) *Offices in a Regional Centre: Follow-up Studies of Infrastructure and Linkages,* Research Paper No. 3, Location of Offices Bureau, London.

EFTA (1973) *National Settlement Strategies: A framework for Regional Development,* EFTA, Geneva.

Engström, M. A. and B. Sahlberg (1974) *Travel Demand and Transport Facilities,* Lund Studies in Geography (B), No. 40, Gleerup, Lund.

Friedly, P. H. (1974) *National Policy Responses to Urban Growth,* Saxon House, Farnborough.

Gibson, W. A. (1959) "Three multivariate models compared: factor analysis, latent structure analysis and latent profile analysis", *Psychometrika,* **24**, 54-76.

Goddard, J. B. (1970) "Greater London Development Plan: Central London, a key to strategic planning", *Area,* **3**, 52-5.

Goddard, J. B. (1971) "Office communications and office location: a review of current research", *Regional Studies,* **5**, 263-80.

Goddard, J. B. (1973a) *Office Linkages and Location: a Study of Communications and Spatial Pattern in Central London,* Pergamon Press, Oxford.

Goddard, J. B. (1973b) "Civil Service for the Regions", *Town and Country Planning,* **41,** 451-4.

Goddard, J. B. (1975) *Office Location in Urban and Regional Development,* Clarendon Press, Oxford.

Goddard, J. B. and D. M. Morris (1975) *The Communications Factor in Office Location,* Pergamon Press, Oxford.

Greater London Council (1970) *Greater London Development Plan: Statement,* G.L.C., London.

Lazerfeld, P. P. and M. W. Henry (1968) "The application of latent structure analysis to quantitative ecological data". in F. Massarik and P. Ratoosh (eds.), *Mathematical Explorations in the Behavioural Sciences,* Dorcey Press, Illinois.

Location of Offices Bureau (1968) *A Study of Non-Movers,* LOB, London (mimeo).

Location of Offices Bureau (1974) *Annual Report,* LOB, London.

Persson, C. (1974) *Kontaktarbete och Framtida Localiserings Föränringar,* Geographiska Institution, University of Lund.

Rhodes, J. and A. Kan (1971) *Office Dispersal and Regional Policy,* Dept. of Applied Economics, University of Cambridge, Occasional Paper 30, Cambridge University Press, Cambridge.

Sahlberg, B. (1970) *Interregionala Kontäkmönster,* Gleerup, Lund.

Thorngren, B. (1967) "Regional economic interaction and flows of information", in *Proceedings of the Second Poland-Norden Regional Science Seminar,* Committee for Space Economy and Regional Planning of the Polish Academy of Sciences, PWN, Warsaw.

Thorngren, B. (1968) "External economies and the urban core", in M. Van Hulten (ed.) *Urban Core and Inner City,* Brill, Leiden.

Thorngren, B. (1970) "How do contact systems affect regional development?", *Environment and Planning,* **2,** 409-27.

Thorngren, B. (1971) Komm 71: *Kommunikation-Sunddersöking vid Statliga Myndigheter,* Economic Research Institute, Stockholm School of Economics (mimeo).

Thorngren, B. (1973) "Swedish office dispersal", in M. Bannon (ed.) *Office Location and Regional Development,* An Foras Forbartha, Dublin.

Törnqvist, G. (1970) *Contact Systems and Regional Development,* Lund Studies in Geography (B), No. 35, Gleerup, Lund.

United Kingdom (1973) *The Dispersal of Government Work from London,* Cmnd. 5322, H.M.S.O., London.

CHAPTER 9

THE SPATIAL DIMENSIONS OF
POLLUTION POLICY

D. N. M. STARKIE
University of Reading

PROLEGOMENA

Apart from the view, strongly held by some, that pollution (here defined in the usual conventional terms as damage producing waste matter or surplus energy originating from human activity) is increasingly pervasive in modern society, at least two other possible inter-related factors combine to imbue good environments with political import. Increased spending on the luxury of less pollution, as a consequence of satisfying our basic needs for food, clothing and shelter, is one factor (House of Commons, 1974, Col.104). Another is that social values are supposedly changing and good environments are moving upwards in the list of social priorities (Royal Commission on Environmental Pollution, 1971).

Not all commentators, impartial or otherwise, share the views of such august authorities. N. Gunningham (1974), for instance, rejects the idea of a change in the fundamental values of society and, instead, attributes the recent concern with environmental pollution to the machinations of the communications media. Although recent content analyses do not refute Gunningham's argument (A. Auliciems and I. Burton, 1970), his views still beg the question as to why newspapers, radio and television should react in the way they do, if not to reflect the underlying views of society. It would be a mistake, however, to conclude that the quality of life in the widest sense of the term is a twentieth-century obsession. On the contrary, a distinct continuity with nineteenth-century legislation on public health can be discovered in recent enactments regarding pollution. Indeed, public health acts form the basis of a great deal of contemporary legislation on pollution in the United Kingdom, with the enforcement of pollution laws very much in the hands of local authority public health inspectors and the Alkali Inspectorate, the latter established in 1863. Notable of past legislation in this regard is the Public Health Act of 1936, which firmly established the concept of statutory nuisances, whereby nuisances were defined in law.

CHANGING PERSPECTIVES AND POLICIES

Whether or not basic societal values have changed, there has nevertheless been a shift of emphasis over time in the general focus of pollution policy. Thus, for example, in the United Kingdom the emphasis of post-war policy has drifted steadily from the abatement of air pollution (with its obvious physiological manifestations) to the more subtle psychological pollutant, noise, described as "one of the curses of modern society" (House of Commons, 1974, Col.101). Reasons for this shift are varied. It reflects partly the success of past legislation in overcoming particular problems of pollution, and partly the emergence of new problem areas. With increasing affluence, the diversification of products and services available, and purchased, focuses the problem afresh on the concomitant pollution. The car, the jet aircraft, the package holiday and packaging in general, particularly of the plastic kind, are all symbolic in this context. Moreover, "the diversification of products and industrial processes often throws up new and potentially dangerous or troublesome forms of waste" (House of Commons, 1974, Col.98). Subsequently, the perceived nature of the pollution problem changes (even if its overall importance does not).

Another feature of contemporary pollution policy has been its tendency increasingly to incorporate the public sector within its rubric of statutory nuisances. Both statutory undertakings and public works have long enjoyed a privileged position in this regard, possibly reflecting the idea that there is a distinction between pollution from publicly owned property and that from private property.

Yet the rapid growth of the public sector and development of the mixed economy have made such exclusiveness more difficult to justify. The 1965 Airports Authority Act and the Land Compensation Act of 1973 incorporate fundamental changes in this respect, in so far as they modify the rule "followed since 1845 and possibly before" (V. Moore, 1974) that where no interest in land is acquired, compensation for injurious affection (from pollution) should exclude damage resulting from the *use* of public works. The former Act modified this rule with respect to aircraft noise in the vicinity of certain airports, while the latter represented an important extension of the same modification to all other public works (including highways constructed after mid-1969) resulting in injurious affection from noise, vibration, smell, fumes, smoke, artificial lighting and the discharge onto land of any solid or liquid substance (Section I, 1973 Act). It should be noted that injury caused by the visible presence of the public works is never compensatable; in addition, common law action has never protected a view and therefore it can be argued that "officially" there is no such thing as "visual pollution".

Another notable feature of recent anti-pollution policy has been its *international* character. Parallel legislation is frequently to be found in different countries. Thus, to take air pollution by way of example, the 1956 Clean Air Act in the United Kingdom was mirrored by the 1963 Clean Air Act in the United States (with both Acts providing grants for programmes to control air pollution) and by the 1965 Federal legislation in Germany. Conversely, the 1974 Control of Pollution Act in the United Kingdom emulated 1971 legislation in the United States, by establishing powers to regulate the composition of motor fuels.

It is not entirely coincidental that such parallel developments have occurred. The pollution problems of advanced industrial nations, locked together in the international trading economy and symbolised by multi-national conglomerate industries, are naturally similar, in spite of differences in the capacity of different countries to assimilate various levels of pollution. But, quite apart from the tendency for different nations to be producing and consuming fundamentally similar manufactures, there are more subtle aspects to the international perspective. Firstly, there is the issue of trans-boundary pollution; the eco-system through which pollution is transmitted is disrespectful of national boundaries. Consequently, the Dutch are forced to import the polluted water of the Rhine (A. Cairncross *et al.*, 1974, p. 165), while Scandinavia supposedly suffers in a similar manner by sharing an air-shed with industrial Europe. Secondly, there is the problem that competitive pressures may lead to the cutting of internal standards to gain an advantage in international trade. Conversely, if pressure is applied by one country to achieve higher standards, employment will be endangered, with perhaps the eventual move of the organisation elsewhere (House of Commons, 1974, Col. 116). The overall problem has been summarised in the following succinct terms:

> Within one country ideal adjustment requires both pollutor and sufferer to change their output and inputs. These adjustments require population migration and the relocation of production. With international problems . . . the adjustment mechanisms show up in the balance of payments . . . as changes in the flows of goods, of capital, and of labour.
>
> (A. D. Scott, 1972, p. 256)

It is not surprising, therefore, that steps have been taken to reach international agreements and to establish international standards of pollution control.

Perhaps the most successful of such agreements reached to date concerns aircraft noise. This is the International Civil Aviation Organisation's (ICAO) recommended standards for the noise certification of aircraft. These recommendations, ratified in 1971 (as an Annexe to the Chicago Convention), were already embodied, albeit in a slightly more stringent form, in the United States Federal regulations of 1969 and were anticipated in the United Kingdom by the Air Navigation (Noise Certification) Order of 1970 (enabled by the Civil Aviation Act of 1968).

Not all attempts at international agreement have been so successfully concluded. The European Economic Community, for example, has yet to reach full agreement with respect to vehicle noise. But this is often for good reason. Nations differ with respect to their natural endowment, and thus their capacity for harmless assimilation of pollution; with respect to their economic and social priorities; and with respect to their levels of development (J. H. Cumberland, 1972, p. 252).

Finally, one of the factors giving rise to international problems of pollution, viz., the transmission of pollution through the eco-system, is increasingly providing an incentive for the establishment of federal and national agencies to combat pollution problems. The United States' approach to standards of ambient air quality is notable in this regard, while in England and Wales the Water Act 1973 establishes the ecological basin approach to the administration and control of water pollution.

A SPATIAL TAXONOMY OF POLLUTION

Within this general framework of policy issues and events, the spatial elements are three-fold. First, there is the analysis of the attenuation of pollutants with distance from their source; secondly, recording and mapping the distribution of pollution over space, as an aid to monitoring the effects of abatement legislation or aiding decision makers with respect to the formulation of new environmental legislation; and, thirdly, the analysis of the effects of pollution on locational decisions, both of a residential and of an industrial nature.

To view the situation in this way is implicitly to make a distinction in both scale and time. Thus, the spatial decay functions relating to individual sources, when amalgamated, form distributions in macro-space. It is basically in response to this overall pattern of pollution, and the perception of it, that pollution-determined locational adjustments take place. Moreover, to observe the coalescence of pollution flows forming a pollution-scape is to see the process of diffusion within the eco-system; again locational adjustments are essentially a postscript to this diffusion process.

DISTANCE DECAY

Fundamental to the process of formulating policy and reaching decisions where issues of pollution are involved is an appreciation of how pollution attenuates with distance from its source. Partly as a consequence of legislation, such as the 1973 Land Compensation Act, such an appreciation is now crucial, for example, in the planning of new roads and motorways.

All pollutants attenuate in intensity with increasing distance from their source(s), as a consequence of their source energy dissipating in the atmosphere. Figure 9.1 illustrates this process for transport sources and suggests that the fall-off with distance approximates closely to an exponential decay.

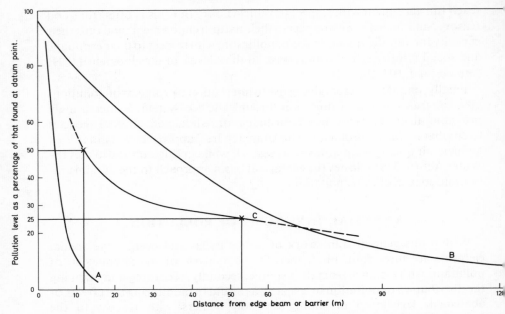

Fig. 9.1. Distance decay functions for lead concentrations (A and B) and noise (C).(A m soil, as % of that on edge of hard shoulder M4 motorway, B m atmosphere as % of that in central reservation; C, noise level at 8 m as % of their new 3 m barrier, single carriageway. Source: Lassière 1974)

Not all pollutants, however, attenuate at the same rate. This is partly because of difference in the nature of the energy source. Indeed, a specific pollutant, noise for example, will vary in its attenuation properties for the same reason. Such distinctions are illustrated well by noise from motor vehicles. Although there are several sources of noise on an individual vehicle (such as engine, exhaust and tyres), it is conventionally treated as if it were a *point source*. Cars in a stream of vehicles (each an individual source of noise) passing on a road, however, are at varying distances from the receiver. Here the conventional simplification is to treat the traffic stream as a *line source* (A. Lassière and P. Bowers, 1972, pp. 81-3), with the consequence that the sound pressure level falls at half the rate of that for a point source for each doubling of distance between source and listener (3 decibels vis-à-vis 6 decibels).

In addition, such rates of attenuation will be affected by the nature of the ground over which the pollution passes (attenuation of noise over grass is much more than that over hard ground); by wind direction; and by wind and temperature gradients. With increasing height the surface attenuation effect declines rapidly, so that noise sources some distance from the ground are little, if at all, affected by such factors (Lassière, 1974, pp. 5.25-6.26). However, with an increase in height a new factor, atmospheric turbulence, comes into play and is particularly important in the case of air-borne gas or solids pollution, especially when associated with high emission stacks. It has also proved to be a difficult factor to model and take into effect in the distance decay functions (R. Scorer, 1968).

Spatial attenuation, therefore, is a complex and too little understood process. Present research is attempting to expand this knowledge, particularly in fields such as attenuation of aircraft noise and the attenuation of motorway "dust" pollution (J. Spence, 1972), thus enabling the environmental impacts to be assessed with a greater degree of certainty.

THE SPATIAL DISTRIBUTION OF POLLUTION

Models of distance decay provide a vital ingredient in the analysis of the possible pollution impact of proposed roads, railways, power stations and the like. In this forecasting context, it is necessary to simulate these impacts with the assistance of the attenuation functions. *Pollution maps* simulated in this way were instrumental, for example, in the decision on the precise location and orientation of runways for the proposed Third London Airport at Maplin Sands (Fig. 9.2), though this is not now to be built.

Mapping the distribution of *existing* pollution is not, of course, dependent upon an understanding of the process of spatial attenuation. It is, however, costly in terms of data requirements, particularly where a comprehensive picture over time is required and where—as with noise, for example—the pollution is of an ephemeral nature. In spite of this, several analyses have been completed. For instance, noise indices have been mapped for a number of existing airports in the United Kingdom, such as Manchester, Luton, Heathrow and Gatwick. In the last case, such maps were instrumental in the formulation of land-use policies by Surrey County Council (E. Sibert, 1969). Maps of exposure to aircraft noise have been used also for determining "minimum noise routes", which enable aircraft departing and arriving at airports to be channelled, thus minimising the number of persons overflown (P. E. Hart, 1973). Around Manchester, Luton, Gatwick and Heathrow airports they have been used also for delimiting areas eligible for subsidised sound insulation, under the terms of the 1965 Airports Authority Act (D.N.M. Starkie and D. M. Johnson, 1975). Better examples of the use of pollution maps in the latter context now arise as a consequence of the compensation clauses of the 1973 Land Compensation Act, and several such maps have been drafted for major road projects completed since mid-1969.

Apart from assisting in the implementation of standards, analysing the geographical spread of pollution also provides a valuable monitoring tool, particularly for checking potential health hazards or for assessing the impact of various control or abatement policies. In both these contexts, the spatial analysis of air-borne pollution figures prominently. For example, there are

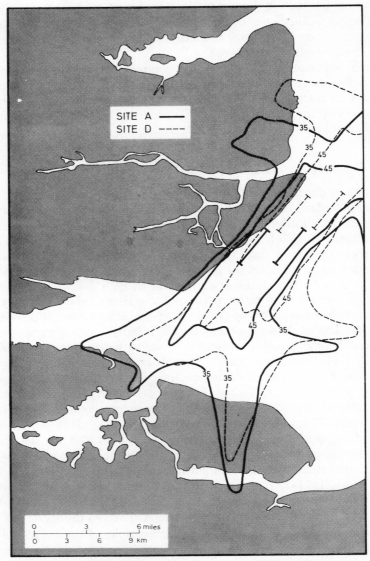

Fig. 9.2. Estimated day noise contours for proposed Maplin Airport, 1990
Source: Dept. of the Environment (1972)

several cases where the subject of analysis has been the contamination of areas
around industrial smelting complexes. A celebrated and recent example of this
concerns the Avonmouth industrial complex of Severnside, which includes
the largest lead and zinc smelting plant in the world. An example of one form

of contamination in the area surrounding the plant (which was variously represented by the levels of zinc, lead and cadmium in leaf and soil samples) is shown in Fig. 9.3, and indicates that the distribution is strongly affected by prevailing wind conditions (P. Little and A. H. Martin, 1972).

Perhaps because of the comparatively long and frequent use of spatial analyses in the context of air pollution policies, such analyses also illustrate well the use of various "geographical" techniques. The Avonmouth analysis, for example, was based upon the well-established technique of *geobotanical prospecting,* namely the analysis of plants, particularly mosses, as indicators of aerial pollution.

Aerial photography has also been used in this context. For instance, infra-red "false-colour" films, which show healthy natural vegetation as red, have been used to assess the damage to vegetation caused by SO_2 in the air. Another technique with aerial photographs is to use semi-conductor infra-red detectors to break down the "picture" into single spot sequences, which are then stored on magnetic tape. This information can be retrieved and printed out in the form of different shades of grey, with every shade indicating a definite temperature. It is thus useful for the analysis of thermal water pollution, detection of burning waste tips and decomposing refuse tips and the like.

A more down-to-earth, distinctly geographical, technique for analysing spatial spread, and one used in the context of air pollution is *trend surface analysis.* This is basically a way of fitting a surface to spatial data, in this case a pollution surface, by methods closely allied to regression analysis, and its use in the analysis of urban air pollution in the West Midlands conurbation is illustrated in P. Anderson's 1970 paper. Its particular advantage in the context of pollution policy is that it reduces the data required to build up a pollution picture because of its inherent ability to extrapolate and interpolate from certain spatial "fixes". Its potential for use in the noise pollution field is undoubtedly considerable (although little-explored) in view of the expense previously noted of collecting this type of pollution data.

Finally, in regard to technique, another employed in geographical research, but not yet used to paint the pollutionscape as seen by the affected public, is *cognitive mapping* (P. Gould and R. White, 1974). A large measure of "paternalism" has always been evident and important in the field of pollution policy (W. R. D. Sewell, 1974; Sewell and P. Little, 1973) and therefore, perhaps because of this and in spite of the inherently subjective nature of many pollutants (noise, for example, is described by the Committee on the Problem of Noise (1963), as "unwanted sound") the issue of measured public perception has, surprisingly, played little direct role in the formulation of policy. It has not been entirely absent. Noise indices, which have had some influence on policy, such as the Noise Number Index and the Traffic Noise Index, were derived by relating (not always very successfully) community

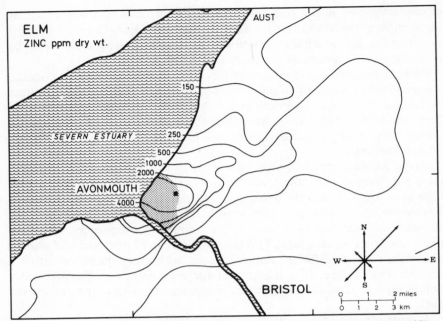

Fig. 9.3. The distribution of zinc in unwashed elm leaves, Avonmouth area, autumn, 1971 (The stipple marks the Avonmouth industrial area and the black square the smelter. After Little and Martin, 1972)

annoyance to the characteristics and the frequency with which sounds occur. But, cognitive mapping of pollution, that is persons reacting by sketching "mental maps" of noise, dust, vibration and smells, has yet to play a role in the formulation of pollution policy.

LOCATIONAL ADJUSTMENTS

(a) Industry

The third spatial dimension specified here—the effects of pollution policy on location decisions of firms, businesses and households—is one about which little is known at present, but it is of particular significance because it impinges upon wider political issues of regional policy, international relations and balance of payments.

It will always cost something to get rid of pollution; therefore, pollution of all kinds is always economically beneficial to some people to some extent. When a factory discharges untreated waste into a river it is done, presumably, because that is the cheapest way of getting rid of waste and, therefore, the prices of its products will be lower than they would otherwise be (J. H. Dales, 1968). Conversely, if abatement policies require the treatment of the wastes, the firm will have to undertake capital expenditure on new technology and perhaps incur higher operating costs too. If these additional expenditures are other than trivial, it will profit the industry concerned to consider relocation and locating additional productive capacity elsewhere, so as to avoid such expenditure.

Recent surveys in the United States have shown that for the abatement policies currently entertained by policy makers, the expenditures in many industries are far from trivial. In a McGraw-Hill survey (quoted in M. E. Ray, 1974, pp. 21-2), thirteen of the eighteen industries included were committing in excess of 5 per cent of total capital expenditures for pollution abatement equipment in 1973. For all manufacturing, 10·1 per cent was to be committed, the most seriously affected industries being paper (42·5 per cent), non-ferrous metals (22·5 per cent), iron and steel (13·6 per cent) and chemicals (12·3 per cent).

The basic theory of locational response by industry faced with such expense is to be found in R. E. Kohn's (1973) work. Kohn has developed a model which is behavioural in construct, using a Von Thünen-type location model as an analogue. Thus, the prime focus is a series of bid-rent curves for centrally-located production sites by different (polluting) industries, bid-rent curves which are modified as a consequence of the abatement costs associated with the standards of air quality. The closer industry locates to the (central) market, the greater will be the concentration of pollutants and the higher the level of abatement costs imposed upon it by the government (for any given quality standard). This will increase industry's costs and reduce the rental it can afford to pay for land. But, and this is the crux of the issue, industry emitting serious pollution will find that its cost will increase more than other industry and so, accordingly, via the rental mechanism, there will be a readjustment of industrial land use, both within industry itself and between industry and other economic sectors competing for land.

To test out some of these ideas, Kohn used the example of the Granite City Steel Company. Applying linear programming with production and air quality constraints for the St. Louis air-shed (and minimum control costs as the objective function), Kohn simulated the company's abatement costs and emission fees *per acre of site* at various locations, and hence distances, from a monitoring point (the total area of site was assumed to remain constant, regardless of location and rent).

One of a number of interesting conclusions reached was that there was a strong inverse geometric relationship of emission fees plus abatement costs per acre to distance. With these costs deducted from the maximum rental which a firm could pay for land in any particular location, this spatial relationship suggests the possibility that some rental gradients may be concave—downwards, in which case the industry concerned is unlikely to locate centrally. Still other shapes for the rental surface were thought possible;

for an emission source with very tall stacks, concentration will increase from a point some distance from the source, so that a rental gradient consisting of upward and downward concavities was thought conceivable.

The Kohn model is not scale-specific and the basic ideas apply equally at the urban, intra-regional or inter-regional levels. Moreover, just as M. D. I. Chisholm (1962) showed that in the agricultural land-use context the relevance of Von Thünen's ideas could be traced at a global scale, Kohn's application of these ideas to polluting industry also has an international relevance seen, for example, in the decentralisation of "dirty" Japanese industry within South East Asia.

An alternative, or complementary, policy to the use of source abatement standards or emission fees, is to use planning controls to allocate industrial land uses in such a way as to disperse and minimise pollution. A model by D. Scheffer and J. M. Guldmann (1973) illustrates an application of this type of policy. It also focuses upon the locational implications of a given set of area-wide standards of air quality, but differs from Kohn's behavioural approach because of its essentially *normative* nature. Sheffer and Guldmann's model seeks the optimal location-abatement pattern of industry at the intra-regional level for various standards of ambient air quality. The model, applied to the Haifa region of Israel, is of the linear programming genre. The objective function is to minimise total fuel costs with constraints in the form of total production targets; no relocation (but allocating new capacity); the availability of land in various zones; and an *air quality* constraint (based on SO_2). Eight significantly distinct industrial types were specified, each with fuel needs based upon energy requirements per employee. These energy requirements could be satisfied in the model by three separate fuels of varying costs, calorific value and sulphur content.

An interesting input, in view of earlier discussion, was the coefficient of the distance decay function (referred to in the study as the air pollution transfer coefficient) which was defined for specific wind speeds, directions and for atmospheric stability.

The model was then used to allocate industry spatially for three different pollution policies, viz. keeping air quality at its 1969 level; varying uniformly standards of some specific zones; and testing the impact of a uniform standard of air quality.

LOCATIONAL ADJUSTMENTS

(b) Residences

The traditional theory of residential location set out in the early 1960s by L. Wingo (1961) and W. Alonso (1964) is a theory also derivative of Von Thünen. Households substitute commuting costs—which are regarded as a steadily increasing function of distance from centrally located jobs—for rent (a payment of proximity), with the rate of substitution governed by the households' preference for high or low density housing. Choice of residential site is thus determined by a trade-off of satisfaction derived from more living space versus satisfaction from high accessibility.

In this classic framework, preference for less polluted living plays no explicit part. Recently, however, perhaps encouraged by the idea that with increasing affluence environmental quality is gaining added significance in households' preference functions, environmental considerations have received more attention in general models of residential location.

H. W. Richardson's (1971) revision of classical theory is a case in point, and one that inclines towards the opposite extreme of giving pre-eminence to environmental factors in locational decisions. Housing preferences are considered a function of size of house/plot requirements and *environmental tastes,* and preferences are maximised within an ability to pay constraint (transport costs are relevant only in so far as they have a bearing on the ability to pay).

The implications of these "elements of new model" are that they prescribe urban rent gradients and density profiles which are, in part, conditioned and moulded by consideration of environmental pollution and, thus, by policies with respect to pollution abatement.

It is generally the case that urban pollution surfaces peak towards focii of employment (see Fig. 9.4). These (disutility) surfaces, therefore, are highly and positively correlated with accessibility to job opportunities, shopping opportunities, and the like, and the one factor (pollution) will thus tend to offset the other (access) in structuring urban rents and densities of residential

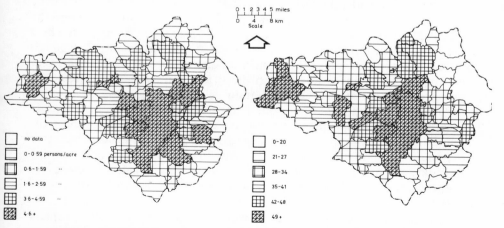

Fig. 9.4. Manufacturing employment densities, 1966 (left), and composite pollution indices (right) in Greater Manchester (after Wood *et al.,* 1974)

living. We would, therefore, expect, *ceteris paribus,* successful area-wide policies of pollution abatement to lead to adjustments of residential location which result in more sharply falling density (and rent) profiles.

Furthermore, there are also policies that are selective in a distinctly areal sense, policies such as the implementation of smoke control zones; the designation of noise abatement zones (permitted by the 1974 United Kingdom Control of Pollution Act); and policies creating a *Cordon Sanitaire* around sources of pollution (Department of the Environment, 1973, Appendix 2). Spatially discriminating measures such as these may lead to distortions, irregularities or lack of symmetry in pollution surfaces, and in rent and density surfaces too.

The presumption that households will adjust to pollution by altering their location has been a fundamental tenet in attempts to attach a monetary value to the nuisances and damage caused by pollution. The importance and attention given to obtaining such a value has increased in recent years, for a number of reasons. Increasing weight has been given to both pollution and cost-benefit analyses in public investment decisions (see, for example, Department of the Environment, 1973, para. 21; Starkie, 1973, Ch. 3), while the argument for adopting a policy of making the pollutor pay have also been advanced with vigour (Lord Zuckerman and W. Beckerman, 1972).

The Roskill Commission's search for a Third London Airport site provides the most celebrated attempt so far to value pollution in the context of public policy. At the fulcrum of Roskill's "noise cost model" (summarised in A. D. J. Flowerdew, 1972) was a decision process on the part of households whereby they either stayed in their existing location and persevered with the newly-imposed airport noise or moved to a quieter neighbourhood to avoid the noise pollution. Incomers occupying houses left by "disturbed" movers (or by those moving for other reasons) would, it was presumed, correctly assess the effects of noise on housing utility and, thus, expect to be compensated by a lower purchase price. Therefore, proceeded the argument, a (spatial) differential between areas of high and low noise would develop in the price of housing, and continue to develop until the differential accurately reflected the perceived areal variation in noise pollution.

Although it constituted only one item in the total disbenefits of noise calculated by the Roskill research team (the costs of moving were another), the house price differential has now assumed symbolic significance as an indicator of pollution costs in studies by environmental economists. A seminal study by R. Ridker and Associates in the mid-1960s successfully revealed differences in property prices in St. Louis, according to property location with respect to air pollution.

A more recent study of the effect of water pollution abatement on property prices by D. M. Dornbusch and S. M. Barrager (1973) achieved basically similar findings. The Dornbusch study was based on riparian, tide-water and lakeside sites in various parts of the United States. An analysis of changes in property prices with improvement in water quality over a 10-year period revealed a most significant relationship between distance from the pollution source and the degree of temporal change in prices, a relationship which, interestingly in view of the earlier discussion of distance decay functions, approximated an exponential decay.

Unfortunately, studies in the United Kingdom have been singularly unsuccessful in *observing and measuring* differences in house prices caused by pollution; the Roskill research team, for example, used values derived from the judgment of estate agents. It is possible that collinearity of the pollution and accessibility surfaces, noted above, has created a problem here, and that a more determined attempt to view the problem in the broader context of residential location theory may improve the situation.

The absence of hard evidence on this matter of locational (and, subsequently, rent) adjustments led D. N. M. Starkie and D. M. Johnson (1975) to advance an alternative approach to the valuation of pollution, the *exclusion facilities* approach, based on the idea of *in situ* adjustments by households to pollution damage. The basic notion is that the principal adjustment that households make when faced with pollution is to purchase "equipment" for eliminating or mitigating the nuisance, an expenditure from which an appropriate value of willingness to pay might be derived. Thus, blinds or heavy curtains could be used to cure the nuisance of intruding artificial lighting; aromatic sprays or dispensers could off-set smell pollution. Similarly, a household living in an area of air pollution could nullify the adverse effects by installing air conditioning, while Starkie and Johnson (1975) used sound insulation to value the reduction in noise pollution.

Although basically aspatial, the exclusion facilities approach has close affinities with studies of *in situ* damage-reducing adjustments to natural hazards, carried out by the Chicago School and other geographers (R. W. Kates, 1967; P. Wilkinson, 1972). Nevertheless, though attempts to value benefits of hazard-reducing measures have been made, these have focused (none too successfully) upon house price differentials or on the costs of re-instating damage (E. F. Renshaw, 1961), to the total neglect of the exclusion facilities type of approach.

CONCLUSIONS

In this brief review of the situation, it can be appreciated that the spatial dimensions of pollution policy are important, indeed, significant enough to require a thorough understanding if policies are to be successfully concluded.

Three spatial elements have been specified. These elements might at first glance appear as disparate strands of a general subject matter. However, more detailed analysis reveals that they are inter-related to a considerable extent. Thus, acceptance by local authorities of such advice as:

> Predictions of the effects of traffic noise on sites proposed for noise-sensitive development will need to be available to the planning authority in the form of a map.
>
> (Department of the Environment, 1973)

requires accurate functions describing the attenuation of noises with distance from their sources. Similarly, modification, by controls or taxes, of the overall pollution-scape, built up from a myriad of pollution sources and their associated decay functions, may in the longer term have repercussions on the location of economic activity, significant on both a national and an international scale. Recent deliberations suggest that these spatial dimensions have not been overlooked by those who formulate appropriate policies of pollution control.

REFERENCES

Alonso, W. (1964) *Location and Land Use: Towards a General Theory of Land Rent,* Harvard University Press, Harvard.

Anderson, P. (1970) "The uses and limitation of trend surface analysis in studies of urban air pollution", *Atmospheric Environment,* **4,** 129-47.

Auliciems, A. and I. Burton (1970) *Perception and Awareness of Air Pollution in Toronto,* Working Paper Series No. 13, Natural Hazards Research Series, University of Toronto.

Bevan, M. G. *et al.* (1974) *Measurement of Particulate Lead on the M4 Motorway at Harlington, Report 626,* Transport and Road Research Laboratory, Crowthorne.

Cairncross, A. *et al.* (1974) *Economic Policy for the European Community: The Way Forward,* Macmillan, London.

Chisholm, M. D. I. (1962) *Rural Settlement and Land Use: An Essay in Location,* Hutchinsons, London.

Clark, C. (1951) "Urban population densities", *Journal of the Royal Statistical Society,* Series A, **114,** 490-6.

Commission on The Third London Airport (1971) *Report,* H.M.S.O., London.

Committee on The Problem of Noise (1963) *Noise, Final Report,* Cmnd. 2056, H.M.S.O., London.

Cumberland, J. H. (1972) "The role of uniform standards in international environmental management" in *Problems of Environmental Economics,* O.E.C.D., Paris, pp. 239-54.

Dales, J. H. (1968) *Pollution, Property and Prices: an Essay in Policy-making and Economics,* University of Toronto Press, Toronto.

Department of the Environment (1973) "Planning and Noise", *Circular 10/73,* H.M.S.O., London.

Dornbusch, D. M. and S. M. Barrager (1973) *Benefits of Water Pollution Control on Property Values,* Socio-economic Environmental Studies Series, U.S. Environmental Protection Agency, Washington.

Flowerdew, A. D. J. (1972) "Choosing a site for the Third London Airport: The Roskill Commission's approach", in R. Layard (ed.) *Cost Benefit Analysis,* Penguin Books, Harmondsworth.

Gould, P. and R. White (1974) *Mental Maps,* Penguin Books, Harmondsworth.

Gunningham, N. (1974) *Pollution, Social Interest and the Law,* Law in Society Series, Martin Robertson, London.

Hart, P. E. (1973) "Population densities and optimal aircraft flight paths", *Regional Studies,* **7** (2), 137-51.

Haynes, K. E. and M. I. Rube (1974) "Environmental quality and urban population densities", in M. Yates (ed.) *Proceedings of the 1972 Meeting of the IGU Commission on Quantitative Geography,* McGill-Queen's University, Canada.

House of Commons (1974) *Hansard,* 17 June 1974, H.M.S.O., London.

Kates, R. W. (1967) "The perception of storm hazards on the shores of Megalopolis", in D. Lowenthal (ed.), *Environmental Perception and Behaviour,* Department of Geography, Research Paper No. 109, University of Chicago, Chicago.

Kohn, R. E. (1973) "Urban air pollution and the Von Thünen rental gradient", Paper to Environmental Economics Study Group, London.

Lassière, A. and P. Bowers (1972) *Studies on the Social Costs of Urban Road Transport (Noise and Pollution),* European Conference of Ministers of Transport, Paris.

Lassière, A. (1974) *The Environmental Evaluation of Transport Plans at the Strategic Level* (First Draft), Department of the Environment, London.

Little, P. and A. H. Martin (1972) "Survey of zinc, lead and cadmium in soil and natural vegetation around a smelting complex", *Environmental Pollution,* 3, 241-4.

Moore, V. (1974) "Guide to the Land Compensation Act 1973", *Estates Gazette,* London.

Ray, M. E. (1974) *The Environmental Crisis and Corporate Department Policy,* Lexington Books, Massachusetts.

Renshaw, E. F. (1961) "Relationship between flood control losses and flood control benefits", in G. White (ed.) *Papers on Flood Problems,* Department of Geography, Research Paper No. 70, University of Chicago, Chicago.

Richardson, H. W. (1971) *Urban Economics,* Modern Economics Series, Penguin Books, Harmondsworth.

Ridker, R. (1967) *The Economic Costs of Air Pollution,* F. A. Praeger, New York.

Royal Commission on Environmental Pollution (1971) *First Report,* Cmnd. 4585, H.M.S.O., London.

Scorer, R. (1968) *Air Pollution,* Pergamon, Oxford.

Scott, A. D. (1972) "The economics of international transmission of pollution", in *Problems of Environmental Economics,* O.E.C.D., Paris, pp. 255-75.

Sewell, W. R. D. (1974) "The role of perceptions of professionals in environmental decision-making", in J. T. Coppock and C. B. Wilson (eds.) *Environmental Quality,* Scottish Academic Press, Edinburgh.

Sewell, W. R. D. and P. Little (1973) "Specialists, laymen and the process of environmental appraisal", *Regional Studies,* 7 (2), 161-71.

Sheffer, D. and J. M. Guldmann (1973) "A model of air quality impact on industrial land use allocation", *Working Paper No. 25,* Centre for Urban and Regional Studies, Israel Institute of Technology, Haifa.

Sibert, E. (1969) "Aircraft noise and development control—the policy for Gatwick Airport", *Journal of the Town Planning Institute,* 55 (4), 149-52.

Spence, J. (1972) *Pollution by Dust in Urban Areas,* Contract T.R.R.L. EH/GR/842/111, Department of Geography, University of Reading.

Starkie, D. N. M. (1973) *Transportation Planning and Public Policy,* Pergamon Press, Oxford.

Starkie, D. N. M. and D. M. Johnson (1975) *The Economic Value of Peace and Quiet,* Saxon House Series, D. C. Heath, Farnborough.

Wilkinson, P. (1972) "The adoption of damage-reducing adjustments in relation to experience and expectation of natural hazards in London, Ontario", in W. P. Adams and F. M. Helleiner (eds.) *International Geography 1972,* University of Toronto Press, Toronto.

Wingo, L. (1961) *Transportation and Urban Land,* Resources for the Future, Washington.

Wood, C. M. *et al.* (1974) *The Geography of Pollution: a Study of Greater Manchester,* Manchester University Press, Manchester.

Zuckerman, Lord and W. Beckerman (1972) Minority Report, in Royal Commission on Environmental Pollution, Third Report, *Pollution in Some British Estuaries and Coastal Waters,* Cmnd. 5054, H.M.S.O., London.

CHAPTER 10

ENERGY POLICIES IN WESTERN EUROPE AND THE GEOGRAPHY OF OIL AND NATURAL GAS

P. R. ODELL
Erasmus University

Paradoxically for a continent which rose to economic pre-eminence in the nineteenth century as a result of the development and use of its coal resources, Europe has shown a surprising indifference over the last 25 years towards the role of indigenous energy resources in the process of economic development.

This indifference may be contrasted with the attitudes of the United States and the Soviet Union which have remained *largely* independent of foreign supplies of energy, not only because they happened to have resources at home, but also because they deliberately pursued autarkic *policies* which gave preference to domestic supplies and/or kept out imports of lower cost oil. It was only in the period 1971-3 that the United States "flirted" with the idea of free trade in energy—and then only because "environmentalism" at home had temporarily inhibited the ability of the American energy industry to deliver the energy in the quantity required. In post-war Western Europe, on the other hand, so-called "cheap energy" became the central aim of energy policy makers. Thus, there was established an institutional framework and a state of mind in the continent which enabled the European energy market to be opened up to oil supplies from regions where the commodity was not only inherently low-cost to produce (M. A. Adelman, 1972, Ch. 2) but also guaranteed because of the state of the power-political relationships between the international oil companies and the countries concerned. The companies, backed by the United States and, to a lesser degree, by the United Kingdom, the Netherlands and France, ensured that these low-cost resources could be used for the benefit of the increasingly affluent energy consumers of Western Europe and of Japan (see P. R. Odell, 1974, for a background to this development). The international oil companies themselves, of course, were not simply institutions which took advantage of this European view. The high levels of profits they achieved in the late 1940s and the 1950s (as a consequence of the post-war shortages of energy and their abilities to organise the markets at that

The editor and author wish to apologise for a series of errors which have either crept into this chapter or which were not eliminated at the pre-publication stage. Given that this is a contribution concerned with the European-ness of one of the main sectors of the economy it may be seen either as doubly unfortunate or as appropriate—depending on the view of the reader towards the question of "Europe" —that it was the checking of this chapter which was upset by that well-known phenomenon and its even better-known effect viz. "Fog in the Channel; Continent Isolated". The author in Rotterdam was isolated from the editor in Edinburgh at critical moments in the production of the book and serious mistakes and omissions have ensued. The following are the more important ones:

p. 165, line 16: Close brackets after the word 'development'.

p. 168, line 14: After "In such circumstances" add the following text,
"the traditional economic base for policy decisions on the supply and price of energy becomes well-nigh irrelevant particularly in respect of the traditional attitudes towards free trade and the comparative advantages arising from it."
line 18: After "15 years", add, "on the international oil industry—".

p. 169, Fig. 10: Caption should continue "—as predicted in 1969".
Key: the section of the key describing the inter-connected circles on the map is missing. This is the planned evolution of the distribution and marketing system for Groningen gas. See Odell (1969) for a correct version.

p. 171, The reference in the text and in Table 10.2 to "Likely Actuals as estimated in December 1974" should have been updated. The actual 1975 figures are, however, not greatly different from those given here. An up-to-date version of the Table will be supplied to anyone interested on request to the author.

p. 175, Fig. 10.4: The names of the natural gas producing areas in Western Europe have been omitted. A correct copy is available from the author.

p. 176, Fig. 10.5: An up-to-date version of this map should have been included. Again, a copy is available from the author.

p. 180, Fig. 10.6: The 'arrows' emerging from Rotterdam Europoort represent oil pipeline connections to other parts of W. Europe. A correct version also available from the author.

p. 182, Fig. 10.7: This is generally confusing as drawn and reproduced. Note especially that there should be no "tanker route for Russian oil" from west to east in the English Channel and that "Atlantic Oil in mammoth tankers" is not supposed to cut the "Atlantic Oil in small tankers" route. Correct version also available.

p. 184, 2nd paragraph: After "Figure 10.8" read "and 9".
2nd paragraph, last line: "Figure 10.9" should read "Figure 10.10".
Figure 10.10 which is a map of all off-shore areas of petroleum potential around Western Europe is, however, not included in the publication. The author will be pleased to supply a copy on request.

p. 186, "Odell, P. R. (forthcoming)" should be "Odell, P. R. (1975)".

time so as to ensure a high profit per ton of oil sold) enabled them to expand as they chose and to undertake all the research and development efforts they liked. As a consequence they secured a technological lead which made competition from alternative energy sources difficult—most notably, of course, as far as European coal was concerned. This had to face, on the one hand, the joint difficulties arising from the war-time de-capitalisation and/or destruction of the industry and, on the other, the labour-cost implications of full employment economies for an industry which remained highly labour intensive (with labour costs accounting for about 50 per cent of total costs).

The oil companies thus took a leading role in persuading Europe that dependence on cheap, imported oil was the most reasonable—perhaps even the only—way to ensure development. Moreover, they initiated or encouraged the development of all aspects of the economic system which increased the intensity of energy use (e.g. in road transport facilities, air travel, high standards of heating coupled with low standards of insulation, air conditioning and energy-intensive product development) based on what throughout the period seemed to them the limitless availability of crude oil resources from their massively successful efforts at exploration and development in areas of low-cost production—notably, of course, the Middle East and North Africa. European governments (and populations) in their turn chose to accept these essentially irresponsible views (which were, indeed, welcomed as an important means whereby the now general revolution of rising expectations could be achieved). Thus, the inherent political instability of the regions of the world on which Europe came to depend for its energy was almost entirely discounted—an attitude which was not considered unreasonable in the light of the very limited and short interruptions to Europe's oil supplies which had, in fact, been occasioned by wars in the Middle East in 1956/7 and 1967 and by other traumatic political events, including the overthrow of traditional governments and their replacement by revolutionary factions in important oil-producing countries such as Iraq and Libya.

Given these powerful motivations both by the suppliers of oil and by the consumers of energy, it is not surprising that indigenous resources were either ignored or excluded from a major and continuing role in development of energy policy. Table 10.1 shows that, even as recently as 1973, the conventional expectation of developments in the energy economy over the next decade implied acceptance of the continuation of the post-1950 trends—with a continued worsening of the relationships between the contribution of indigenous and imported energy to the total supply.

Today, in light of the "oil" crisis (Odell, 1974, Ch. 9), which has not only quadrupled the price of energy, but has also made its continuing availability open to considerable doubt, the irresponsibility of Western Europe's attitude towards energy resources is clear. Such irresponsibility lies in the treatment of the supply of energy as though it were just another commodity which it is

TABLE 10.1. Conventional and alternative views on Europe's energy supply 1973-98

| | 1973 Approximate actual use | | 1980 estimates | | | | 1985 estimates | | | | 1998 estimates | | | |
| | | | Conventional | | Alternative | | Conventional | | Alternative | | Conventional | | Alternative | |
	mmtce*	%**	mmtce	%	mmtce	%	mmtce	%	mmtce	%	mmtce	%	mmtce	%
Total energy	1550	100	2255	100	1900	100	2870	100	2350	100	5425	100	3500	100
Oil - Total	970	63	1500	66	835	43	1845	64	840	36			1400	40
(i) Indigenous	30	2	50	2	500	26	195	7	640	27			1150	33
(ii) Imported	940	61	1450	64	335	17	1650	57	200	9			250	7
Gas - Total	135	9	265	12	575	30	385	14	790	34			1100	32
(i) Indigenous	125	8	215	10	500	26	300	11	640	27			850	25
(ii) Imported	10	1	50	2	75	4	85	3	150	6			250	7
Coal - Total	400	26	280	12	310	16	310	11	350	15			500	14
(i) Indigenous	360	23	205	9	230	12	220	8	250	11			400	11
(ii) Imported	40	3	75	3	80	4	90	3	100	4			100	3
Primary electricity	45	3	210	10	180	9	330	12	370	15			500	14
Total indigenous	560	36	680	31	1410	74	1045	37	1900	81			2900	83
Total imported	990	64	1575	69	490	26	1825	63	450	19			600	17

(1998 Conventional columns other than Total energy: not available)

Sources: Organisation for Economic Cooperation and Development (OECD), European Economic Community (EEC) and various national estimates prior to the oil crisis of future energy supply patterns form the basis of the conventional estimates. The alternative estimates are the author's own.
* million metric tons coal equivalent
** Columns do not necessarily add to 100 because of "rounding".

worthwhile to import even if it can be obtained only at fractionally lower cost than indigenous resources, as was the case, for example, in comparing the cost of making electricity from imported oil on the one hand and indigenous coal on the other. What such irresponsibility in policy attitudes chose to ignore was two important factors: firstly, that the consequential loss of a capacity to produce energy at home was not something that could be reversed overnight (if anything should happen to imports) because such capacity, once abandoned, is costly and time-consuming to recreate; and secondly, that the use of energy cannot be eliminated—or even reduced—without affecting all other sectors of the economy and, indeed, many other aspects of accepted patterns of societal organisations. Because of these factors policy attitudes to energy (as towards the production of food) need to be qualitatively different from attitudes to other commodities and goods which can either be substituted in the short-term or foregone in event of difficulties, without the changes having a traumatic effect on the economy and society.

There is, of course, no point in simply holding a post-mortem about the causes of the present energy crisis for Western Europe, or trying to attach blame to the various interest groups involved. In any case, one must remember that the cheap energy policy did, indeed, bring enormous economic benefits to the continent. It can perhaps be isolated as one of the single most important factors which contributed to the rapid growth in *per capita* well-being over the decade and a half from 1955—in marked contrast with the United States, where economic development over the same period was much less strong and where a higher-cost autarkic energy policy was certainly seen to be one of the hindrances to growth.

Irrespective of such considerations, however, public policy makers in Europe have now been brought up against a fundamentally changed world energy situation, one, that is, in which external suppliers of energy are no longer willing to supply either cheap energy or, indeed, as much energy as it was generally assumed we would require to sustain future economic growth along established lines. In the short term—with a very constrained indigenous potential to produce energy—this means that policies have to be restructured so as at least to reduce the rate of growth energy use or even to cut back on the amount of energy we have become accustomed to using (Odell, forthcoming).

Conservation of energy will in any case be difficult—involving not only the acceptance of technological change (such as a more efficient use of energy in industrial processes and the use of more effective insulating materials in houses), but also the acceptance of changes in the organisation of society (J. A. Over and A. C. Sjoerdsma, 1974, chap 3-6) such as a reduction in personal mobility as energy-intensive road and air transport have to be restrained in favour of slower and/or less convenient modes of transport. It is because changes of this kind seem likely to be generally unacceptable (except to a modest degree and/or for a limited period of time) that there arises the strongest possible motivation for governmental policies which are much more oriented to the search for, and the development of, indigenous resources of energy, especially for resources of oil and natural gas which can be most easily and cheaply incorporated into the economic and social systems to which we have become used.

Public policy needs emerging from these considerations are, however, strongly reinforced by the increasingly recognised need for Western Europe to divorce itself from dependence on imports of an essential commodity such as energy. This need is particularly great when the dependence is on a group of countries whose instability is self-evident and whose decisions on whether or not to export oil—and, if so, then at what price—are so influenced by considerations of hostility to the Western world. In such circumstances the traditional *economic* base for policy decisions on the supply and price of energy become almost irrelevant, particularly in respect of the traditional attitudes towards free trade and the comparative advantages arising from it. Thus undermined, for example, are the sorts of policy recommendations which arise out of the analyses of the international oil industry which Adelman has made over the last 15 years' work which has demonstrated not only the existence, but also the likely continued existence of an international long-term *supply* price for oil of under $1 per barrel (Adelman, 1972, chapters 6 and 7). Insecurity of supply makes it impossible to depend on such oil in spite of its economic attractions.

Given this international economic situation there is an additional motivation to develop indigenous resources independent of any special considerations arising from the temporary state of the international market— the variations in which produce an obviously undesirable degree of instability into the price and availability of energy, so making reasonable forward planning by both governments and industry impossible. Thus the evaluation of the indigenous energy resource base needs to be treated as a matter apart, so making the economic geography of the development of energy resources in Europe a function of internal production and transport cost differentials between different possible supply points for different sorts of energy into different markets—and requiring, of course, the willingness to produce those resources with the production and/or transport cost advantages at the fastest rate possible compatible with the technically optimum rates of their depletion. This apparently self-evident proposition has not been realised, as is shown for example, in Dutch and Norwegian policies over indigenous gas and oil production respectively. The idea of "conserving" these resources for the long-term future has become a central theme in decisions on rates of production.

It was this approach which lay behind an earlier attempt by the author to describe and define appropriate policy attitudes in Western Europe towards the utilisation of the natural gas resources which have already been discovered

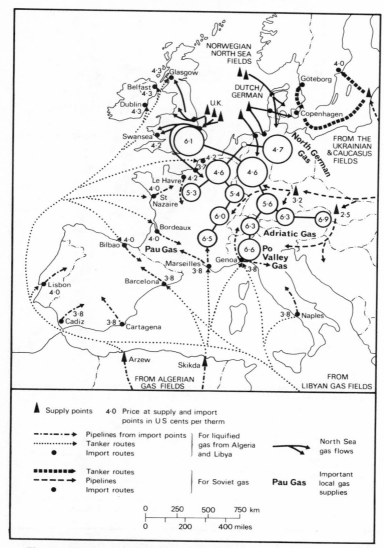

Fig. 10.1 Western Europe's potential natural gas supplies in the mid-1970s

by the late 1960s (Odell, 1969). This involved a gas supply potential (both internal and from abroad) as shown in Fig. 10.1, and out of this potential there emerged a possible geography of natural gas use in Western Europe in 1975, as illustrated in Fig. 10.2. Though various restraints have in the meantime been allowed to develop, and have served to inhibit the exploitation of some of the gas reserves, the actual pattern of gas use as it has, in fact, emerged by 1975 is

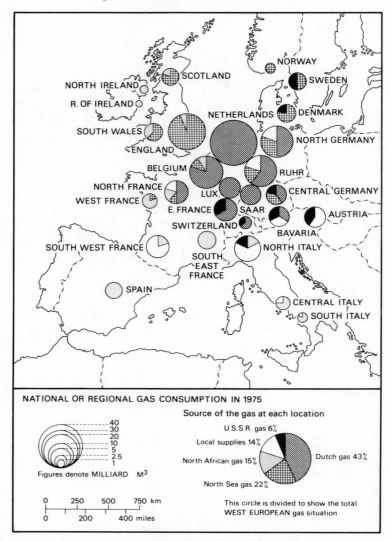

Fig. 10.2. Western Europe: a 1969 prediction of natural gas consumption in 1975

not too much at variance with the mid-1970s future projected from 1969. The 1975 market for gas was then described in the following terms:

Western Europe will by 1975 be consuming some 275 milliard m³ of natural gas per year. Of this, the Netherlands will supply about 43% with the Groningen field itself producing up to its limit of 100 milliard m³ and the rest coming from other fields both on land and under the Dutch sector of the North Sea. Other indigenous Western European supplies will come from the British/Danish sectors of the North Sea (35 milliard m³). German production will amount to about 25 milliard m³ whilst local production in France will be just under 10 milliard m³ and that from Italy up to twice this amount mainly from the newly discovered Adriatic fields. In total, indigenous gas supplies will account for nearly 80% of Western European consumption whilst the remainder, split roughly in the ratio of 3:1 will be imported from North Africa and the Soviet Union respectively (Odell, 1969, pp. 22-4).

The contrast between that 6 year old geographical prediction and what (in December 1974) seems likely to be the pattern of supply of natural gas in Western Europe in 1975 is shown in Table 10.2. The 1975 "actual figures" are based on industry/government expectations as at December 1974 in the light of known contrasts between suppliers and customers. They could be up to 5 per cent larger in the event of colder than normal weather and further increases in oil prices.

If the 1969 prediction is compared with the likely pattern in 1975 the only significant difference (except in imports) is in Dutch gas where the rate of production is 25 per cent less than predicted. This "shortfall" is not, in fact, due to the non-availability of reserves but rather to certain institutional restraints which inhibited the growth of production. Firstly, there was the unwillingness of NAM (a Shell/Esso combine) to develop the ten or so off-shore gas fields which they discovered in the early 1970s in a situation in which they calculated that any additional gas from these fields would serve

TABLE 10.2. *Western Europe: estimates of natural gas production and imports in 1975*

County or region	Author's estimate in 1969[1]	Forecasts for 1975 Official estimates in 1969[2]	Likely actual as estimated in Dec. 1974[3]
		(in milliards of m³)	
The Netherlands	125	55	100
(of which, Gronigen)	(100)	(55)	(85)
Western Germany	25	15	20
South North Sea	35	30	45
(excluding Dutch sector)			
Italy	20	12	15
France and other	10	8	10
European countries			
(Sub-total—indigenous production)	(215)	(120)	(190)
Imports	60	12	20
(of which U.S.S.R.	(45)	(8)	(9)
N. Africa)	(15)	(4)	(11)
Overall total	275	132	210

Sources:
[1] P. R. Odell, *Natural Gas in Western Europe*, 1969, pp. 22-4.
[2] From EEC/OECD/country estimates made in 1969 of the 1975 gas supply position.
[3] Based on company and governmental estimates in November/December 1974 of likely deliveries of gas in 1975.

further to undermine the energy market which was, of course, in over-supply until 1973, not only from the increasing availability of natural gas in Western Europe but—and even more important—from low-cost oil from overseas. Secondly, there was the question of the policy attitudes developed by the Dutch government which, in the early 1970s, was much influenced by Club-of-Rome type warnings about the long-term scarcity of energy sources and resolved therefore to ensure that known resources of gas in the country were not depleted too quickly. Thus the rate of increase in the supply of gas from the Netherlands was constrained. Apart from this it is the contrast between the predicted flow of gas from the Soviet Union and the now likely 1975 flow which stands out in Table 10.2—a contrast which arises not from a lack of gas or of a motivation to sell it in Western Europe but partly because the construction of the pipelines required to deliver the gas from the Soviet Union to Western Europe has been delayed and partly because of some continuing political pressures on Western European countries not to import too much Soviet gas.

It is perhaps interesting to look also at the official ECE/EEC/OECD 1968/9 forecasting of 1975 gas supplies in Western Europe. These were, as shown in Table 10.1, of the order of 130 milliard m³. Their pessimistic outlook arose because the official investigations failed to recognise the dynamics which underlie resource development in a strong demand situation and also the strong preference by consumers for this indigenous and clean source of

TABLE 10.3. *Western Europe: an estimate of its natural gas resources and production potential in the early 1980s*

	Recoverable reserves		Early 1980s annual production potential	Million tons of coal equivalent
	As declared in 1973	As developed by 1980		
	($\times 10^9 m^3$)		($\times 10^9 m^3$)	
On-shore Netherlands	2250	2750	135	150
South North Sea—British Sector	1000	1250	60	75
South North Sea—Other Sectors	250	1250	40	50
On-shore West Germany	400	650	35	40
Austria, France, Italy, etc.	400	600	35	45
Middle North Sea Basin—UK/Norway	750	1600	80	90
North North Sea Basin—UK/Norway	500	2300	80	90
Rest of European Continental Shelf	—	350	15	20
	5050	10,450	480	560

Source: 1973 estimates from *Oil and Gas Journal,* 25 December 1973; 1980 estimates are the author's own (see Odell, 1975).

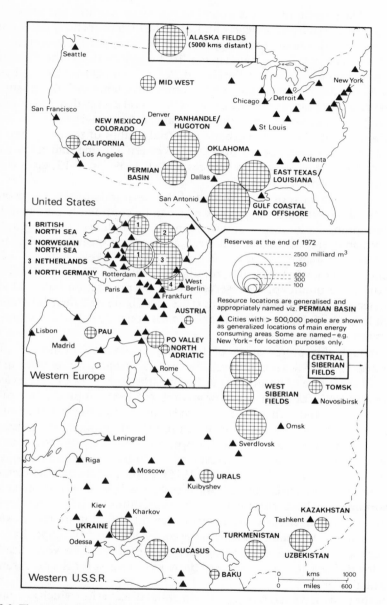

Fig. 10.3. The geographical relationship of principal natural gas producing locations with main energy consuming areas in the United States, the Soviet Union and Western Europe

energy. The geography of the potential supply of gas and the demand for energy in Western Europe clearly indicated the high propensity for this new, preferred energy source to be incorporated in the European economy at a very rapid rate. This idea is illustrated in Fig. 10.3 which contrasts the situation in Western Europe with those in the United States and the Soviet Union. In both of those countries natural gas, on becoming available in large quantities, enjoyed a growth rate well above the growth in total energy demand in spite of the long distances—and hence the high transport costs—involved in getting the gas to the markets of the urban/industrial regions of the countries. This severe friction of distance is absent in Western Europe and adds to the advantages for gas over energy sources (Odell, 1969, pp. 6-13, gives a more detailed discussion of this point).

Today—on a basis of a knowledge of the geography of the gas resources discovered—or of those resources which can be confidently predicted from the continuing exploration—and from an understanding of the geography of energy demand and the role that natural gas can play in meeting this demand, it is similarly possible to make predictions about likely patterns of gas production and use in Western Europe in the early 1980s. Table 10.3 shows the evolution of estimates of the reserves and of the production potential which will emerge by the beginning of the next decade. Figure 10.4 then illustrates the possible flows of this quantity of gas—almost 500 milliard m³ per year—into the energy markets.

Although this presentation of the possible level of utilisation of gas resources by the 1980s remains well above the continuing rather static official views of the future of natural gas in Europe (the June 1974 EEC forecasts of energy for 1985, for example, show an expected 1985 gas production of only 300 milliard m³ and even this is considered to be "optimistic" by other official bodies), it does not, in fact, require much more than a modest extrapolation of firmly established trends in the European gas market and the continued expansion of the gas reserves as a result of continuing exploration—especially in parts of the North Sea basin (Odell, 1975). Important though this element is in terms of Western Europe's future energy policy, it is now even more important to make as careful as possible an evaluation of the development potential for indigenous oil reserves—given the situation in which external sources of this dominant element in the continent's energy supply have now become so unreliable and in a recognition of the fact that the North Sea basin has already been proved to be one of the world's largest for the occurrence of high quality oil.

On the basis of what is already known about discoveries (which are mapped by size on Fig. 10.5) and on the assumption that the oil which has been discovered will be brought into production as soon as possible, then one can estimate a potential annual production amounting to 300 million tons per year by the early 1980s and to over 400 million tons in 1985 (Odell, 1975). This

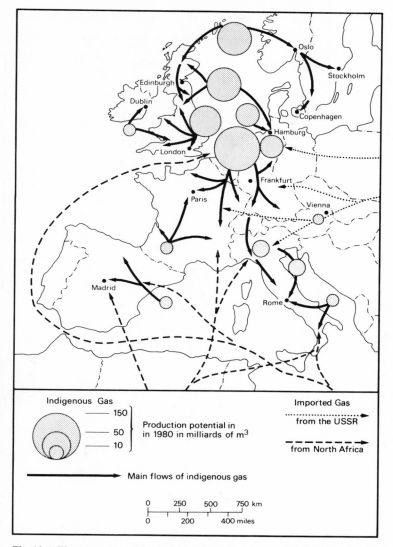

Fig. 10.4. The geography of Western Europe's natural gas supply by the early 1980s

amount of energy from the North Sea will make a quite fundamental difference to the overall structure of the energy supply for the continent as compared with previous expectation for the 1980s—particularly as we are entering a period in which higher energy prices and other restraints on energy use will serve to reduce the demand for energy well below the trend of the

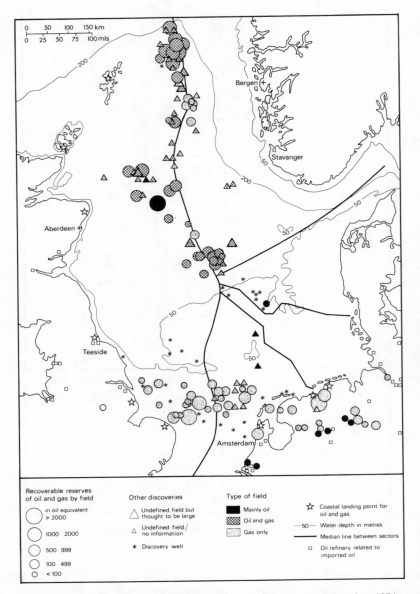

Fig. 10.5. The North Sea Oil and Gas Province: discoveries up to December, 1974

post-1950 period and so make North Sea oil relatively even more important. The spatial aspects of this development lie partly in terms of the impact that the production and the landing of the off-shore oil will have upon the regions and communities which are affected. This is seen in the attention that is being paid to the influence of oil-related developments on the so-called off-shore capital of the world—Aberdeen (A. Hogg, 1975) and on other settlements along the East coast of Scotland in the Orkneys and Shetlands (J. Francis and N. Swan, 1973, Sec. 3-5; and anon., 1974). It is seen even more strongly in the importance attached by the Norwegian government to the protection of the regional industries and regional qualities of life in these sparsely populated areas of the west coast where oil-related developments are also of rapidly-growing importance (Norwegian Government Publications, 1973-4, Ch. 6).

The dangers, of course, for these peripheral regions of Europe, with their small populations and their great concern for environmental considerations, arise from the traumatic effects that oil developments must have in such small communities. This is so not only because of their relatively heavy demands for labour and the ability of the oil industry to outbid other employers for the limited amount of labour available (and the consequential in-migration and inevitable social problems to which such conditions lead), but also from their impact in overburdening relatively undeveloped transport systems and in changing the very appearance of places through the introduction of new sorts of activities. In brief, the activities of the oil industry lead to a near instant incorporation of such regions into the world of "big business" and "large scale" activities for the first time. In such societies there is thus a need for control and regulation in order to safeguard the qualities of life, the protection of the environment and the use of land. And indeed, many geographers and others are involved in such impact studies on which policy guide lines can be based.

But there is also a danger that the seeming inevitability of change arising out of massive oil developments (such as the 200 million tons crude oil terminal under construction at Sullom Voe in the Shetland Islands where the possibility is also being held open for associated refining and other processing activities), will create very great pressures for the developments to be stopped—as, of course, has already happened in several instances in Scotland at sites for oil production platform construction and associated facilities, e.g. at Drumbuie (anon., 1974, Sec. 4). Undue restraints and/or delays in building essential on-shore facilities for successful North Sea exploration and development work would, however, have a severely disadvantageous result for the economy of the United Kingdom in particular, and for Western Europe in general. This clearly indicates that the sort of land use/environmental impact policy evaluations in which many geographers get involved must not be seen as having an absolute validity—as unfortunately sometimes appears to be the case with such policy-orientated geographical studies of local areas and regions. The validity of the studies in themselves is not in question—what must be appreciated is that their conclusions have to be considered in the light of the important macro-geographical policy issues concerned with the supply of energy to Western Europe.

In this larger geographical context—and on the assumption that neither local political nor local milieu and environmental/societal constraints unduly hold back the rate of exploitation of the North Sea's oil reserves—then a basis will be established for a quite fundamental change in the geography of Western Europe's main source of energy. This, in turn, makes it necessary to consider the consequential likely changes in patterns of oil transportation and refining in Western Europe and the influence of these changes on those oil centres of the continent which have been associated with the pattern of oil supply to Western Europe as it has developed over the last 30 years. All this does, indeed, constitute a sizeable agenda for policy-oriented geographical research on a subject which, in addition to its very obvious economic aspects, also has important social and political variables which need to be taken into account.

In this chapter there is no opportunity to do more than to state the problem —and briefly to describe the main elements in the changing situation which need to be researched. The following components appear to be important in such policy-oriented research on the development of the future oil supply and refining patterns:

(a) The availability—and the consequential use (given its preferred status)—of rapidly increasing amounts of natural gas will steadily reduce the demand for fuel oils in the energy economy of northwest Europe. This will not only alter the overall pattern of the demand for oil products, with a consequential effect on refining activities (an aspect which is discussed under (b) below), but also implies changes in demand which will be highly uneven geographically, given the spatially variable degree to which natural gas will be incorporated into patterns of energy use. In this context one must note the impact of the friction of distance in establishing the geography of gas use, especially when this is viewed in relation to the lower unit costs involved in transporting oil. This friction suggests geographical contrasts in the relative use of gas and oil depending upon distance from the points of supply—points of supply which, of course, coincide in part because of the joint nature of the production of oil and gas from much of the North Sea basin (Fig. 10.5). Other considerations must, however, be taken into account. Most notable amongst these are, firstly, the high degree of public ownership and/or control which is exercised over the gas industry and the consequential national pressures to eliminate regional differentials in the price at which natural gas is marketed; and secondly, the pressures emerging from the idea that the use of gas must be restricted to "premium markets"—meaning essentially a limitation on the degree to which it is allowed to compete with fuel oils. Both of these factors could so limit consumption in the areas geographically closest to the on-shore landing points for off-shore gas production that they will create a propensity for a more dispersed pattern of gas use than would otherwise arise, and thus become important components in any modelling of the developing use of natural gas in Western Europe.

(b) Given competition from an increasing availability of natural gas and the consequential much reduced demand for fuel oil in North-west Europe in particular, then the light, low-sulphur North Sea oil will become eminently suitable for the main crude oil stream required by refineries around the whole of the North Sea basin. Thus, refineries in this region—including those in the most important refining centres in Rotterdam, Antwerp, Thameside and Southampton—will have to be technically restructured by means of new investments in facilities designed to produce higher percentages of middle distillates and light products than can be produced from the existing facilities. It is these investments—rather than investments in new refining capacity—which thus appear likely to become the main new inputs into any continued growth in the oil sector in such locations, so creating, of course, a change in outlook for those locations in North-west Europe which enjoyed continued expansion throughout the post-1950 period, as in the case of Rotterdam where refinery growth has gradually spread downstream from its original location (Fig. 10.6).

(c) Most refineries in the United Kingdom and in other parts of North-west Europe are at the "wrong end" of the North Sea for handling the production of most of the North Sea oilfields (Fig. 10.5). As a result much initial investment will be required in crude oil delivery systems (pipelines and tankers) to take the production from the fields or from intermediate storage at coastal landing points near existing refineries—the sort of development, in fact, that is already under construction at Peterhead (in Aberdeenshire) to handle oil from a group of fields in the East Shetland graben. However, we can hypothesise that both economics and politics will, on balance, eventually require the expansion of refinery capacity—and associated petro-chemical and other oil and gas based industry—at locations which are much more closely related to the supply points of North Sea oil. Conflicting locational forces are at work in determining the strength and speed of this development and may be summarised as follows:

(i) There are forces at work designed to stop facilities being built in Scotland and Norway because of fears for the environment and for the existing structure of local societies and economies. Effective opposition to the industrialisation which could be based on the local availability of oil and gas could keep the local multiplier effect to a minimum.

(ii) There are also forces at work trying to ensure that the oil and gas produced can be freely transported to pre-existing refinery/processing

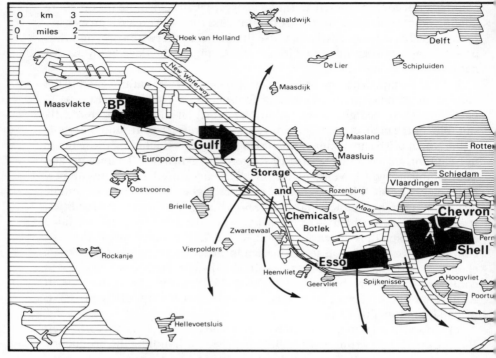

Fig. 10.6. Oil industry development in Rotterdam

and other energy-using locations (in other parts of Europe or even other parts of the world). Such pressure would be appropriate from most of the major oil companies which are developing large-scale North Sea oil production in that they already have existing refineries in North-west Europe. Such pre-existing refineries will, given the now expected much reduced rate of growth in the demand for oil in Western Europe, provide them with more than enough refining capacity to meet their anticipated needs for some years ahead. It is thus only in respect of long-term expansion plans that such companies will give a high priority to refineries associated geographically with the crude oil terminals for North Sea oil—in the absence, that is, of governmental and/or political pressures for the construction of such facilities.

(iii) Some of the producers of the North Sea oil, on the other hand, are relatively new to the European region and have very limited, or even no, pre-existing refining capacity in the region through which to run their productions of North Sea oil. For these companies the economics of refinery location within the North-west European demand area may well suggest the construction of refineries at the terminal points of the crude oil delivery lines from the North Sea oil fields. In as far as many of these companies hope to supply markets outside Europe with some oil products made from North Sea oil (notably in terms of light products and middle distillates to be supplied to the United States), such a resource-based pattern of location for their refineries would appear to offer advantages over the more traditional local market orientated refinery locations in Western Europe.

(iv) Such decisions by oil companies to build refineries on "green-field" sites in Scotland, Norway and elsewhere will be powerfully supported by political and economic pressures within those countries and regions for such developments—in order to achieve the important multiplier effects which can thereby be obtained for the local economies. Governmental pressure on companies to take such decisions seem likely, moreover, to be supplemented by national enterprise in this field—as, indeed, is already required by Norway through Statoil (the newly formed state oil company) and as will be required of the British National Oil Corporation. Thus Statoil has been given the right and the obligation to participate in refining and petro-chemical activities and instructed to relate these developments geographically to the regions of Norway most closely associated with oil production.

(d) With North Sea oil steadily achieving pride of place in the total pattern of European oil supply there will inevitably be consequential changes in the geography of oil activities elsewhere in Europe. Figure 10.7 indicates a possible new over pattern of supply by the early 1980s—arising out of an availability by then of 300 million tons of preferred indigenous oil from the North Sea and within the framework of a total demand for oil in Western Europe by then of about 630 million tons. This is rather less than total oil use in 1973—the last year of very cheap oil, but the fivefold increase in price since then, governmental efforts to restrain demand for energy use in general and the substitution of oil by other fuels have eliminated the expectation of any further growth in the use of oil over the next decade (see Odell, 1975, for a full discussion of the emerging demand situation). The availability of North Sea oil for the refineries of the whole area around the North Sea basin and the enhanced use of the south to north crude oil pipelines from the Mediterranean import points for North African and European Mediterranean (including trans-Suez) oil all but eliminate the need for massive flows of oil in mammoth tankers around the western coast of Europe to the series of large oil ports and refining centres stretching from Le Havre and Southampton to Thames-side, Dunkerque, Antwerp, Rotterdam and Hamburg/Wilhelmshaven. Thus, the economic validity of such terminals will be undermined and there is no further need to search for a solution to the problem of getting these mammoth tankers through the relatively shallow and congested waters of the English Channel.

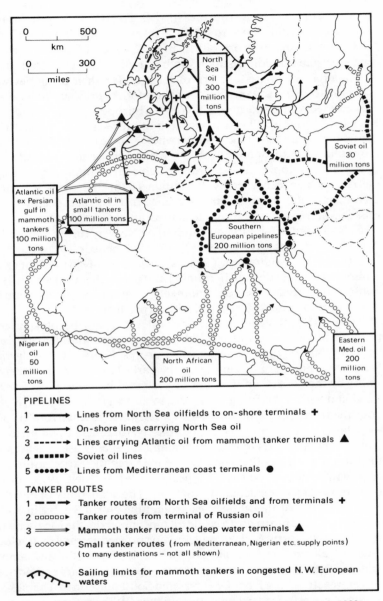

Fig. 10.7. The geography of Western Europe's oil supply in the early 1980s

This potential development signals an important retreat from the concern for "bigness" which has pervaded economic thought about tanker and terminal size over the last 25 years. The limited amount of oil moving into North-west Europe by tanker will, indeed, probably be best moved in small tankers, for the oil-exporting countries plan to develop their own refining capacity so as to supply products rather than crude oil to their overseas customers. North Sea oil will also by then be moving partly by small product tankers (from the Scottish and Norwegian refineries) and partly as crude oil to existing refineries. However, given a distance of only a few hundred miles from the loading terminals to the refining centres, there will be no transport cost advantage to be gained in using tankers of more than 70,000 to 100,000 tons for such crude oil movements, though, in all likelihood, tankers larger than this will be used on these short runs simply because larger tankers will be available and smaller ones unavailable. Their use, however, will be nothing to do with the relative economies of large as against smaller vessels and the average size of tankers will fall as new tankers of 70-100,000 tons are built to serve this trade and, given their cost advantages, take over from the larger vessels. Thus, not only is the economic *raison d'etre* of the large, deep-water centres for receiving and refining crude oils essentially undermined—but there also opens up the possibility of a more dispersed pattern of future location of refineries in Western Europe, a result of the fact that refinery location will become much less critically related to depth of the channel in the approaches to oil ports as the size of the tanker diminishes.

CONCLUSIONS

The development of the energy sector in Western Europe for the rest of the century thus depends on the inter-relationships of many variables which are essentially geographical, variables which are, indeed, only understandable in the context of economic geography rather than the generally space-less world of economics or even the non-political and non-socially influenced world of regional and spatial economics. All this is becoming increasingly clear in the context of the rapidly changing energy situation in Western Europe where we are already far removed from the simplistic economics based on concern for how best to obtain and use the cheapest possible energy within an internationally free-trading system, hitherto organised to ensure the advantages for the industrial nations.

This chapter has attempted to show just how geographical variables—such as the distribution of resources and their location relative to demand, as well as the spatial variations in political and social factors—provide a basis on which policy decisions may be taken: and how the policy decisions themselves then become an input into the continuing re-evaluation of the geography of supply and demand. The latter part of the chapter posed many questions which are essentially geographical and answers to which are also relevant to wise policy decisions in the energy sector. In the limited space available it has only been possible to illustrate the relevance of geography to policy making in this part of modern society and, as will be apparent, the analysis has by no means been exhaustive.

Figure 10.8 indicates a continuity of growth in the productivity of the North Sea basin for almost two decades into the future and shows that there are even more extreme and surprising policy options which should be under consideration from the geographical point of view (Odell and K. E. Rosing, 1974). Even longer-term and more extraordinary in its likely effect on the geography of Europe's energy supply—and even on the more general geography of its economy—is the likely continuation of exploration activities for off-shore oil and gas in the many areas of possible interest which exist around the continent. Figure 10.9 demonstrates the scope of the possibilities involved.

This large potential availability from the off-shore waters of the continent of very conventional oil and gas for meeting the future energy requirements of the Western European economy raises the question of the validity of the proposed programmes for the massive development of nuclear power in Western Europe over the next 10 to 20 years. The extraordinary high capital cost of nuclear development compared with the limited investment in off-shore oil and gas makes it a "bad buy". Preliminary results of research currently under way in the Economic Geography Institute in Rotterdam indicate that investment in off-shore oil is 3·3 times more productive—in terms of useful energy produced—than investment in the present generation

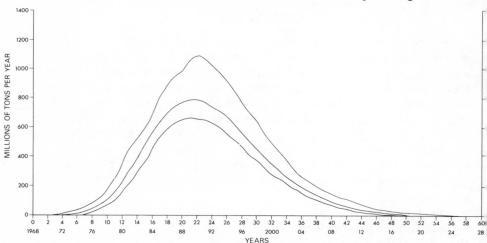

Fig. 10.8. Production potential from the North Sea Oil Province 1969-2028 (bottom curve, 90% probability of at least this annual production; top curve, 1% probability of production reaching this level; middle curve, mean production potential from 100 operations of model)

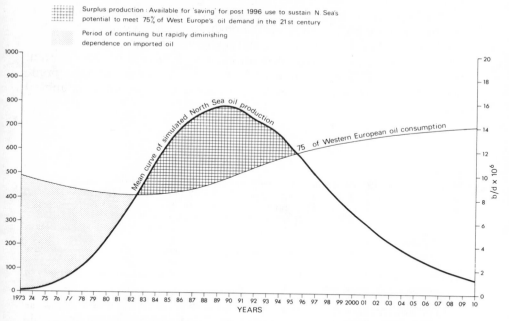

Fig. 10.9. The mean curve of simulated North Sea production potential compared with the curve of 75 per cent of expected Western European demand for oil 1973-2010

of nuclear power stations. This comparison is valid even when it is assumed that the energy economies based on the alternative possibilities are the same in terms of type of final energy used—and, in particular, in terms of the degree to which electrification is required in an economy. However, the conventionally fuelled economy need not be so "electrical" in terms of final use as must the nuclear economy and hence the former is still less capital intensive since it is electricity production which absorbs capital resources most effectively. Furthermore, the economy based on oil and gas as the conventional fuels can be made more efficient by associating electricity production with the utilisation of the waste heat produced in the manufacture of electricity. What this means is a new geography of electricity generation, a move away from the development, well nigh exclusively, of large central power stations (from which the heat produced as a by-product of electricity generation must be dispersed to the atmosphere or via cooling water and hence serves no useful purpose) to the establishment of a geographically dispersed pattern of electricity production in thousands of locations where a local demand for the "waste" heat exists and which can thus be incorporated into a more efficient energy economy.

This important component in the discussion of the future of electricity is yet another that is in part geographical (though, of course, a component which has to be combined with economic and engineering aspects) and emphasises the way in which public policy decisions in this whole field of the important energy sector of the economy must be subjected to the use of appropriate geographical analysis and based, in the final analysis, on geographical understanding.

REFERENCES

Adelman, M. A. (1972) *The World Petroleum Market,* Johns Hopkin's Press, Baltimore.

Anon. (1974) "Offshore oil: a cause for regret", *Architect's Journal,* **26** (159), June, 1371-2.

Hogg, A. (1975) "The North East and Tayside", in A. M. Hutcheson and A. Hogg (eds.), *Scotland and Oil,* Oliver and Boyd, Edinburgh, 2nd edition, pp. 80-97.

Francis, J. and N. Swan (1973) *Scotland in Turmoil,* Church of Scotland Home Board, Edinburgh.

Norwegian Government (1973-4) *Petroleum Industry in Norwegian Society*, Parliamentary Report No. 25.

Odell, P. R. (1969) *Natural Gas in Western Europe: a Case Study in the Economic Geography of Energy Resources,* Erven F. Bohn, Haarlem.

Odell, P. R. (1974) *Oil and World Power,* 3rd edition, Penguin Books, London.

Odell, P. R. (forthcoming) "European alternatives to oil imports from OPEC countries: an energy economy based on indigenous oil and gas", in F. A. M. Alting van Geusau (ed.) *Energy Policy Planning in the European Community.*

Odell, P. R. and K. E. Rosing (1974) "The North Sea Oil Province: a Simulation Model of its Development", *Energy Policy,* **2** (4), 316-29.

Over, J. A. and A. C. Sjoerdsma (eds.) (1974) *Energy Conservation, Ways and Means* , Stichting Toekomstbeeld der Techniek, The Hague.

CHAPTER 11

A GEOGRAPHER IN THE ENVIRONMENTAL MOVEMENT IN NEW ZEALAND

R. G. LISTER

University of Otago

Throughout the 1960s New Zealanders observed the progress of active environmental groups in the countries of the northern hemisphere but not until the later years of the decade had an indigenous movement emerged in this country. There were some strong early indications of the coming development of environmental forces when, in 1959, the Government accepted a proposal from an international aluminium consortium for harnessing the waters of Lake Manapouri (Fig. 11.1) to provide electric power for a major smelter, only to find the Royal New Zealand Forest and Bird Protection Society launching a vigorous protest. This powerful society raised the alarm and mustered 25,000 supporters for its petition to Parliament but failed to rally the widespread support in the community that would have been necessary to offset the appeal of the consortium's offer, which reached the Government at the time when British entry to the European Economic Community was being first strongly advocated and the realisation of the possible loss of the British market had come as a shock to New Zealanders.

EMERGENCE OF A NATIONAL ENVIRONMENTAL "CONSCIENCE"

During the following 4 or 5 years, however, many strands linked to emphasise the dangers of ignoring environmental considerations in national development programmes for New Zealand's economic growth. A number of overseas examples received widespread publicity and helped to convince thinking New Zealanders of the need to be constantly alert against threats of economic or strictly technical domination of the country's way of life. Oil spills, the Aberfan tragedy, the threat of extinction of the whale and the fight

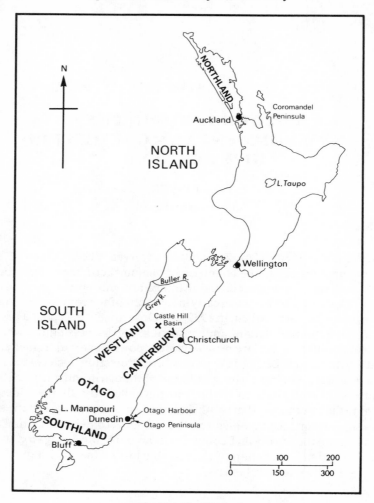

Fig. 11.1. New Zealand

in the United States against supersonic aircraft all contributed in different ways to the formation of strong feelings against overdevelopment in New Zealand.

When therefore, in 1967, the aluminium consortium gave notice to the Government that it wished to take up its option of power from Lake Manapouri in the terms provisionally agreed 8 years before, public indifference was no longer evident. The New Zealand community had clearly moved a long way since 1959 on the path of environmental awareness. The Government took the necessary steps to build the power station, as agreed, to provide the energy for the large smelter at Bluff but found its plans meeting growing resistance over the issue of raising the level of the lake in order to maximise the power that Manapouri could produce. During 1968 the "Save Manapouri" campaign enlisted widespread support among professional people as well as amateur naturalists, and this movement provided the first focus for a new environmental "conscience" that had been created in New Zealand through the impact of numerous events during the intervening years. Geographers played their part alongside botanists, geologists and other scientists in helping to gather evidence and formulate scientific support for the argument that power from Lake Manapouri should not involve the raising of lake levels. The Otago branch of the Royal Society was moved to produce a soundly-based submission highlighting the scientific issues involved, (1970) to demonstrate that raising the level of Lake Manapouri was not a critical element in the success of the smelter whereas raising it would certainly prove to be critical for despoiling the scenic value of this beautiful lake. The principle of undertaking major engineering projects within a National Park also provided a key argument, since the National Parks Act 1953 had set the criteria for areas of outstanding scenic beauty and the inclusion of Lake Manapouri within the Fiordland National Park had necessarily involved its designation as an area to be preserved unspoiled in perpetuity.

The Otago submission was formally presented to the Commission of Enquiry which the Government set up in response to what had, by 1969, proved to be the most successful parliamentary petition of all time in New Zealand in support of the "Save Manapouri" campaign. The Commission sat for almost 3 months during that year taking evidence from a wide variety of persons and organisations. Despite the Government's legal obligation to the consortium to complete the task of raising the lake, and a rather non-committal report from the Commission (1970), which indicated broad acceptance of the reasoning of the campaigners but left the issue of its legal commitment to the Government, the Cabinet finally bowed to the campaign to the extent of deciding not to raise the level of the lake "in the meantime". The solution proferred was to build a dam only up to the level of the mean height, at 583 ft (178 m) above sea level. This left the ultimate decision on whether to raise the lake to some future administration. This was possible within the terms of the Government's legal commitment because the consortium's plans did not include the need for the extra power produced by raising the lake until almost 20 years later, in 1986, when the final phase of expansion of aluminium output was scheduled.

This long-drawn-out controversy stimulated New Zealand's interest in the wide range of issues involved. It served to emphasise the need for scientific understanding of the environment so as to appreciate accurately the nature of the damage that could be done to scenic beauty for the sake of economic gain.

It thus brought field scientists into a movement in which their expertise was shown to be important for the solution of political problems. At the same time it demonstrated the need for interdisciplinary work because no single discipline could provide the answer to the questions raised. Economists, politicians and natural scientists involved themselves in vigorous public debate and, through the popularity of the campaign, found themselves caught up into the eventual success story of the Manapouri controversy, as measured by progress towards official recognition of the significance of environmental issues.

But there was more to this than a conflict between advocates of technical progress and protectors of the natural environment, because the consortium using the Manapouri dam for power was essentially foreign-owned and clearly intent on utilising a major New Zealand resource in order to place its products to the best economic advantage on world markets. Many New Zealanders therefore saw the campaign as one involving exploitation of their country's resources for profits that would be taken out of the country, notably to Australia and Japan. This type of situation was therefore one in which an overall appreciation of the elements of the landscape and a grasp of the principles of economic geography were useful tools in approaching the issues at stake.

Meanwhile, quite apart from the popular enthusiasm generated by the Manapouri question, a parallel movement was at work leading towards similar objectives. Members of the professional Institution of Engineers had become concerned over the trend being reflected in current goals for economic growth in New Zealand. The country had failed to boost its productive capacity during the post-war decade as successfully as many people had hoped and, as a result, the Government became convinced that some more formal programme was required in order to achieve the growth rate necessary for sustaining rising standards of living. New Zealand was falling behind a number of other Western countries in registering an annual increase of little more than 2 per cent in its gross national product. In common with other advanced countries that were achieving figures of this order, the New Zealand Government took further initiatives in an attempt to improve this position. The threat of the United Kingdom joining the European Economic Community and thus divorcing itself from New Zealand as a special trading partner, gave the necessary focus for an examination of agricultural output and markets. In 1962 an Agricultural Development Conference sponsored by the Government recommended that the time had come for indicative planning across the whole field of farm production, processing and marketing. The aim was an increase of 4 per cent annually in agricultural output of the country. The Government accepted these goals and established an Agricultural Development Council to oversee the planning and subsequent progress. It was soon realised that this move was a successful one.

With similar objectives in mind, therefore, conferences were held in 1964 and in later years in order to examine other sectors of the economy in depth. As a result further Councils were established to set targets and keep an eye on the progress of similar indicative planning for output in the manufacturing, forestry, fishing and mineral sectors while a further Council was set up to review the field of transport.

The Institution of Engineers regarded these developments with some dismay since it was apparently assumed that the country could absorb this continued growth and that the necessary measures to achieve it in all sectors could be put into effect without detriment to the environment both naturally and socially. Politicians certainly saw no need to question the desirability of development towards higher production targets and simply assumed that New Zealanders would be able to adapt appropriate technical means of achieving them. However, it was clear to a growing number of informed persons that increased output in agriculture and forestry could well lead to acute problems in the environment and that these might be produced so quickly that the country would be ill prepared to rectify the damage that might in fact be caused. It was noted that in the United Kingdom the Duke of Edinburgh's Conference on "The Countryside in 1980" had generated widespread interest in long-term views of development and the Institution of Engineers in New Zealand adopted this same approach in calling attention to longer-term issues in relation to growth in the national economy.

In 1967 the Institution therefore took the initiative in sponsoring a conference of invited persons to consider in some depth what might be done to resolve such broad issues. The conference passed a number of resolutions that represented a first attempt to grapple with environmental problems on a national administrative level. It recommended that administrative machinery be set up both nationally and regionally to examine and coordinate environmental matters, linked particularly with conservation and land use; and it suggested that coordination and direction be exercised by a new department of state acting as the agent for a national environment board. The conference resolved that a continuing working party be set up by the Institution of Engineers, to pursue these questions further in consultation with the Institute of Architects, the Municipal Association, the Counties Association, Federated Farmers and the Town and Country Planning Institute, and that representatives of other interested organisations be co-opted as required. The working party recommended that the Government should itself take responsibility for examining the kind of physical environment in which New Zealanders live and work. The Government was persuaded to set up a "Physical Environment Committee" in 1968 to consider the present and potential availability of land for competing productive, residential and recreational purposes. Its task also included a review of pollution problems, and of the contribution that might be made by the Town and Country Planning

Branch of the Ministry of Works to balanced future development and to the preservation of natural scenic beauty in relation to the country's economic and social development. This Committee in turn sponsored a number of working parties into these questions which were thus reviewed over the next 2 years by widely representative groups involving government agencies, professional societies, academics and other individuals.

THE PHYSICAL ENVIRONMENT CONFERENCE 1970

Their findings were reported to the Physical Environment Conference which the Government called in May 1970. This Conference was summoned to assess existing policies and legislation in New Zealand as they affected the environment and to advise the National Development Council upon the measures and resources required to implement a sound environmental policy in relation to the country's economic growth targets.

The Physical Environment Conference was thus envisaged as a landmark in New Zealand's development. Those attending represented a wide cross-section of central government, of local authorities, particularly engineers and local councillors, together with academics and a number of other individuals known to be concerned with environmental and development problems. Some 300 persons attended this conference in Wellington. It was opened by the Prime Minister, Sir Keith Holyoake, and was well publicised through press and radio. It was not a public forum, since attendance was by representation or by invitation.

It was therefore evident that, by the close of the decade, the Government was taking the whole issue of environmental policy and administration seriously. By the frequent comments from the platform and from the floor on the Manapouri issue it was also clear that the lessons revealed by this campaign were being learned. The working parties had prepared papers with formal recommendations to place before the Conference and these provided the substance of the matters dealt with in the three days of discussions. The homework which these reports represented had been well done and, given the good will apparent on all sides, the Conference emerged as an important step forward in the history of New Zealand's growing sense of responsibility towards its own environment.

Geographers from most of the University departments in the country attended and were included amongst those who presented the leading papers and amongst those who contributed to the discussions. It was noteworthy that in the final plenary session, a warning note was sounded by Sir Guy Powles, New Zealand's first Ombudsman, to the effect that New Zealand appeared to be moving towards more official direction and technical control by persons who had not been subjected to the democratic process of elections. He feared that, however desirable the goals of environmental significance might be, the procedures being recommended for dealing with them were in fact a retreat from democracy. His impassioned plea produced no apparent effect in relation to the recommendations of the conference, but it was no doubt heeded by many present.

Perhaps the most significant result that came from the recommendations of the conference was the confirmation that further progress would depend upon the establishment of permanent machinery to monitor changes and to administer environmental measures. The precise form of such a continuing element in central government was not worked out in detail at the Conference, but it was agreed to recommend to the Government that an Environmental Council be set up to survey the existing structure of central and local government measures related to the environment and make its own recommendations upon measures that might be necessary to improve the kind of environment to which New Zealanders aspire.

In due course the standing committee of the Conference sifted the many recommendations and passed on to the Government its suggestions for implementing them.

THE ENVIRONMENTAL COUNCIL

The method adopted for creating the proposed Environmental Council was to invite all those organisations which were represented at the conference—and there were more than 100 of them—to nominate suitable persons as members for the Council. The final selection was made in the light of these nominations. The members were thus not directly elected.

Towards the end of 1970 those selected were invited to attend an inaugural meeting of the new Environmental Council which the Government had decided to build into the structure of the National Development Council (N.D.C.). This Council had grown from its first sector council, for agriculture, in 1962 to become a body of some fourteen sector councils, each setting growth targets in its own field and reporting to a central body, the National Development Council, which had in this way become the focal point of what might be termed indicative national planning in New Zealand.

This central body met first in 1968 and again at 2-year intervals. The terms of reference for the new Environmental Council made it clear that its task included a review of the development plans brought forward by each of the sector councils and the preparation of a report to the National Development Council in relation to the environmental issues which might be raised.

The Environmental Council was chaired by a barrister, (a Q.C.) and comprised eight official and six private members. The officials were the permanent heads or deputy-heads of government departments of Lands and Survey, Health, Works, Forests and Treasury, together with another senior member of Treasury acting in his capacity as Principal Executive Officer of the National Development Council. The Counties Association nominated one member (a chairman of a County Council in Canterbury) as also did the Municipal Association, represented by a Wellington City Councillor who was an architect in the city. The Regional Planning Authorities had one representative who was on the Auckland Authority. Private members were an East Coast farmer with special experience of farm education and training as well as of Federated Farmers administrative matters, a natural scientist from the Department of Scientific and Industrial Research, the managing director of a large mining industry, a consulting engineer from Auckland, the author as a geographer and one woman member whose contribution in community and social affairs had been widely recognised. Two permanent staff members were attached to the Council. Apart from an inaugural meeting with Ministers at the end of 1970, the Council began its business meetings in the New Year, 1971.

Members of the Environmental Council did not therefore represent organisations or electorates, but were expected to confer as independent persons. Their task was to report both directly to the Minister and, through the framework of the National Development Council, to the Cabinet on such environmental problems as were referred to them or such items as the Council itself chose to consider. As with other sector councils of the N.D.C., the Environmental Council had been given no executive authority to carry out a policy, for it was an advisory body. It would need to make its own way and build its own influence. The Council was attached to the Ministry of Works for administrative purposes. This attachment offered a number of advantages since this Ministry was in fact responsible for spending a substantial proportion of the national budget and incidentally commanded a wide range of such facilities as might be needed for the typing, preparation and printing of reports and the like, and was also able to provide a wide range of data and advice on environmental matters in which its various divisions were directly concerned. However, it had the possible disadvantage of also being the department of state whose members were responsible for some of the most massive, and often popularly regarded as the most detrimental programmes of interference with the environment of the country, and it was difficult to see how the new Council could hope to appear to be completely independent if it were in any way seen to be associated with its operations. However, the arrangement worked well initially and during the subsequent months it became clear to even the most critical individuals on the Council that its administrative attachment to the Ministry of Works carried with it no strings of any kind.

The author's own background in the environmental field had been one which included experience with community organisations in Otago and with local government through the Regional Planning Authority in the Metropolitan area of Dunedin. In the mid-1960s the Regional Planning Authority had decided to broaden its base of operations in respect of environmental matters and had invited the author to take charge of a new sub-committee of the authority to be responsible for recreation and scenic amenities. This committee was set up in 1966 and had demonstrated its value to the local bodies in the region principally through a series of reports, appearing approximately annually, on major areas of importance in the field with which it was concerned. The first of these reports dealt with the scenic resources and development potential of the Otago Peninsula (Fig. 11.1), with special emphasis on its role as a new type of "Regional Park". This report had been well received and its objectives became largely incorporated in the district scheme. He had been further involved in assisting the establishment of a voluntary organisation, the Otago Peninsula Trust, uniting a range of members of service clubs and the public who were interested in and concerned with the scenic values of the Peninsula. Subsequent reports on regional issues helped to define policy and offered recommendations for action, notably in the Town Belt—a scenic area set aside in the earliest plans for Dunedin City which were laid down originally in Scotland before the foundation of the Otago settlement in the 1840s. The Town Belt concept had been jealously guarded but in practice it had left much to be desired in respect of development on the ground. Another report reviewed Dunedin's Ocean Frontage and a fourth considered the Otago Harbour as a Regional Recreational Resource. Each of these reports had led to effective results within the region and, moreover, had helped to develop a wider appreciation by the public of the outstanding scenic attractions of the city and its surrounding region.

During 1971 the Environmental Council had before it some 150 recommendations passed to it from the 1970 Conference. These were sifted, analysed and sent on to appropriate government departments for action or for further investigation, while some of them clearly fell into the area of concern of the Council itself. Subcommittees were set up among council members to deal with these recommendations and bring down reports for appropriate government action.

THE ENVIRONMENTAL COUNCIL'S TASKS AND RESPONSIBILITIES

Under the terms of reference laid down by the National Development Council, the Environmental Council has been responsible for keeping under review:

(i) the objectives of preserving and developing the quality of the environment, established following the Conference on the Physical Environment in May 1970;

(ii) the policies, measures and resources necessary to their attainment;

(iii) the environmental effects of the programmes suggested by other sector councils.

The council's terms of reference formally required it to advise both the Minister and the National Development Council:

(i) on the changes which may be required from time to time to the objectives and to the policies, measures and resources required for their attainment including the status and powers of the Environmental Council itself;

(ii) on any matters concerning the efficiency in the use of resources required to maintain, preserve and develop a high environmental standard;

(iii) on any other matters which may be referred to it from time to time or which it may consider merit its attention.

Several examples will illustrate the way in which the Council has pursued its tasks under these three headings.

SOUTH ISLAND INDIGENOUS FORESTS

Possibly the most important programme of development to come before the Council during its first 3 years has been the proposal from the Forestry Development Council for the utilisation of the remaining indigenous beech forests in South Island. These represent one of the few major natural resources still available in New Zealand for exploitation at the present stage of technical knowledge. The Forest Service proposed (1971) that large-scale development of the South Island beech forests be undertaken in order to achieve sustained yield from the forests, and suggesting that this programme be supplemented by a carefully defined scheme of clear felling and re-planting with exotic pines. The Silver Beech (*Nothofagus menziesii*) is one of the few native species capable of providing an economic return as most other indigenous timber trees have a very long growing period. While the Silver Beech reaches maturity at an age between 80 and 120 years, the Rimu (*Dacrydium cupressinum*) which was for many decades the most widely-used and popular structural timber in New Zealand, is not mature until about 300 years of age. Whereas in the North Island, *Pinus radiata* has for some years been the principal building timber,

Rimu is still preferred in the South Island owing to its relative abundance on the West Coast.

During the 1960s it had become clear that because of the continuing inroads being made into the forests of the West Coast, the numerous and mainly small timber mills of the region would be unable to continue in economic timber production for any substantial future period while operating on their present basis. Current milling production involves selective cutting, to extract the marketable timber while leaving the "rubbish" to regenerate. This wasteful type of exploitation has continued for over a century and the areas of cutover forests on the West Coast have become very considerable. Only in South Westland are there still extensive areas of unexploited forest.

The proposals for sustained yield beech forest development include clear felling of much of the cutover bush in and around the Grey Valley in Northern Westland so as to provide an area of concentrated forest development focussing on the lower Grey Valley. To achieve a relatively quick turnover from these areas first cleared, it is proposed to plant *Pinus radiata* in place of some 60,000 hectares (148,000 acres) of beech-podocarp forest (of which about 21,000 hectares (52,000 acres) represent already cutover bush). The *Pinus radiata* forests, on the basis of experimental plantings on the Coast, would be mature and ready for felling after some 35 years. The first regenerated Silver Beech forest, with appropriate thinning and management operations, would not be ready for felling in less than 80 years. By incorporating the *Pinus Radiata* plantings, particularly in the initial phases of the scheme in the Grey Valley, there would be advantages in utilising cutover country in the heart of the area in order to provide the quantities of timber required to sustain the proposed pulp mill.

During 1971-2 the New Zealand Forest Service had published its proposals, circulating them widely for comment and inviting suggestions and counter-proposals from interested bodies and individuals. Some conservationists regard the replacement of native beech by *Pinus radiata* as an abandonment of New Zealand's heritage in respect of an important natural resource. Hence there was strong criticism of the Forest Service's proposals on this account.

The correspondence which arose from this process was referred amongst other documents to the Environment Council for its assessment of the scheme and for its recommendation to the National Development Council as to its acceptability on environmental grounds. The Council was invited to comment on any terms or conditions which it might consider necessary in order to provide a satisfactory basis for the scheme's acceptance by government. After receiving the documents and reviewing them the Council visited the West Coast on a study visit to the area concerned and to view experimental *Pinus radiata* plantings that had been undertaken during the last two decades; a visit was also made to trial areas in which beech was regenerating under management. Members of the Council were flown around the development area and over adjacent forest districts and were conducted on the ground into a range of forest sites, both indigenous and exotic, in and around the Grey Valley (Fig. 12.1).

Much of the cutover country in the Grey Valley has poor quality stands of native timber, owing to the irregular selective felling in the past. In this area of the middle Grey and Buller valleys, there are well-drained dissected terraces providing good sites for pine forests, unlike much of the ill-drained "pakihi" terrace top land of much of Westland which cannot be used to raise planted pine forests or to regenerate good beech stands.

In any event, no beech forests will be affected on mountain slopes above 1000 metres, because they are classed as protection forests under arrangements with the catchment authority. Care has been taken to examine the scheme in order to designate scenic areas and scientific reserves of suitable extent and in appropriate localities. Because of the importance of the Grey Valley as a tourist route for travel between Canterbury and the West Coast, scenic areas are being liberally designated. Indigenous flora and fauna reserves are also being set aside, and this policy will continue as investigations proceed and more detailed field results become available. A standing Scientific Committee is being set up as an integral part of the scheme.

Mountain ranges flanking the Grey Valley to both east and west include fingers of comparatively narrow valleys occupied by Silver Beech. The Environmental Council stressed that these valleys should not be exploited for their timber but should be regarded as integral parts of the scenic and recreational area of the mountains, and should therefore be deleted from the scheme area.

In all there are 3·4 million hectares (8·4 million acres) of indigenous forests in the South Island, of which some 1·6 million hectares (4·0 million acres) are lowland forest. Within this total, the development scheme envisages the use of 70,000 hectares (178,000 acres) in Westland and 80,000 (200,000 acres) in Western Southland for the planting of pine and 215,000 hectares (530,000 acres) in the programme of sustained-yield beech regeneration.

The Council found that the proposals had been carefully prepared in relation to environmental considerations and, subject to a number of minor modifications related to scenic areas and scientific checks, recommended accordingly to the Government that the beech forest scheme be proceeded with. However, the Government accepted none of the tenders submitted in 1975 by several large consortia and requested a further study of the possible combined use of existing pine forests in Nelson with West Coast beech forests.

CASTLE HILL BASIN PROPOSAL

From time to time specific problems arise in relation to environmental aspects of development proposals which bring contentious issues sharply before the public eye. During the latter part of the 1960s the public generally became acutely aware of the need for vigilance to ensure the survival of much that New Zealanders value in the character and quality of their natural landscape.

In mid-1972 it was announced that a development company intended to purchase the Castle Hill Basin in Canterbury as it had come on to the market because of the decision by the holder of this sheep station to sell his "run". The property comprised some 400 hectares (1000 acres) of valley flats together with about 20,000 hectares (50,000 acres) of foothill and mountain country around the Basin. On all mountain country sheep runs both are used in an essentially related way. In a very real sense the capacity of the hill country to carry its stock numbers depends upon the ability of the valley flats to provide winter feed for the sheep. However, the developer was offering to buy the 400 hectares of valley floor in order to build a resort town of "second homes", for purposes of mountain recreation, particularly for the people of Christchurch, 100 kilometres (60 miles) to the east. Plans of the proposed town in the mountains showed a well-laid-out suburban pattern of streets and standard subdivisions, with a number of tall blocks of flats grouped around a conspicuous outcrop of striking limestone hills which rise from the valley floor. The valley is almost entirely an open landscape and is cultivated for winter feed crops and high-yielding pastures.

The local county council had produced no District Scheme and hence had shown no planning requirement in relation to such a proposal.

The Scenery Preservation Society, established a little more than a decade earlier in Christchurch when Lake Manapouri first became a lively issue, took a strong stand over the Castle Hill Basin proposal, insisting that it was incompatible with the environment of the mountain scenery of the Basin.

The whole issue was referred to the Environmental Council, with the request that a recommendation be made to the Minister.

The Council took the view that this new recreational town, the first of its kind in New Zealand mountain country, would in effect set an important precedent in this country. It was strongly felt that the Castle Hill Basin itself should be viewed as one element in a succession of scenically attractive landscapes occurring along the major tourist route between Christchurch and the West Coast. In fact, this road should be regarded as one of New Zealand's outstanding scenic corridors.

Lincoln College at the University of Canterbury took an active interest in this issue and arrangements were made for a study in depth of the Castle Hill situation, viewing the development area in relation to its total setting as well as a desirable centre in itself for the recreation of the citizens of Christchurch who were likely to seek tramping, skiing, horse riding, fishing, swimming and mountain climbing facilities in this area. Staff and research students

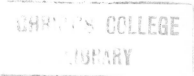

collaborated in the field study and the Environmental Council assisted in publishing the results.

In brief, the solution proposed was to recommend development in the Basin only under certain specified conditions. The whole central area of the Basin was visually important to the main route and no suburban atmosphere should therefore spoil the mountain scene enjoyed by travellers on this route. Moreover, around the limestone hill an important small reserve had been set aside to conserve the very rare buttercup, *Ranunculus paucifolius,* restricted to the Basin and justifying particular care in ensuring that no development of housing was undertaken in proximity to it. Recreational facilities in the mountains warrant a different planning approach from that of a suburban type in Christchurch and therefore a more appropriate layout should be an essential element in any such scheme. Engineering advice indicated that small clusters of holiday homes of 70 to 120 houses would each justify an economic sewerage treatment unit and could be designed and sited around the margins of the Basin where small pockets of beech forest would provide a most attractive situation. Moreover, houses could be shaded and in part concealed among the beech trees. In this way the impact of a recreational facility for a population of several thousand people could be made environmentally acceptable within the setting of the Basin.

While this study was proceeding the Council advised the Minister to veto the development pending the findings and publication of the report. The developer himself took a considerable interest in the investigations and it is expected that new proposals will emerge along the lines formulated in the study. The Report (J. A. Hayward and F. D. Boffa, 1972) sets out a disciplined and refined methodological approach to environmental planning, within which specific projects may be developed along sound lines.

COASTAL DEVELOPMENT

Since the Second World War New Zealanders have been multiplying their popular recreational development of holiday homes many times over and the rush to secure attractive coastal sites has reached somewhat alarming proportions, particularly so in the north of the North Island. It has long been a feature of the New Zealand way of life to buy a site and build a "bach" or a "crib". While this "do-it-yourself" style remained an individual objective for the more energetic, prosperous or successful members of the community, it occurred within acceptable proportions. In recent years, however, large-scale developers have moved on to the scene and purchases of substantial areas of attractive coastline for development and subdivision have been increasing year by year. Many observers realise that some limitation of this type of development would become necessary but it has been virtually impossible for any local authority to take action and, in the democratic society of which New Zealanders are most proud, it was held that it was no part of the State's responsibility to intervene.

By the end of the 1960s, however, popular opinion itself began to call attention to some of the more serious anomalies in the situation and during 1971-2 the Environmental Council became involved in a number of cases which were referred to it for advice. For example, a developer in the Coromandel Peninsula, about 180 kilometres east of the Auckland metropolitan area, proposed to lay out a seaside town beside the beach at Waikawau Bay, with a major shopping centre behind the sand dunes and some 2000 holiday homes, with ready access to this centre, built on the slopes behind the limited flat land around the township.

It so happens that this Waikawau beach is the last bay of any size on the east coast of the Peninsula that had not previously been developed for recreational purposes. Its unspoilt farmland backed by native bush overlooks almost 2000 metres (1·2 miles) of the sweep of silver sands, and provides a glorious scene which recalls the wilder beauty of Coromandel at its best. Sporadic development of holiday homes had already taken place on both east and west coasts (though by no means taking up all available sites), so leaving no comparable beach scene. If any such bay were to remain on Coromandel, it was clear that this was the only remaining possibility. Environmental groups in Auckland and elsewhere favoured the retention of this outstanding rural scene as the culmination of the coastal drive up the coasts on the east or on the west side. Developers, however, were quick to point out that there was an almost insatiable demand for holiday homes in this area and that they were simply meeting popular demand in providing for such a township. They were supported by the local county council which had suffered from a declining rural population for much of the past half century. It would welcome this possibility of a new source of rates after so long a period of struggle to meet its commitments.

In the circumstances the Environmental Council took the view that the county council, though the responsible local authority in the matter, could not be expected to take into account wider regional considerations, nor could this body in its financial situation be expected to forego the opportunity which such a proposal offered. It would be no legacy, however, to future New Zealanders to allow every beach on the Coromandel Peninsula to undergo similar development even though there might be a demand and the developer might provide considerable variety. It was therefore recommended that the Minister should, in his capacity as Minister in charge of Land Settlement subdivision, decline the proposal for cutting up the property at Waikawau Bay and in the meantime advise Coromandel County Council that such a development was unacceptable on national and regional grounds. The Minister took this advice and development proposals were shelved in the meantime. He declined to consider the Environmental Council's further recommendation that a moratorium might be imposed pending a review of problems of coastal development.

It was well known that such a situation was paralleled by many others east and north of Auckland in particular, and on a lesser scale elsewhere in New Zealand. It was important to demonstrate that environmental considerations deserved strong support so that future developments would be more wisely approached.

The Council appreciates that the structure of local government in New Zealand must carry much of the blame for the lack of a broad view in such matters. Many small rural counties have not been able to maintain the standard of services and amenities required for a modern community demanding continual upgrading of facilities. The Local Government Commission had been producing recommendations for the restructuring of the metropolitan areas of New Zealand in order to identify regional forces at work and match them by a suitably revised structure of regional government. Its recommendations, however, had no force of law and during the 1960s it had become apparent that no local bodies were likely voluntarily to accept proposals for regional reorganisation. There was, however, a growing body of opinion favouring more vigorous central government action in this matter. In particular, regional planning was becoming urgent and regional thinking was overdue in the motor car age. The Council therefore had reason to expect that during the next few years regional policies in some form or another would be likely to emerge and its action in attempting to stem the tide at Waikawau Bay served to give notice that such regional thinking needed to replace the more local loyalties of the counties as they stood.

Subdivisions in Northland over the following few years have continued to emphasise the need for a revision of local government, particularly in respect of coastal subdivision. In November 1974 a new Local Bodies Bill was passed by Parliament reinforcing the powers of the Local Government Commission and requiring it to produce schemes of regional government for the whole of New Zealand by 1980. This new structure will ensure that wider views prevail in matters related to regional planning and it is expected that pressures on coastal land will be better controlled as a result.

Meanwhile, since 1972, the national Budget has included an allocation of a million dollars annually for purchase of coastal land of outstanding scenic and recreational value. A start is thus being made towards the reservation of important areas of the coast. The Department of Lands and Survey is charged with assessing the scenic and recreational value of the whole of the coast line, carrying out this review by county units and so enabling the head office of the Department to place appropriate priorities for coastal and lakeside purchases of the reserves each year. Because of rising prices, progress with a million dollars annually has not been as dramatic as might have been expected but this has proved a popular move and the sums involved may well be increased. A start has therefore been made to reversing the apparently irresistible advance of the developers along the New Zealand coasts.

The Wetlands of New Zealand, both coastal and other marshland areas, constitute a wildlife asset of irreplaceable value in that they provide the habitat of numerous native and migrant birds. A number of significant habitat areas have been officially designated as scientific reserves but the pace of reclamation has accelerated during the past decade, as techniques available for reclamation have improved and subsidies for farmers undertaking such work have become more readily available.

Accordingly, a critical stage has been reached requiring urgent action to set aside more of the wetlands as wildlife habitats, and the Environmental Council has recommended to the Government that a scheme comparable to that for the annual purchase of coastland and lakeshore recreational and scenic reserves, be established, though on a smaller scale of expenditure. At the time of writing, no such scheme has yet been announced by the Government.

INTERNATIONAL LINKS

The Environmental Council was charged with the responsibility for international contacts in environmental matters. It was therefore recognised as the appropriate body to participate in the Stockholm Conference on the Human Environment in 1972, which the author attended as one of New Zealand's official representatives.

Following Maurice Strong's visit to New Zealand about a year before the Conference, the Council decided that it should produce a report on New Zealand's environment. This was the first time that such a document had been attempted in this country and it served to draw attention to the major issues affecting New Zealand in respect of a range of environmental problems. The Council invited a number of authorities within the field to assess the situation as at 1972 and thus many of the central government agencies became involved in a useful exercise in coordination (Environmental Council, 1972a).

In addition to the preparation of the national environmental report, the Council accepted Maurice Strong's invitation to prepare a case study of environmental change in some part of New Zealand. He recognised that New Zealand presented unusually favourable opportunities for assessing the impact of man's changing techniques upon the landscape, since in New Zealand almost all major development had taken place during the past century and most of the process was well-documented. Moreover, recent policies had begun to emerge from the growing impact of progressive environmental thinking upon official views. Accordingly, the Council selected the Lake

Taupo catchment area in the centre of the North Island as the subject of this case study (Environmental Council, 1972b) and a brief history of development was prepared outlining the course of the dramatic landscape changes that had been effected. This area involved native forests, exotic pine plantations developed from natural scrub cover, and pasture establishment on an extensive scale for livestock farming, following the discovery that critical trace element deficiencies in the volcanic soils could be rectified. Maori land disputes had been involved and recent recreational pressures around Lake Taupo had arisen since the Second World War, as the motor car enabled Aucklanders and Wellingtonians to reach the shores of the Country's largest lake for weekend relaxation. This mosaic of problems has in recent years been tackled through the coordinated efforts of an officials committee representing all the government departments involved. In practice, most of the land of the Taupo catchment is owned by the Crown and comes under the jurisdiction of one or other of the principal State agencies for land development. Investigations are proceeding and the basis of sound policies which give a useful lead for land-use policy has been established.

The second major occasion when the Council's international responsibilities were exercised was in connection with a preparatory New Zealand statement to be presented to the Population Conference at Bucharest in 1974. In this instance the Council received a request from the Prime Minister asking that a survey of public opinion be undertaken by the Council in cooperation with the Social Council, to test the feeling of individuals and interested organisations in respect of population issues. The Council prepared an outline series of brief questions which were widely publicised early in 1974. The result was encouraging, as a wide range of bodies responded, representing professional groups, environmental societies, scientific bodies and responsible individuals (and remarkably few "cranks"). The final document, prepared by the Environmental Council (1975), was an assessment of the answers received and attempts to provide the first steps towards the formulation of a population policy for New Zealand.

It remains to be seen how deeply the issues highlighted by the Bucharest Conference will influence New Zealanders' thinking, but the Environmental Council has now committed itself to a role in this field. It is clear to the Council that environmental matters and the maintenance of high environmental standards are closely related to population change in one form or another and that it is in New Zealand's interest to evolve a positive population policy in the light of its own national objectives. The Environmental Council's population report prepared for the use of the Bucharest delegation from New Zealand is to appear as a published document as one of the Council's Occasional Papers (1975).

Towards the end of 1974 the Environmental Council formally set up three sub-committees which had previously been evolving in practice: on urban objectives; on energy; and on population. Each of these three committees is to take responsibility for coordinating the views of New Zealanders both in government and in public life, towards better environmental standards in so far as they affect and are affected by these important spheres of national development. The author's own position as Chairman of the Population Committee is a particularly interesting one for utilising his geographic experiences. In this way national policies may be formulated and higher environmental standards achieved for this country.

CONCLUSION

While the role and responsibilities of the Environmental Council were emerging through its work during the past 3 years, public appreciation of the significance of environmental values was growing and has been in turn reflected in administrative acceptance of its importance. Nationally this was recognised by the appointment of a Minister for the Environment in 1972. He was to act as coordinator of environmental matters affecting all Departments, and was given a small executive staff with the right to question the full range of development programmes coming before Cabinet. The first portfolio for the Environment was held by Duncan McIntyre, who had already held the portfolios of Lands, Forests, Maori Affairs and Island Territories, but subsequent Ministers, under the Labour administration, have linked the Environmental portfolio with Recreation and Sport (another new Ministry since 1972) and with Tourism. The Environmental Council itself, at its own suggestion, became attached for administrative purposes to the Minister for the Environment and severed its direct links with the Ministry of Works.

In 1973 the Labour government in the Kirk administration introduced the legal requirement of Environmental Impact Statements, to be prepared for all major government works. In order to audit these Statements, a well-qualified staff was vital, and accordingly a Commissioner for the Environment was established, acting virtually as permanent head of the newly-developed Ministry for the Environment and concerned principally as the executive officer for environmental questions. His role has developed as an important one, exercising liaison between all government departments whose work impinges upon environmental issues—and this in practice means virtually all departments of state.

The Commissioner's office has become the point in government to which local issues may be referred, despite the lack of any requirement for environmental impact statements from local authorities at present. Accordingly, the Commissioner's influence is becoming steadily more widespread and his role is becoming recognised as a most significant one, in much the same way as that of the Ombudsman, in relation to matters raised by citizens against the heavy

powerful influence, whether cases come before them or not, since local and central government officers and private developers formulate programmes in the knowledge that the Commissioner is constantly ready and willing to act if requested to do so in any matter likely to lead to environmental deterioration.

In some respects, New Zealand has been fortunate, owing to its isolated situation, in being able to avoid many of the afflictions of modern industrial societies. In other ways, through an enlightened attitude to management, and an often *ad hoc* approach to environmental issues, it has been learning from other countries' experience, establishing administrative procedures, and forming controlling and advisory bodies nationally, regionally and locally. It has been generally recognised that a geographical approach has played a significant part and it has been a rewarding experience to be involved at each of these levels, as well as in international aspects, in moving towards solutions to matters that are becoming recognised as of over-riding importance for New Zealand's future well-being.

REFERENCES

Commission to enquire into the Proposal to Raise the level of Lake Manapouri for the Purpose of Generating Electricity (1970), *Report*, Government Printer, Wellington.

Dunedin Metropolitan Regional Planning Authority (1968-73), *Reports:* Otago Peninsula: Recreation and Scenic Amenities (1968); Dunedin Town Belt (1969); Dunedin's Ocean Frontage (1971); and Otago Harbour as a Regional Recreation Resource (1973).

Environmental Council (1970) The Physical Environment Conference 1970. *Reports, Papers and Proceedings.* Government Printer, Wellington.

Environmental Council (1972a) *The New Zealand Environment,* National Report of the U.N. Preparatory Committee for the 1972 Conference on the Human Environment, Government Printer, Wellington.

Environmental Council (1972b) *The Taupo Basin: a New Zealand Study in Environmental Management,* Government Printer, Wellington.

Environmental Council (1973) *Report of the Environmental Council on the Proposed Utilisation of the South Island (West Coast) Beech Forests,* Wellington.

Environmental Council (1975) *Report of the Environmental Council and the Social Development Council on Public Submissions on Population Matters,* Occasional Paper No. 1, Wellington.

Hayward, J. A. and Boffa, F. (1972) *Recreation in the Waimakariri Basin,* Lincoln Paper in Resource Management No. 3, Lincoln College Press, Christchurch.

New Zealand Forest Service (1971). *Utilisation of the South Island Beech Forests,* White Paper, Government Printer, Wellington.

New Zealand Institution of Engineers (1967) *New Zealand Countryside in 1980,* Proceedings of Study Conference, Auckland.

Royal Society of New Zealand Otago Branch, (1970) The Case for Conserving the Natural Shoreline Environment of Lakes Manapouri and Te Anau. *Report,* Dunedin.

CHAPTER 12

THE POPULATION CENSUS OF NIGERIA, 1973

A. L. MABOGUNJE

University of Ibadan

Outside of the municipality of Lagos, the 1973 Population Census of Nigeria was the third actual census ever taken in most parts of the country. The first nation-wide census dates only from 1952 and was followed by a second in 1963. Before these dates, all censuses of the population of the country were based on estimates derived from various sources, notably district tax records. The earliest of these estimates was made in 1911, 10 years after the area now known as Nigeria had been declared a British colony. Similar estimates were computed for 1921 and 1931. The Second World War made it impractical to undertake such an assessment of the population in 1941 so that not until the 1950s was new interest shown in finding out the size of the Nigerian population.

Even from these earliest estimates, it was obvious that this portion of Africa contained some of the greatest concentration of population on the continent (R. R. Kuczynski, 1948). The 1911 estimate gave the population as 16 million and over the next 60 years this figure more than quadrupled. Table 12.1 shows the population of Nigeria from 1911 to 1973. It reveals a situation which is unparalleled in the history of population growth in most countries of the world. Given that the area of the country has not changed to any substantial extent during the period, the incredible rates of growth, especially since 1952, can be said to be due largely to problems of coverage control exacerbated by excessive political enthusiasm over the results of the census for different parts of the country. This chapter is concerned with the geographical contribution to coverage control for the 1973 census.

Coverage control in this connection refers to that aspect of census management which seeks to ensure that all individuals, residences and areas are enumerated. Along with ascertaining the accuracy of responses to the questionnaire, it constitutes one of the most important factors determining the quality of census returns generally. Failure to establish an effective coverage control in a census could give rise to either an undercount or an overcount of the population, from both of which Nigeria censuses would

207

appear to have suffered. Indeed, up to 1952, it would appear that the population of the country had been greatly underestimated. In 1911, for instance, the Acting Governor of the Northern Provinces of Nigeria, in forwarding the returns of the census for those provinces to the Secretary of State, expressed the opinion that the population of certain provinces had been underestimated by as much as 1·16 million (C. K. Meek, 1925, p. 169). Similarly, it was suggested that the population of the southern provinces in the 1921 census was underestimated by as much as 10 per cent (P. A. Talbot, 1926, p. 3). The report of the 1931 census indicated an undercount of about 5 per cent for the northern provinces and of about 10 per cent for most of the southern

TABLE 12.1. *Population of Nigeria 1911-73*

Census year	Population (million)	Percentage increase	Rate of growth (per cent per annum)
1911	15·97	—	—
1921	18·37	15·7	1·4
1931	19·93	8·5	0·8
1952	30·33	52·2	3·9
1963	55·67	83·5	5·7
1973	79·76	43·3	3·7

Sources: For the 1911 and 1921 census, P. A. Talbot (1926) and C. K. Meek (1925, vol. 2, p. 177); for the 1931 census, S. M. Jacob (1931, vol. 1, 1933, p. 10).

provinces reaching as high as 15 to 20 per cent for the provinces of Onitsha, Owerri and Calabar (Nigeria, 1933, Vol. I, p. 6). For the 1952 census, the error of undercount has been estimated to be of the order of 11 per cent. By contrast, the 1963 census is regarded as involving an overcount of as much as 14 per cent whilst an overcount of between 20 and 25 per cent is already being suggested for the 1973 census.

This persistence of a high degree of error in all Nigerian censuses underlines the inadequacy of coverage control to date and provides the back-drop against which to view the activities of the geographic profession during the preparation for the 1973 census. In what follows, an attempt is made to discuss first, the nature of the preparations for previous censuses as a background for evaluating their differences from those for the 1973 census; second, problems of coverage control for the 1973 census of Nigeria; third, the actual details of this control in terms of the demarcation of enumeration areas; fourth, the extension of control through house listing and house numbering just before the census; fifth, the evaluation of the effectiveness of the various coverage control activities; and finally, the prospect for transforming the present geographic contribution of the 1973 census into the basis for a spatially-oriented and easily-sustainable information system for the country.

THE NATURE OF CENSUS PREPARATION IN NIGERIA

Until the 1973 census, attempts have always been made to undertake census counts on the cheap. The cost of the 1921 census, for instance, was put at £9457 (excluding salaries and passages) or just about 0·12 pence per head of population, whilst that for 1931 was only £7600 or about 0·09 pence per head of population (Nigeria, 1933, p. 92). The Government Statistician who conducted the latter census congratulated his administration for the very economical way the census was carried out. For the 1952 census, the operation in the Northern Region was reported as costing approximately £39,000, that is, slightly more than ½d per person (Nigeria, 1956a, p. 7). In the Eastern Region the cost was £44,000 or about 1·3 pence per head (Nigeria, 1956b, p. 14) whilst in the West total expenditure came to £31,000 or about 1·2 pence per head (Nigeria, 1956a, p. 61). For the whole country, the cost of the 1952 census thus came to £114,000 or about 0·9 pence per head of population. According to T. M. Yesufu (1968, p. 111) the 1963 census, along with that of the 1962 count which was rejected, cost the country over £4 million, or about 17·1 pence per head. By contrast the 1973 count is already close to £20 million (i.e. approximately £12 million) or about 36·0 pence per head.

There is, of course, no virtue as such in engaging in very expensive census operations. Nonetheless, the amount of money allocated does affect how detailed the preparation for a census can be, especially in terms of coverage. Because of the limited funds provided, both the 1921 and 1931 censuses were undertaken in two parts, namely by townships and by provinces. Townships were small enclave settlements occupied largely by foreigners who were enumerated through mail questionnaires. This population constituted less than 0·05 per cent of the total. The great majority of the population were enumerated through a procedure of asking the native authorities to indicate the villages and towns under their jurisdiction and provide some estimates of the population and their characteristics. These were compiled for each province by the Resident who then despatched them to the Census Officer for the Northern and the Southern groups of provinces respectively.

These data were not provided for units of settlement below the level of provinces and divisions. In 1921, the country was divided into 24 provinces and had, besides, 20 townships. For the 12 provinces in the southern portion of the country figures were also provided for the 39 divisions of which they are comprised. In 1931, the number of provinces in the country had been reduced to 23. Eleven of these were in the north and comprised some 39 divisions. Outside the gross aggregate for these units, information was provided for what were regarded as the 40 largest towns in Nigeria. In short, the objective of these two censuses was considerably circumscribed and was concerned with getting no more than a rough picture of the demographic situation in Nigeria, largely for administrative purposes.

The 1952 census thus represents a major departure in the process of census taking in Nigeria since for the first time attempts were made at actually enumerating individual households. This bold step was possible partly because of the relatively higher level of development in the country by this time but particularly because of the post-war change in the objective of colonial administration whereby greater emphasis came to be paid to social and economic development (Nigeria, 1946). The enumeration of individual households was not, however, based on any formal system of coverage control. The procedure adopted took the following form. The three regions into which Nigeria was then divided were each recognised as a Census region presided over by a Regional Census Officer. In the Northern region, provinces were recognised as census spatial units and provincial census officers were appointed. Census officers were also appointed for the smaller spatial units of divisions and districts. The Western region decided to ignore the provincial level and appointed census officers at only the divisional and district levels. In Eastern Nigeria, because the native authorities tended to be much smaller and more numerous, census officers were appointed mainly at the district level.

The major function of these various categories of census officers was to plan for the effective enumeration of the area under their jurisdiction. This involved not only publicity amongst the general populace but also the training and disposition of enumerators to ensure full coverage. How the latter was done is best illustrated from the report on census operation in the Eastern Region. To quote:

> Once the general line of policy had been settled, each District Officer was asked to make a plan to suit his own division. This involved dividing it up into enumerators' tasks—an estimated count of 1,500 people or seven days' work—and census districts, in each of which a supervisor controlled about twenty enumerators. The tasks were, if possible, to correspond with some natural division—a village or quarter, and the districts if possible with a clan or well-known area (Nigeria, 1956b, pp. 5-6).

In short, although full coverage was attempted, there was no basis for controlling ensuring that this was achieved. Inadequacy of map coverage on a suitable scale was a major reason for this short-coming since it was not possible to allocate to enumerators a set of mutually exclusive and non-overlapping enumeration areas which can be shown to cover exhaustively each whole district.

The situation in the 1963 census was somewhat more complicated. This census was in fact a substitute for one carried out in 1962, the results of which were rejected by the government of the day. The background story to this rejection underlines the importance attaching to coverage control in the management of censuses and therefore needs to be told in some detail. In 1960, the neighbouring Republic of Ghana undertook its decennial census and invited a United Nations team to undertake preliminary activities of coverage control and questionnaire testing as well as overseeing the census count and the processing of the results. Their coverage control activities, which involved the demarcation of the whole of Ghana into enumeration areas, was of real and novel significance in Black Africa. It was therefore decided that officials of the Nigerian government, both federal and regional, should go to Ghana to observe the demarcation with a view to their engaging in similar exercises in their regions in preparation for the 1962 census of Nigeria.

On returning to Nigeria, officials from both the Northern and the Eastern region decided that such a demarcation of enumeration areas was too ambitious and impractical for the circumstances of their region and they were prepared to operate as they did during the 1952-3 census. Only in the Western region were deliberate efforts made to divide every rural district and urban centre into enumeration areas so as to ensure complete coverage (C. Okonjo, 1968, pp. 82-3). In the event, when the three regions indicated that they had completed all preparatory activities and were ready to begin the census count, the Eastern Regional government suddenly announced that it had just discovered a new settlement of some 20,000 persons in Eket Division of whose existence it had not previously been aware (Nigeria, 1962, p. 1; R. K. Udo, 1968, p. 101). It is immaterial to add that the villagers involved expressed surprise at the announcement since they claimed that they had always paid tax to the government. At any rate, the harm had been done. In the charged political atmosphere of the period, allegations that the announcement was a means of preparing the mind of the public for massive inflation of census figures were openly levelled at the Eastern Regional Government. Eventually, when the census was held and its results presented to the Federal Government, they were rejected and a decision made to undertake a fresh count in 1963.

The period between the announcement of the rejection and the date for a new census was too short for any serious improvement to be made to the preparations for coverage in any of the regions. The 1963 census was therefore undertaken with the same ineffective national coverage control as the 1962 census. The result was a situation in which the census figures became a matter of political negotiation rather than of statistical calculation. This meant that only aggregate figures could be produced indicating the population of each region, province and division and giving some details of demographic characteristics at this level. Detailed breakdown to the level of individual settlements, whether urban or rural, was not possible except for a list of settlements with population of over 5000 which was later published.

COVERAGE CONTROL AND THE 1973 CENSUS

The fiasco of the 1962/1963 census underlined quite starkly not only the importance of coverage control but also the vital role of the geographic profession in the successful execution of a census. The critical issue is not simply one of ensuring complete coverage but of devising a control system such that the reliability of census operations can be ascertained and, if possible, rectified. Such a system was particularly vital in a country where census taking is a very live political issue and where attempts at inflating results for socio-political ends cannot always be ruled out. It is thus against this background that the role of geographic advice to the National Census Office during the preparation for the 1973 census must be seen.

Under the auspices of the Nigerian Geographical Association, a programme was initiated in 1971 to persuade the National Census Office of the wisdom of adopting a modern, spatially-oriented geo-coordinate grid system for the identification of settlements in its plan for ensuring coverage control during the 1973 census. The proposal involved conceiving a census as a major information gathering exercise and accepting the importance of designing *ab initio* a system which would facilitate not only the collection but also the storage, organisation, retrieval and analysis of the data. In short, the attempt was to seize the opportunity of the 1973 census to instal for Nigeria an efficient and durable information system.

The arguments for and against the adoption of this new system raged fiercely and eventually required a decision by the National Census Board. That decision read:

> The Board noted that while the "grid" system was an ideal method and was suitable in sophisticated and developed countries, it was, however, not operationally feasible in our country at present because of our peculiar circumstances, the available manpower and financial resources (National Census Board, 1973, p. 5).

This view, however, was not shared by the universities although the Demographic Section of the National Census Office and the Federal Survey Department felt that time was no longer available for establishing such a completely new system. As a compromise, the author was then invited as Census Adviser to take charge of the demarcation of enumeration areas throughout the country.

Given the federal and multi-lingual structure of the country, the organisation for the demarcation of enumeration areas was decentralised, with each state undertaking the operation and the National Census Office providing uniform guidelines and supervising and coordinating state activities. Figure 12.1 shows the division of Nigeria into twelve states as well as the position of the state capitals. It emphasises the problem of supervision, both from the federal capital of Lagos and within each of the states. This problem arises in particular from the somewhat eccentric location of many state capitals within their respective states—a situation which impairs quick and effective communication. The most extreme case, is, of course, that of the North-east State where the distance from Maiduguri, the state capital, to the farthest settlement in the state is as great as the north-south length of Nigeria itself.

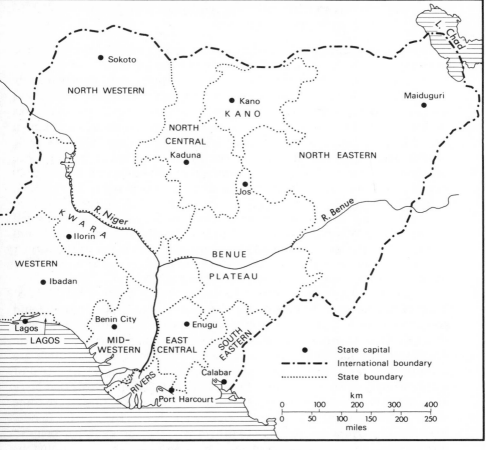

Fig. 12.1. Nigeria: the twelve states and their capitals

In spite of this organisational difficulty, the need to ensure efficient management from the federal capital meant that a strategy of coverage control had to be designed which would minimise the necessity to refer frequently back to the field when any problem arose. The activities involved in this control strategy were essentially fourfold, namely:

(i) demarcation of each state into enumeration areas;
(ii) assessment of the building content of each enumeration area;
(iii) assessment of the household membership of each building unit; and
(iv) estimation of the population of each enumeration area.

THE NATURE OF THE DEMARCATION OF ENUMERATION AREAS

The demarcation of any district or settlement into enumeration areas essentially involved one or the other of two tasks: either the grouping together of small settlements to form units of population of approximately 500 or the breaking down of larger compact settlements into units areas assumed to contain a population of approximately 1000. These two tasks were often referred to as the demarcation of rural or urban areas, although large villages in rural areas were treated as if they were urban. The basic logic of this decision is that it was believed that, assuming an average size household comprises 5 persons, an enumerator should be able to count 40 households in one day or·200 households (that is, 1000 persons) in 5 days if all households were in close proximity to one another. This figure was halved for rural areas to allow for time spent trekking or cycling from one small settlement to another. In fact, the various sample censuses of urban and rural households in the country showed that whilst over 70 per cent of the former tended to be under 5 persons, over 40 per cent of the latter were over 5 persons (e.g., National Manpower Board, pp. 13, 29).

The success of such an operation depended heavily on the availability of maps of suitable scale. For the rural areas, a scale of at least 1:50,000 would appear to be most appropriate, whilst for the urban areas any scale smaller than 1:5,000 will start to pose serious problems. The map coverage of Nigeria on these scales has improved considerably in recent years but there are considerable areas which are still unmapped. Figure 12.2 shows the extent of areas currently covered by maps of a scale of 1:50,000. It reveals that large parts of the North-eastern states were not covered and that there were some rather awkward gaps in a few other states, notably in Kwara and Benue-Plateau states. Although funds were provided to the Survey Department to provide maps for these areas from aerial photography, it was soon obvious that this could not be accomplished in time for the census. As such, alternative arrangements had to be made. These were based essentially on using smaller-scale maps and filling in the gaps from actual work in the field. For the large, urban centres, the position was even more serious. Figure 12.3 shows the distribution of urban centres which have been mapped on scales varying from 1:1,200 to 1:12,500. There are roughly 72 such centres in a country where at least 180 centres are known to have had a population of at least 20,000 in 1963.

Even for areas with map coverage at the appropriate scale, much field work was found to be necessary, partly because the maps did not include all names of settlements and partly because in many areas and urban centres they were no longer up-to-date. Moreover, other activities in the strategy of coverage control made such field visits vital. The field visits were organised

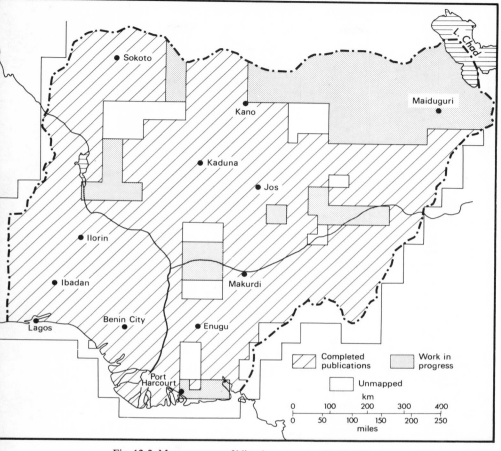

Fig. 12.2. Map coverage of Nigeria on a scale of 1:50,000

by teams in each of the states. In the rural areas, the activities of an Enumeration Area Demarcation (EAD) team comprised the following:

(i)   identification of the name of each settlement and of any other name by which it was known;
(ii) counting of the number of houses in each settlement;
(iii) choosing a sample of houses for rapid enumeration of households and individuals;
(iv) from the average of population per house attempting a rough estimate of the total population of the settlement;

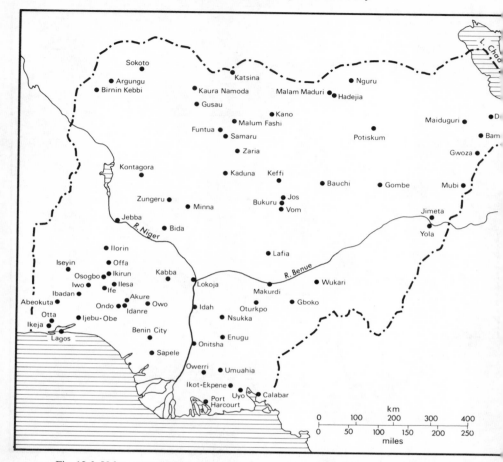

Fig. 12.3. Urban centres in Nigeria with map coverage on scales between 1:2,000 and 1:12,500

(v) on the basis of this estimate, deciding whether the settlement should constitute a single enumeration area or be divided into more than one or be grouped together with others to form one enumeration area, bearing in mind the principle of contiguity.

In the urban areas and in large rural settlements the activities were slightly different. On arrival, the first task of the team when it had a cadastral map was to ascertain the names of all streams, lanes and streets, and to sketch in new extensions of the town or the whole town plan where there was no map. For each block bounded by streets, lanes or streams the same procedure of estimating the population as indicated above for rural areas was then followed and a decision made whether such a block should constitute one enumeration area, be broken into two or more, or merged with another block to form a single enumeration area. Once this decision had been taken, the block or blocks forming the enumeration area had to be sketched so that the boundary streets, lanes or streams and their name were clearly shown. Houses at the corners of the block were also to be identified by the names of their owners.

For both the rural and urban areas a verbal description of the boundaries of an enumeration area or the settlements that comprise it was also meant to be indicated on the form containing the sketch. These forms, when duly completed, were sent to the state headquarters which made a copy and forwarded the original to the National Census Office in Lagos, together with the large base map showing the contiguous relation of all enumeration areas. The duplicate kept in the state capital were meant to serve as an insurance against loss as well as to facilitate communication of editorial comments and queries from Lagos.

At the Lagos headquarters, the organisation for coverage control was divided into five sections: editing, cartography, typing, coding and printing. The maps and forms from the states were checked in the editing section to ensure that no settlement on the map was unaccounted for, that all settlements listed in the form were indicated on the map, that the annotation of sketches was intelligible and that the estimated population for each enumeration area conformed with the prescribed sizes. If there were queries, these were listed on special forms and sent back to the states. Once editing was satisfactorily completed, the sketch from the field was sent to the cartographic section where it was carefully traced in the appropriate part of a specially provided foolscape size sheet. This was then sent to the typing pool to have the description of the enumeration area typed on. When this was completed, the coding section assigned a fourteen-digit code number to the enumeration area indicating its state (2-digits), division (2), district or local council area (2), its rural or urban status (1), its code as a settlement or part of a settlement (3) and its code as an enumeration area (3). The completed form was then sent to be printed. Twelve copies were usually made, six of which were sent back to the states for eventual distribution to the enumerators during the census period and to all other officials overseeing various stages of the operation. A copy of this form, designated National Census Office document No. 19 or simply NCO 19, is indicated in Figure 12.4.

At the completion of this demarcation exercise, the whole of Nigeria was divided into 112,614 enumeration areas. Details of this geographical subdivision of the country by states is shown in Table 12.2 along with their 1963 populations. It is clear that whilst, by and large, there is some relation between size of population and number of enumeration areas, the position is not always consistent. Clearly, there is some effect exercised by the nature of administrative divisions, and by the pattern of settlements. This is particu-

FEDERAL OFFICE STATISTICS
DEMOGRAPHIC UNIT
CENSUS OF 1973

EA Code No. U/0004

Local or District Council. Ondo

Province. Ondo

State. West

DESCRIPTION

Starting from the junction Sara and Akunnara streets along Akunnara to the corner with Oreretu st. along Oreretu to the corner with Sara st. along Sara to the starting point.

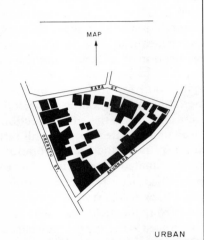

URBAN

FEDERAL OFFICE STATISTICS
DEMOGRAPHIC UNIT
CENSUS OF 1973

EA Code No. R/005

Local or District Council. Nkalagu

Province. Enugu

State. Central-East

DESCRIPTION

Starting from the bridge where the main road between Enugu and Abakaliki crosses River Aboine, follow this river to its confluence with River Ude, along River Ude to its junction with the path from Obiagu to Ezillo, follow the path to Ezillo on the main road between Enugu and Abalakaliki, and then follow the main r... back to the starting point.

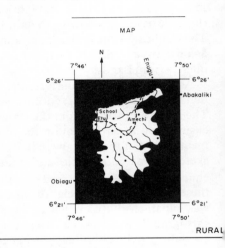

RURAL

Fig. 12.4. Nigeria 1973 census: Enumeration Area sketch

TABLE 12.2. *Nigeria: division into enumeration areas*

State	1963 pop. (in millions)	No. of divisions	No. of districts*	No. of enumeration areas
Lagos	1·44	5	7	2,544
Western	9·49	25	108	16,759
Mid-West	2·54	14	31	4,288
Rivers	1·54	5	17	4,529
East Central	7·24	35	639*	20,325
South-Eastern	3·62	14	58	8,493
Benue-Plateau	4·01	15	142	6,664
Kwara	2·40	11	80	5,235
North-Western	5·73	10	13	8,413
North-Central	4·10	11	53	9,250
Kano	5·77	9	45	9,711
North-Eastern	7·79	14	141	16,403
Total	55·67	168	1,434	112,614

*Community Council Areas

larly the case with respect to the East-Central State where the acceptance of community council areas as basic administrative units is largely responsible for the high number of enumeration areas.

Enumeration Areas were not allowed to cross administrative boundaries and hence it is likely that, with many such boundaries, the number of under-size enumeration areas would increase.

HOUSE NUMBERING AND CENSUS ENUMERATION

In order to increase further the effectiveness of coverage control the census operation itself was divided into two parts separated by an interval of 3 weeks. The first part was a housing census which, in effect, was a more detailed recording of the procedure followed during the demarcation of enumeration areas; the second part was the actual count of population.

The objectives of the housing census were manifold. Ostensibly, its purpose was to number every house and list the households in each house. In essence, however, it was to provide a control list at the level of both individual houses and households. Figure 12.5 provides some idea of the type of information collected at this stage. A basic distinction was made between the building or compound and the census house. A building was defined as

NCO. 5

FEDERAL REPUBLIC OF NIGERIA

1973 POPULATION CENSUS

HOUSE LIST

te-------------------
ision-------------------

District/Community-------------
County/Local Council
Town/Village/Locality/----------
E.A. -------------------------

E.A. No.

State	Division	Council	Locality	Rural/ Urban (Ward)	E.A.

Building Compound Number	Census House Number	Predominant - material of Census House		Purpose for which census house is used	House-hold number	Name of Head of household	Type of water supply	Type of lighting	No. of rooms occupied by Household	Does head or any member of this household operate farm or kept live-stock? Yes/No
		Material of walls	Material of roof							
1	2	3	4	5	6	7	8	9	10	11

Fig. 12.5. Nigeria 1973 census: form for house list

any independent, free-standing structure comprising one or more component units covered by a roof and enclosed within external walls or dividing walls. The component units may be used as dwelling place or as establishments such as shops workshops, factories, garages, stores, cattle-sheds or as combinations such as shop-cum-dwelling or workshop-cum-dwelling. A compound exists where one or more of such structural units is enclosed by a wall. A census house, on the other hand, is a building or a compound or a part thereof having a separate main entrance from the road or a common courtyard or staircase and used or recognised as a separate unit. It may be occupied or vacant and may be used for residential or non-residential purposes or both.

For such a census house, information was collected on a special form (NCO 5), not only about its quality and the level of amenities provided, but also about the number of resident households and the name of the head of each of these households. Each census house and each household were given a special code number. These three items of information, namely the census house number, the household number and the name of the house head, were then abstracted onto another form (NCO 6). The main form was collected and sent to Lagos before the actual census began whilst the abstract was retained for use during the enumeration proper.

On the day of the actual census, the enumerator carried into the field in his special satchel five main documents. These were:

    (i)   the enumerator's instruction manual (NCO 8);
   (ii)   the basic census questionnaire forms which he was expected to fill for each household (NCO 1);
  (iii)   a list of historical events in his district to help with a more accurate assessment of age;
  (iv)   the enumeration area sketch map (NCO 19); and
   (v)   the abstract of the list of census houses and census households (NCO 6).

Two other forms were carried by the enumerator. One (NCO 20) was to enable him to summarise at the end of each day the content of each household questionnaire in terms of males, females and total. The second (NCO 10) was to be completed at the end of the 7-day census operation and was meant to provide a total of the population information for each enumeration area as summarised in the NCO 20 forms for the day-to-day entries.

It is clear from this description that an enumerator in the field carried with him two basic coverage control documents—the sketch map (NCO 19) which defined the limits of his activities and the household abstract (NCO 6) which indicated the number of households he was expected to count. One of the duties of an enumerator on reaching a house was to insert in the place indicated on the basic questionnaire form (NCO 1) both the census house and the household number as listed in the abstract.

The 1973 census of Nigeria lasted 7 days from 25 November to 1 December. At the end of the fifth day, it was found that counting in a few very large cities such as Lagos and Kano was not likely to be completed in the period and so a 1-day extension was granted. At the end of the census, each of the state governments expressed satisfaction at its conduct. The Logistics Unit of the National Census Office retrieved all documents from the States and brought them to Lagos for checking, storage and later processing.

The initial checking was designed to provide the country as soon as possible with some provisional figures of total national population as well as the break-down by states. For this purpose, only information from the NCO 10 document containing the summary figures for each enumeration area was keyed into the computer. The resulting prints-out were distributed among state census officials who had been assembled in Lagos to check for omissions and duplications in the process of data entry. Omissions were easier to detect and new NCO 10 summaries were reconstituted from the NCO 20 forms and were then fed back into the computer.

Table 12.3 shows the figure for the population of Nigeria as indicated by the provisional analysis of the 1973 census results. It reveals how this total of 79·96 million is distributed among the states. As against the 1963 figure of 55·67 million, this new total gives a growth rate of 3·7 per cent per annum over the 10-year period. In demographic terms, this rate of growth appears excessive, especially when it is considered in conjunction with the annual rate of growth of over 5 per cent for the 1952-63 period. At that time, the remarkable high figure for the 1963 census was excused as being due largely to the extent of undercounting in the 1952 census.

TABLE 12.3. *Comparison of the 1973 provisional figures with previous Nigerian Censuses*

State	1973 Provisional	1963 Census	1952/53 Census	Rate of growth 1963-73
Lagos	2·47	1·44	0·50	5·6
Western	8·92	9·49	4·36	—0·7
Mid-Western	3·24	2·54	1·49	2·5
Rivers	2·23	1·54	0·75	3·8
East Central	8·06	7·24	4·57	1·6
South-Eastern	3·46	3·62	1·90	—0·5
Benue-Plateau	5·17	4·01	2·30	2·6
Kwara	4·64	2·40	1·19	6·8
North-Western	8·50	5·73	3·40	4·0
North-Central	6·79	4·10	2·35	5·2
Kano	10·90	5·77	3·40	6·5
North-Eastern	15·38	7·79	4·20	7·0
Total	79·76	55·67	30·41	3·6

Source: Nigeria, *Sunday Times*, no. 1,287, 7 July 1974.

If the overall national rate of population growth appears demographically excessive, the position becomes virtually untenable when the figure is broken down by states. Whilst some states such as the Western and the South-Eastern States recorded negative growth rates, others such as Kwara, Kano and the North-Eastern States showed rates of growth of over 6 per cent per annum. There are no known major demographic displacements that can be adduced to justify this wide internal variation. Not unexpectedly, therefore, the 1973 provisional census results have been a matter of serious national controversy and there have been calls for their total rejection (e.g. Nigeria, 1974a). It is thus legitimate to ask: What went wrong? How was it that with all the elaborate coverage and other management controls the reliability of the census returns cannot be guaranteed?

EVALUATING THE EFFECTIVENESS OF COVERAGE CONTROL

The answers to these two questions can only be fully appreciated within the framework of the organisation and other arrangements made for the census. Although census-taking is constitutionally a federal affair, the multi-ethnic nature of the country and the absence of a lingua franca necessitates a greater role being given to states and local authorities than otherwise would be the case. The National Census Board set up to provide the policy guidance for the census was composed in such a way as to reflect state interests even though it also included individuals from the universities, trade unions and the armed forces. Moreover, notwithstanding this composition, the vital importance of population size both for political and revenue-sharing constituted a great temptation to states and communities to return inflated figures of their population. Nonetheless, in evaluating the effectiveness of coverage control against this background, it is important to distinguish between the provisional and the final figures.

The provisional figures were made up from the summaries of population of enumeration areas contained in the NCO 10 forms. There is no doubt that, given the pressure and haste under which these provisional totals had to be got, there was no time for rigorous scrutiny to ascertain which of the basic NCO 1 documents that were summarised in these totals could be regarded as valid. Validity in this connection relates, among other things, to the presence of the name of the head of a household claimed to have been counted during the census on the list of census houses and households compiled in the NCO 5 forms 3 weeks before the actual census. This task of validation is now a crucial matter for the reliability and general acceptability of the census. A special committee of experts, known as the 1973 Census Data Review Committee, has been set up to look into this matter and take responsibility for the production of the final figures. The work involved in this review is tremendous but its vital importance is widely recognised. There are already indications that such rigorous re-examination of the census documents against standards carefully worked out before the census can help to identify malpractices and facilitate the achievement of a less contestable result.

In his speech announcing the provisional figures, the Nigerian Head of State remarked *inter alia*:

> The National Census Board has set up a committee of experts to conduct the post-enumeration tests, checks and surveys, the results of which are required for arriving at final and reliable figures . . . the final figures may be even less than the preliminary figures just given to you. In that case, necessary adjustments will have to be made to the figures of the states affected and the magnitude of such adjustments, if any, will be determined by the outcome of the various tests and checks now going on in the National Census Secretariat and the post-enumeration field survey that will follow them. I assure you that the checks and verifications thereof will be carried out vigorously and honestly and with a minimum of delay (Nigeria, 1974a).

In this review, it is now clear that much depends on the effectiveness of coverage control in the preparation of the census for discriminating between real and fictitious entries. The work of testing, checking and validating has only just begun and it will be premature to anticipate the outcome.

In the meantime, a post-enumeration check had had to be conducted to provide "norms" against which to measure further the reliability of figures produced for enumeration areas in each division. This was a check of 6000, or approximately a 5 per cent sample of the 112,614 enumeration areas, selected through a stratified random process such that at least five enumeration areas fell within each administrative division in the country. The check occupied 2 days, 2 and 3 August 1974, and its results are also currently being processed at the National Census Office.

In many respects, the post-enumeration check is different from the usual post-enumeration survey. First, unlike the survey which is usually held within a month of a census in the hope of recapturing most of the census conditions, the post-enumeration check in Nigeria was held 9 months after the census. Second, its objective was not that of coverage control in the usual sense but of providing a means for identifying malpractices. In normal census operations, one of the functions of a post-enumeration survey is to make it possible to compute the margin of error through establishing what proportion of the population was not counted for various reasons during the census period; another objective of such a survey is to be able to ask many more in-depth questions about the demographic circumstances of the sampled households. In the case of the post-enumeration check, on the other hand, the idea was to ask as few questions as possible. All that was material was information concerning names, sex, age, relationship to head of household and indication as to whether the individual concerned was counted in this household during the census or not. It is, of course, a moot question whether such a check can be objective as a means of identifying areas of malpractices, especially where a group is determined to repeat such acts. Again, it is too early to pronounce on the post-enumeration check except to note that it provides another possible means of helping to arrive at more realistic figures.

PROSPECTS FOR THE FUTURE

In spite of hopes to the contrary, it is now generally agreed that not even the rule of the military provided a guarantee that census-taking in Nigeria would be insulated from the political manipulations of the 1962 and 1963 censuses. Indeed, there is already a growing body of opinion in the country suggesting that for some time to come the country should desist from further census-taking. Others are canvassing the view that ways should be found of reducing the importance of populations size in questions of revenue allocation and political representation. No one, in fact, can miss the general sense of gloom that now pervades any discussion of the results of the 1973 census or of the prospects of future censuses in the country.

Yet, from within, it is easy to contend that all is not lost. The tremendous effort put into dividing the country into enumeration areas and establishing a comprehensive list of localities provides a very important foundation on which to build the superstructure of an effective information system. To this end, the Geographic Section of the National Census Board is now engaged with the Federal Survey Department in activities of two broad types. First, there is the activity of recording on a permanent basis what has already been accomplished in the demarcation of enumeration areas for the present census. This involves the production for the first time of a map of Nigeria showing the administrative divisions of the country as at 1973 down to the smallest district or local council level. When completed, this will be a major achievement which should enable a lot of information on the socio-economic conditions of the country to be cartographically displayed at this level of details. The main objective of such a map is, however, to provide the framework for mapping the enumeration areas themselves and showing their code number.

When this first stage is completed, the second stage will begin. This involves using the geodesic system of longitudes and latitudes to establish a national grid or geo-coordinate system which should serve as a framework for ascribing a unique geo-coordinate reference code number to each enumeration area. This is only a first step to extending the system to the localities within each of the enumeration areas. A conversion register will then be established indicating the new code equivalent of the present enumeration area code. When this is completed, Nigeria will have gone a long way to establishing the basis for a modern and efficient information system.

Already, other data collecting activities of the Federal Office of Statistics, notably the various surveys being undertaken for a new system of national accounts, are using the enumeration areas of the census as their frame. It should be possible in the period between now and the next census to improve the information on the housing stock in the country and to conduct various demographic surveys which would help in accumulating a wide range of basic information on the size, structure and dynamics of population in different parts of the country. Already, it is being proposed to transform the present census organisation into a permanent body to design, arrange and undertake the systematic collection of vital statistics throughout the country. If this happens, a major way out of the current *impasse* about ascertaining the population of the country might have been found.

CONCLUSION

The 1973 population census of Nigeria has again underlined the problem of census-taking in plural societies where the information about internal population distribution has critical political and economic implications. Nigeria is, of course, not peculiar in being faced with such a problem. Lebanon, for instance, had stopped taking censuses since 1932 in order not to upset the very delicate political arrangement based on some assumed proportion of Christians and Moslems in the population. Yet, there is a growing appreciation of the vital importance of population statistics for socio-economic planning and of the prudence of not always having to mount special surveys for each planning purpose. For example, the country has recently declared its commitment to introducing universal free primary education in 1976. There was need to have some indication of the size of the population of children likely to be of school-going age at that time. Special registration activity had to be mounted in all states and it is not even clear what degree of reliability attended this effort.

The challenge of the situation in Nigeria today is thus how to establish a basis which facilitates the counting or estimation of the population or sections of it in a manner not easily controverted. There can be no doubt that one important means of attaining this end is through building up carefully and systematically a geographic register of settlements and houses in the country. This has never been done in the country before. The Federal Survey Department issues a series of gazetteers based usually on names of settlements and other natural features currently appearing on their maps. The level of accuracy of the gazetter is severely limited by the scale of the maps used and the date of their revision. There have been in the past too many instances of names appearing in the gazetteer which cannot be identified on the ground or of names of fairly substantial settlement not appearing at all in the gazetteer.

The aftermath of the 1973 census thus provides a unique opportunity for resolving this issue of developing an accurate spatially-oriented information system for Nigeria once and for all. Essentially, what is involved is ensuring a closer relation in the activities of organisations in the country responsible for statistical data collection and those concerned with land survey and mapping. If as a result of this, Nigeria can end up with a more comprehensive gazetteer of places and a census register in which all places mentioned can be located on the ground, then from the shambles of the current controversy surrounding the 1973 census, the framework for a new and efficient information system for the country may at least have been salvaged. It is this mediation resulting in the more intimate involvement of all relevant agencies in the activities of ensuring a spatial dimension to the collection, storage, analysis and retrieval of data that constitutes the major public policy achievement of geography in the recent census operation in Nigeria.

REFERENCES

Jacob, S. M. (1933) *Census of Nigeria, 1931*, Vol. 1, London.
Kuczynski, R. R. (1948) *Demographic Survey of the British Empire,* Vol. 1, West Africa; London.
Meek, C. K. (1925) *The Northern Tribes of Nigeria*, Vol. 2, London.
National Census Board (1973) *First Progress Report of the National Census Board, 1973 Population Census*, Lagos.
National Manpower Board (1972) *Labour Force Sample Survey 1966/7*, Vol. 1, Lagos.
Nigeria (1933) *The Census of Nigeria, 1931*, Vol. 1, London.
Nigeria (1946) *A Ten-Year Plan of Development and Welfare*, Lagos.
Nigeria (1956a) *Population Census of the Northern Region of Nigeria*, 1952, Lagos.
Nigeria (1956b) *Population Census of the Eastern Region of Nigeria*, Lagos.
Nigeria (1956c) *Population Census of the Western Region of Nigeria*, Lagos.
Nigeria (1962) *Nigerian Outlook,* Enugu, 10 May.
Nigeria (1974a) *Daily Times,* No. 20, 609, 9 May.
Nigeria (1974b) *Sunday Times,* No. 1, 287, 7 July.
Okonjo, C. (1968) "A preliminary medium estimate of the 1962 mid-year population of Nigeria", in J. C. Caldwell and C. Okonjo (eds.) *The Population of Tropical Africa,* pp. 78-96, London.
Talbot, P. A. (1926) *The Peoples of Southern Nigeria,* Vol. 4, London.
Udo, R. K. (1968) "Population and politics in Nigeria", in J. C. Caldwell and C. Okonjo (eds.) *The Population of Tropical Africa,* London.
Yesufu, T. M. (1968) "The politics and economics of Nigeria's population census", in J. C. Caldwell and C. Okonjo (eds.) *The Population of Tropical Africa,* London.

CHAPTER 13

THE GEOGRAPHIC IMAGINATION
AND POLITICAL REDISTRICTING

R. L. MORRILL

University of Washington

Political redistricting is a highly constrained form of regionalisation, one in which, at least in the United States, the criterion of equal population is overriding. The geographic imagination has evolved ways of looking at the world territorially and of determining or recognising meaningful regions. More quantitatively-oriented scholars from many fields have tended to take a far more limited view, treating redistricting as a "simple" geometric partitioning following such criteria as minimising aggregate travel to district centroids, while political parties, not surprisingly, concentrate on a different quantitative measure, the partisan balance of possible districts. However, some geographers, planners, political scientists and at times, the Courts, have suggested that districts might be more than arbitrary collections of equal numbers. Unexpectedly, the author was afforded the opportunity of exploring these options, when he was asked to redistrict the legislative and congressional districts of the state of Washington early in 1972, the State Legislature having the constitutional mandate to redistrict (Prince vs Kramer *et al.*, No. 9668; Washington Const. art. II, section 3). The one month granted to the task unfortunately restricted the ability to experiment and compare.

The legal requirements underlying redistricting, including certain geographic constraints, will first be discussed, then political bases or criteria, and finally broader geographic criteria. This will be followed by a short analysis of some methods used or proposed to implement these approaches, a summary of the Washington redistricting and a brief discussion of what appears to be a reasonable stance for a geographer who might be involved in redistricting.

EVOLUTION OF CONSTITUTIONAL
REQUIREMENTS

The United States adopted a territorial basis of representation from England, incorporating the principle into both national and state constitutions

(R. G. Dixon, 1968, pp. 22–50; R. W. Teshera, 1970, pp. 117–23, 156–64). States by U.S. constitutional mandate have frequently been confronted with changed number of congressional representatives as a result of population shifts among states. However, through the nineteenth century, these Congressional districts and, within states, the legislative districts, were traditionally rather variable in population (A. Hacker, 1964; Dixon, 1968, pp. 629–831). The growing urban areas were badly under-represented by the end of the nineteenth century. Gradually, the big cities gained representation in Congress and in lower houses, although almost everywhere enjoying lower representation *per capita* than rural areas (Teshera, 1970, pp. 284–92; Dixon, 1968, pp. 629–831). During the last 30 years (1940–70) suburbs were the locus of most growth and became severely under-represented.

The traditional variability of population—often the largest districts were ten times as populous as the smallest districts—was long justified on such grounds as:

(1) the need to represent area as well as population;
(2) the need to represent local political units, such as counties, as well as population;
(3) the greater problems facing sparsely populated areas in providing services;
(4) and maintaining cohesion; and after the majority of the population became urban, maintaining a rural-urban balance (Teshera, 1970, pp. 79–85, 275–6; Dixon, 1968, pp. 59–82; J. Israel, 1963).

Representation by political unit took the form in several states of a "Federal analogy"—that is, the lower house was apportioned approximately on the basis of population, the upper house by county, parish or town (Dixon, 1968, pp. 82–90, 217–27; R. B. McKay, 1963; T. B. O'Rourke, 1972, pp. 99–108). This led by 1960 to such extreme variability in population represented by a state senator as 25,000 to 6,000,000.

In addition to variability of population, American political districts, local to congressional, have often been highly irregular in shape. The term "gerrymandering" refers to the deliberate structuring of political districts for partisan advantage (Dixon, 1968, p. 459; C. O. Sauer, 1918; W. Bunge, 1966) but may be as often used for the purpose of preserving incumbent representatives (see Fig. 13.1).

Not until 1962 in Baker vs. Carr did the U.S. Supreme Court agree that state legislative districts were a justiciable matter under the constitutional mandate that the United States guarantees each state a "representative form of government", and under the Fourteenth Amendment requirement of "equal protection" (A. Bonfield, 1962; Dixon, 1968, pp. 177–216; O'Rourke, 1972, pp. 256–63). In 1964, the "Federal analogy" was struck down (Maryland Committee for Fair Representation vs. Dawes; Dixon, 1968, pp. 196–226) and in Reynolds vs. Sims (377 US 533), in the same year, the Court held that both

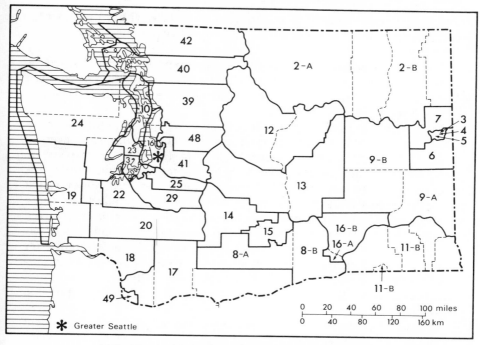

Fig. 13.1. Legislative districts in Washington state in 1971

houses of any legislature must be apportioned strictly on the basis of population. The decision was not accepted meekly, and an almost successful attempt for a constitutional amendment, which would have permitted states to determine their own bases for representation, was made.

The measure of "equal population" gradually narrowed from permitting a variability of about 20 per cent in 1964 to but 1 per cent in 1969; strict population equality was not specified until Kirkpatrick vs. Preisler, 1969 (394 US 526; Dixon, 1968, pp. 444–54); thus, the U.S. Supreme Court, in a redistricting case in Virginia, upheld a plan in which the districts varied by as much as 16 per cent, stating that the precise equality required for Congressional districts was not meant to apply to state legislative districts (Mahan vs. Howell, 93, S. Ct. 979, 1973). The real practical difficulties, after the 1970 census of population, of delimiting legislative districts in smaller states, where 1 per cent of the population was much less than the population of the smallest census enumeration units, led the Court to relax the requirement for legislative districts to between 5 and 10 per cent; since the U.S. census and reapportionment occur only every 10 years, during which at least half of the population has moved and the relative distribution of population changed fairly markedly, and since the census itself is not considered accurate to within 1 per cent (or even 3), particularly in inner cities, a 1 per cent requirement implies false accuracy.

The courts also have held that congressional and legislative districts be contiguous, and increasingly, but not consistently, that districts be compact (see below; Teshera, 1970, pp. 186–90; Dixon, 1968, pp. 460–1; Davis vs. Mann, 1964; D. M. Orr, 1970, pp. 55–6, 68).

The notion that areas of local political units have representation, as well as population, might hold some intuitive appeal to the geographer concerned with the meaning of human territoriality. In the U.S. federal system particularly, the analogy that counties are to states as the states are to the nation still has strong support. The Supreme Court recognised, however, that while the original states were sovereign entities which voluntarily formed a union (residual powers not granted to the federal government being reserved to the state (people), counties are mere administrative conveniences of the state (Dixon, 1968, pp. 82–90, 217–27; O'Rourke, 1972, pp. 99–108). They can readily be added to or abolished, joined or divided, even though this may rarely occur. Powers may be granted or taken away. Altering the pattern of counties could thus theoretically permit any number of arbitrary inequities in representation.

Although they may not be a basis of representation, counties (or equivalent local units) do compel a degree of loyalty, and are the usual units delimiting electoral precincts and conducting elections for all levels. The courts have held that counties, and at a lesser priority, cities, be encompassed within districts to the greatest extent possible, both for the above reasons, and as the principal defence against gerrymandering in non-metropolitan areas; maintaining the integrity of counties tends to foster compactness or regularity, and makes much more difficult partisan ''loading'' of districts (Teshera, 1970, pp. 85–92; Dixon, 1968, pp. 490–9; Orr, 1970, pp. 72–4; H. D. Hamilton, 1966, pp. 16-17).

Arguments may still be advanced in favour of disproportionate representation of sparsely-populated rural areas. Large rural areas may experience particular problems of construction and maintenance of highways, in provision of health and educational services, or management of public lands. They may lack significant internal cohesion, thus making it difficult for one representative to become familiar with his constituency. Such pleas, however, are refuted by lack of objective evidence that rural areas actually have greater *per capita* needs, or more difficult communication between voters and their representatives.

Counties, or less populated regions generally, do have an alternative theoretical basis of representation. Instead of districts of equal population, with one vote each, it would be possible to grant any arbitrary set of areas each a representative, but with a fractional vote equal to their proportion of the total population (Dixon, 1968, pp. 516–20; J. E. Banzhof, 1965, p. 317).

Such a system, not unknown in various special districts (such as sewer or port districts), would accommodate those who believe strongly in the integrity of counties, but also those geographers (and many others) who believe in the reality and meaningfulness of regions (D. Grigg, 1967; Teshera, 1970, pp. 18–49, 101–17; Orr, 1970, pp. 19–36, 92–117). Thus, if it were possible to identify an exhaustive set of "best" regions, reflecting the realities of interaction and perception, these might constitute a semi-permanent set of districts, whose vote would alter as population shifts over time. In the United States, however, the courts have interpreted the plan as fundamentally unrepresentative, since even with a fractional vote, the representative of a smaller unit will have greater exposure and, presumably, influence (WMCS vs. Lomemzo, 238 f. Supp. 916, 923, 1965); although several plans involving fractional voting have been disallowed, there has been no precise ruling on fractional voting.

The principle of territorial representation, while almost universal, is often modified in practice in the United States. This usually takes the form of multi-member districts, for example, in Washington, where two state representatives are elected at large from each senatorial district; or in many cities where entire councils may be elected at large. Although the Supreme Court has recognised that multi-member districts tend to submerge minorities, it has not held that the practice violates the "Equal Protection Clause" (Fortson vs. Dorsey, 1965; Burns vs. Richardson, 1966; Whitcomb vs. Chavis, 1971). Such "at large" voting is normally justified on grounds of avoiding parochialism or "ward politics" (is not that a risk a representative democracy must take?), although in practice, it may be instituted for the less lofty reasons of disenfranchising minorities, or permitting an élite from part of the district to dominate. Surprisingly, the Courts have not disallowed multi-member districts except where it is proved that they were used for systematic disenfranchisement of racial minorities, which has been disallowed (Wright vs. Rockefeller, 376 US 52, 1964; Dixon, 1968, pp. 510–20).

More radical (for the United States) schemes such as proportional representation, either of parties or of cultural groups, as have been called for by some black groups, for example, have never been seriously considered (Dixon, 1968, pp. 525–7), although it would probably be the only way to guarantee some representation to such racial minorities as Native American. The horrendous question of which minorities would qualify and who would belong to which groups exclusively, precludes implementation.

The Fourteenth Amendment requirement of "equal protection under the law", applicable to state and federal jurisdictions, is not only the basis for both equal population and the denial of representation for areas, as well as of multi-member districts which disenfranchise classes of the population, but also for the additional legal criteria of *contiguity* and *compactness* (Teshera,

1970, pp. 186–90; Dixon, 1968, pp. 460–1; Orr, 1970, pp. 55–6, 68; W. Vickery, 1961, pp. 105–10). These geographic/geometric criteria are not explicitly required in the Constitution, and even extreme irregularity is not considered "inherently unequal". Rather it is the fact that parties to suits have been able to show that, first, voters of non-contiguous pieces are effectively disenfranchised, or again, that a district's irregularity was to disenfranchise a minority class (race or colour). It should be understood that irregularity with the effect of disenfranchising the rich or the poor, urban or rural residents, or Democrats or Republicans, or whatever, is not a basis for relief under the Fourteenth Amendment. In the United States, these forms of gerrymandering, which are more common than not, can be prevented only by political compromise, as when the legislature and governor of a state are of differing parties.

The criterion of *compactness* has received some recognition by the courts, having been espoused by more quantitatively-oriented political scientists, planners or geographers, as an objective means to control gerrymandering. Indices of compactness essentially measure the degree of departure from a compact form, usually the circle (J. Schwartzberg, 1966; E. C. Roeck, 1961). Measures include (1) the ratio of the maximum and minimum diameter, (2) the ratio of the perimeter of the districts to the square root of the area (where a circle of that area has a value of "1"), (3) the ratio of the area of the district to the area of a circle formed using the maximum diameter, and (4) the "moment of inertia" of a shape (a measure of the variability of distances from the centroid to the boundary of a district). While apparently objective, strict application of a measure of compactness becomes meaningless, since departure from circularity may well be justified on grounds of the irregular distribution of population, or the shape of the transport network or administrative unit. It is difficult for the statistical measure to distinguish between arbitrary irregularity and the natural irregularity of mountain range crests, rivers or shorelines. Finally, compactness alone does not preclude gerrymandering in the sense of arranging the compact districts so as to "waste" the votes of the opposition party (Dixon, 1968, pp. 458–99; Hacker, 1966; Teshera, 1970, pp. 178–86).

Purposefully discontiguous districts, as to bring together scattered pockets of Native Americans, might be defended on ground of enfranchisement, but, again, discrimination in favour of a particular class is presumably as contrary to the Fourteenth Amendment as discrimination against the class.

POLITICAL CRITERIA

The Court's avoidance of this "political thicket", while constitutionally reasonable, irritates those who would like to see explicitly political criteria for redistricting required, namely, prohibition of gerrymandering or irregularity for partisan benefit, or other critics, who dislike gerrymandering which tends to disenfranchise economic or social, but not racial, minorities (Hamilton, 1966, pp. 30–1; O'Rourke, 1972, pp. 38–48; Dixon, 1968, pp. 458–99; Orr, 1970, pp. 90–2). The significance of these forms of gerrymandering, even with districts of equal population, is not questioned. The typical gerrymandering strategy is to maximise the number of districts with a moderate margin for one's party, while concentrating the opposition party's strength in as few districts as possible (known as "wasted votes"). Thus, in a hypothetical area with equal party strength, part A could normally expect to control two-thirds of the seats by the following arrangement:

.7 B	.3 A	.4 B	.6 A
		.4 B	.6 A
.7 B	.3 A	.4 B	.6 A
		.4 B	.6 A

It has been proposed to prevent this by disallowing redistricting plans which fail a simple test of non-partisanship, basically a measure of relative concentration.

Some political theorists consider that an ideal redistricting plan would maximise the number of "swing" districts, that is with a fairly even balance of parties, in order to foster the greatest responsiveness to voters. On the other hand, one might argue that a degree of continuity of membership is needed in an effective legislative body. In practice, parties and the voters tend to ensure that there is a mixture of a larger number of fairly "safe" districts and a smaller number of "swing" districts. The principal difficulty in using such political criteria is simply the instability and inconsistency of voting behaviour, owing partly to the marked decrease in party loyalty in the United States over the last 25 years.

A legislative body asked to redistrict itself not surprisingly tends to favour an objective of minimising the loss of incumbents. While obviously in its self-interest, and often resulting in unsightly gerrymanders, it may well be that it serves the interest of the voters, who tend to identify with a district and participate in the political process with respect to issues of significance in that district, to avoid unnecessary alteration of the political map.

GEOGRAPHICAL CRITERIA

The criteria of contiguity and compactness have some legal standing, and have been discussed above. The geographic "region" was briefly discussed as the basis of semi-permanent units with representatives granted fractional votes. Local courts have at times required that "natural environmental barriers" be respected (Teshera, 1970, pp. 69–79; Orr, 1970, p. 79), largely as a further defence against gerrymandering. In the case of the redistricting of Washington, the District Court forbade any unnecessary crossing of the Cascade Mountains, Puget Sound, or major rivers or lakes by district lines. More often than not, such a rule may be reasonable, but at times communities of interest may encompass a river or lake basin, or even an entire mountain zone.

Given the overriding constraint of equal population, we may still investigate the extent to which the geographical concern for meaningful regions can be accommodated during redistricting. A restrictive or simplified form of regional criterion has been proposed by several social scientists—namely, to maintain the integrity of cultural groups (Hamilton, 1966, pp. 47–8; Orr, 1970, pp. 75–90; Teshera, 1970, pp. 92–100). Although we might desire a more effective melting pot, many minority groups—blacks, Chicanos, Puerto Ricans and, to a lesser extent, some ethnic groups—perceive spatial concentration and group solidarity to be an effective means of gaining political leverage. Deliberate dilution of such bloc voting on grounds of cultural integration would create a risk of severe frustration and unrest. However, in implementing this criterion by creating a district that is, say, 55 per cent black, one is in a crude sense disenfranchising the 45 per cent who are white. Nevertheless, it is important to remember that the larger proportion of most minority populations is sufficiently dispersed so as not to constitute a voting majority in their districts, however the districts may be drawn.

A desire to assure minority representation raises the more general question of whether districts should be more than arbitrary geometric collections of people, instead possessing some unity, meaning, or reality in the eyes of the resident. Geographers have long been concerned with identification of objectively distinct regions (Grigg, 1967), and it seems reasonable to suggest as a general criterion that each district should constitute the most meaningful region possible to those included therein. Unfortunately, this rational proposition currently is frustrated by two somewhat contradictory conceptions of the proper definition of meaningful regions. The first, adopting the criterion of cultural groups, holds that a region should be homogeneous or uniform with respect to factors such as income, occupational structure, land use, and racial or ethnic composition. In the second, generally preferred by political and economic geographers, it is argued that regions should possess functional unity (Hamilton, 1966, pp. 29–30; O'Rourke, 1972, pp. 42–6; Dixon, 1968, pp. 520–7); for example, a region should encompass a small city as well as its economic hinterland or trade area, or it should embrace both a large shopping centre and the section of the city that it serves. Districts of homogeneous social and economic character tend to embody a community of interest which stimulates homogeneous voting patterns. Considered to be "safe", such districts often have long-term incumbents who presumably reflect the views of the majority of the constituency and offer an argument of desirable stability of representation. Districts of a functional character tend to be more economically and socially diverse, although united by strong patterns of interaction. Such districts are considered to be "swing" districts, which elect fewer long-term incumbents.

Attempts to create districts which are both functional and culturally homogeneous areas should tend to produce regions which are at least fairly meaningful to the residents. The fact that neither uniform nor functional regions divide themselves conveniently into districts of equal population, however, forces us to realise that such regional criteria can be but approximately applied. However, the author's own experience with redistricting and contacts with citizens indicates that people really do appreciate the attempt to delimit districts with which they can identify.

METHODOLOGY OF REDISTRICTING

As a quantitative geographer, the author was enthusiastic about utilising computer programmes to accomplish the redistricting (Dixon, 1968, pp. 527–35; O'Rourke, 1972, pp. 73–98; Hamilton, 1966, pp. 916–24; S. Hess and J. Weaver, 1964; H. Kaiser, 1966; R. S. Garfinkel and G. I. Nemhauser, 1970; E. S. Savas, 1971). As it happened, a severe time constraint prevented preparation and implementation of an adequate programme. In theory, the problem is fairly simple, given the basic criteria of compactness and equal population. The objective is to find "m" centres, out of "n" smaller subdivisions, such that the population assigned to each centre is equal and aggregate travel to the set of centres is minimised. District boundaries are corollary products of the solution. This is generally known as the "capacitated location-allocation problem". Since there is an infinite number of partitions which satisfy the equal-population criterion, evaluation requires a heuristic method. The Goodchild-Massam algorithm is typical of the iterative procedures necessary (B. H. Massam, 1972).

Initial sets of the "m" centres are found, possibly as defined by the present scheme, or by various proposed schemes, or several randomly generated sets of m of the n subdivisions. The reason why several initial sets are needed is that, propaganda notwithstanding, the algorithms produce a variety of sub-optimal solutions in all but simple cases. Populations are assigned to the closest centres, and surplus and deficit populations (from the ideal districts population) found. A "transportation" or "assignment" problem then assigns population from "surplus" to "deficit" centres at the minimum increment in travel. Next, the bivariate median centre (point of minimum aggregate travel) of each of the adjusted districts is found, the population again assigned to the closest of these "first-iteration" centres, surplus and deficits found, and again the surpluses assigned by the transportation algorithm to the closest deficit centres feasible. This iterative process is continued until the assignment of the surplus population is stable,—that is, until no shift in the bivariate median centres occurs.

For small problems the heuristic method works admirably, but for large problems the initial selection is so difficult that a global optimum is perhaps unlikely, since, a realistic problem, such as finding perhaps 100 districts out of 2000 subdivisions, simply exceeds the capacity of our computers. Nevertheless, simplified problems, such as the seven congressional districts of Washington, can be readily solved and result in geometrically pleasing solutions.

Even such simplified problems tend to preclude the use of analytic programming models, which find the optimal solution, but which have to evaluate a moderately high proportion of all possible combinations of areas.

Unfortunately, the distance-minimising location-allocation algorithms do not really permit the inclusion of other variables of interest, such as concern for cultural homogeneity, or functional integrity, or the integrity of political boundaries (cities or counties), although it is possible to incorporate barriers (to maintain some political or natural boundaries) and to minimise travel on a transport network rather than in free space. As a consequence, solutions may look good geometrically, but make insufficient sense socially, economically or geographically.

An alternate approach is that of S. S. Nagel (1965) whose plan begins with existing legislative districts, and gradually trades units of territory and population until criteria of equal population, compactness and "fair political composition" are met. Since the methods minimise change, and tend to preserve incumbents, it has proven acceptable to legislators, but it makes no pretence of achieving an optimal system and is not practical where population changes have been excessive.

THE WASHINGTON REDISTRICTING

After the 1970 census, the existing legislative districts in the State of Washington varied in population from 134,000 (97 per cent too many) to 44,000 (36 per cent too few), as a result of dramatic population shifts, mainly to suburban parts of metropolitan areas. Forty-four of the forty-nine districts were more than 5 per cent over or under par (Fig. 13.1 presents the pre-1972 districts).

The legislature was unable to agree on a compromise between the extremely divergent plans proposed by the Democratic majority in the Senate and the Republican majority in the House of Representatives (Fig. 13.2 presents the Democrat's plan for the state and Fig. 13.3 the Republican's plan, excluding the Seattle–Tacoma metropolitan region).

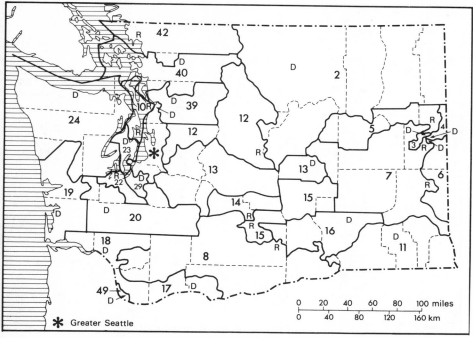

Fig. 13.2. Democratic plan for redistricting Washington state

Confining criteria were laid down:

(1) to allow a maximum of only 1 per cent (plus or minus 685 around 68,445) deviation in population;

(2) to maintain to the greatest extent possible the integrity of counties, cities, census county divisions, and census tracts. Enumeration districts outside urban areas, and blocks in urban areas were the smallest units permissible. Electoral precincts were excluded as possible units, since no census data were collected for them;

(3) to form the districts as compactly as possible and to avoid unnecessary irregularities or sinuosities;

(4) to avoid crossing natural geographical barriers, especially such bodies of water as Lake Washington and Puget Sound; to extend no district across the crest of the Cascade Mountains except along the Columbia River;

(5) so far as possible to reflect some unit of character or interest; in particular, Indian reservations should not be split, and as much of the Seattle "Central Area" (black ghetto) should be included within one district as possible.

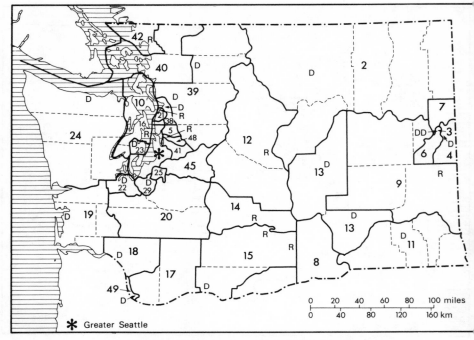

✳ Greater Seattle

Fig. 13.3. Republican plan for redistricting Washington state

The author was forbidden to have any contact with any political figure, or pay any attention to the question of political balance or the location or fate of incumbent legislators. Because of the short time and restrictive criteria, he was unable to experiment extensively with computer solutions, but instead evaluated a small set of plans developed by attempting to apply all the criteria simultaneously (R. Morrill, 1973). The plan judged best and which was adopted by the District Court is presented as Fig. 13.4.

The awkward shape of cities, counties and other census districts, but especially the severe constraint that all districts be within 1 per cent of the ideal, made it impossible to achieve a plan that was aesthetically pleasing, let alone one that delimited really meaningful regions. Yet the attempt to achieve such regional identity as well as reasonable compactness was and is appreciated by legislators and constituents.

The compactness and irregularity of the Court plan, as well as the Republican and Democratic plans have been evaluated (D. Manninen, 1973). Fortunately, the Court plan fared well. The indices of departure from compactness of the Court and Democratic plans are presented as Table 13.1. In general, the Court plan is about one-third better than the Democratic plan,

TABLE 13.1. *Compactness of Court and Democratic plan districts*

		Areal perimeter*	Area (district) / Area (max. diameter of circle)	Moment of inertia**
Court	mean	·2978	·4225	·8422
	minimum	·0646	·2416	·5936
	maximum	·5764	·6329	·9481
Democratic	mean	·1962	·3098	·7221
	minimum	·0414	·1382	·4585
	maximum	·4537	·5202	·8883
Ideal square		·7854	·6370	·9962
Ideal rectangle		·6981	·5099	·8740
Circles: all = 1·0				

*Technically, $\dfrac{\text{Area}\,(4\pi)}{\text{Perimeter}^2} = \dfrac{\text{Area (district)}}{\text{Area (circle with same perimeter)}}$

$$** \frac{\Sigma\, r^2 a}{\cdot 5\pi\, A^2}$$

(r = distance to centroid)

(a = exhaustive set of small subareas)   variance (moment of inertia) of district

(A = area)   variance (moment of inertia) of circle same area or district

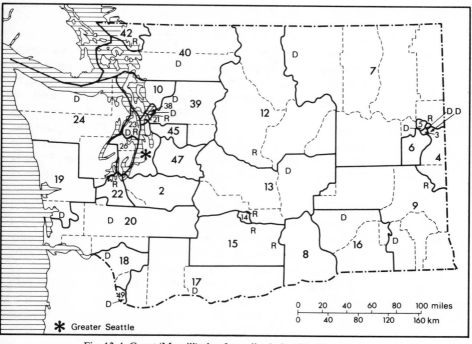

✳ Greater Seattle

Fig. 13.4. Court (Morrill) plan for redistricting Washington state

but rather worse than if all the districts were perfect squares. The greater irregularity of the Democratic plan is well illustrated by its districts 8 and 13 which extend halfway across the state, as well as across the virtually uninhabited central Cascade Mountains. The purpose of the gerrymanders was unabashedly partisan, that is, to preserve incumbents of one's party, while placing two incumbents of the other party in one district.

The Republican plan was similarly motivated, as illustrated by districts 13 and 39. The Court plan, by statistical accident, resulted in about equal numbers of Democratic and Republican incumbents placed against each other.

The Republican and Democratic plans did attempt to concentrate opposition votes in excessively "safe" districts, while again by chance, the Court plan resulted in about a proportional mix of a "safe" and "leaning" (i.e. characteristically small majority) districts for each party, and a larger number of "toss-up" districts than the parties would have preferred.

STANCE OF THE GEOGRAPHER IN REDISTRICTING CASES

Redistricting mainly raises an image of electoral districts, but the problem of population or capacity-constrained districts also includes the delimitation of school districts, and to some extent fire, health, library or other public service districts. Although the task of redistricting is technical, the alteration of electoral or school boundaries is both politically sensitive and has policy implications with respect to the fate of individual and programme, and to educational philosophy and support.

In the delimitation of School districts, in which the author is currently engaged, the problem is more interesting and difficult in the sense that geographical variables such as flows of pedestrian and car traffic, and patterns of acquaintanceship, can and should supplement the essential concerns of sufficient pupils to justify a school and minimisation of walking and bussing time, not to mention to real and vocal concern and involvement of constituents in the process!

A good job of redistricting involves, first, a technical ability to work with census materials and maps. Since almost anyone can add numbers to a requisite total, a more important asset is a sensitivity to what is "reasonably compact" in terms of a district which will be as meaningful as possible to the voters—in short what we know as the "geographical imagination" or knowledge of the landscape, that shifts the problem from defining arbitrary areas to delimiting good regions. It includes, too, a sense of flexibility, knowing when to relax geometric or numerical provision in favour of other human values. While geographers have no monopoly on this capacity, they do, or should, emphasise it. In the real world of policy formulation, a knowledge of the real terrain is a great asset. While arming ourselves with the mathematical tools appropriate to solving the technical aspects, it would be false to our heritage, as well as speciously reductionist, to present ourselves as totally objective. Boundaries are necessary; they influence our lives. We should take advantage of the integrative quality of geography to help society do a better job of the necessary districting.

ACKNOWLEDGEMENT

This chapter is based in part on the author's paper, "Ideal and reality in reapportionment", published in the *Annals of the Association of American Geographers*, 63, pp. 463–77.

REFERENCES

Banzhof, J. E. (1965) "Weighting votes doesn't work: a mathematical analysis", *Rutgers Law Review,* **19**, 317.

Bonfield, A. (1962) "Baker vs. Carr: new light on the constitutional guarantee of republican government", *California Law Review,* **50**, 245.

Bunge, W. (1966) "Gerrymandering, geography and grouping", *Geographical Review,* **56**, 256–63.

Dixon, R. G. (1968) *Demographic Representation: Reapportionment in Law and Practice,* Oxford University Press, New York.

Garfinkel, R. S. and G. I. Nemhauser (1970) "Optional political districting by implicit enumeration techniques", *Management Science,* **16**, 122.

Grigg, D. (1967) "Regions, models and classes", in R. Chorley and P. Haggett (eds.), *Models in Geography,* Methuen, London, pp. 461–509.

Hacker, A. (1964) *Congressional Districting,* Brookings Institution, Washington, D.C.

Hamilton, H. D. (ed.) (1966) *Reapportioning Legislatures: A Consideration of Criteria and Computers,* Charles Merrill Books, Columbus.

Hess, S. and J. Weaver (1964) "Nonpartisan political redistricting by computer", *Operations Research,* **13**, 998–1006.

Israel, J. (1963) "Nonpopulation factors relevant to an acceptable standard of apportionment", *Notre Dame Lawyer,* **38**, 499.

Kaiser, H. (1966) "An effective method for establishing legislative districts", *Midwest Journal of Political Science,* **10**, 200–13.

McKay, R. B. (1963) "Federal analogy: state apportionment standards", *Notre Dame Lawyer,* **38**, 487.

Manninen, D. (1973) *The Role of Computers in the Process of Redistricting,* unpublished M.A. thesis, Geography, University of Washington.

Massam, B. H. (1972) *The Spatial Structure of Administrative Systems,* Commission on College Geography, Research Paper No. 12, Association of American Geographers, Washington, D.C.

Morrill, R. (1973) "Ideal and reality in reapportionment", *Annals of the Association of American Geographers,* **63**, 463–77.

Nagel, S. S. (1965) "Simplified bipartisan computer districting", *Stanford Law Review,* **17**, 863–99.

O'Rourke, T. B. (1972) *Reapportionment: Law, Politics, Computers,* American Enterprise Institute for Public Policy Research, Washington, D.C.

Orr, D. M., Jnr. (1970) *Congressional Redistricting: the North Carolina Experience,* Studies in Geography, No. 2, University of North Carolina, Chapel Hill.

Roeck, E. C., Jnr. (1961) "Measuring computers as a requirement for legislative apportionment", *Midwest Journal of Political Science,* 5, 70-4.

Sauer, C. O. (1918) "Geography and the gerrymander", *American Political Science Review,* 12, 403–26.

Savas, E. S. (1971) "A computer-based system for efficient electoral districts", *Operations Research,* No. 12, 135–55.

Schwartzberg, J. (1966) "Reapportionment, gerrymandering and the notion of compactness", *Minnesota Law Review,* 50, 443.

Teshera, R. W. (1970) *The Territorial Organization of American Intergovernmental Jurisdiction,* unpublished Ph.D. dissertation, University of Washington.

Vickery, W. (1961) "On the prevention of gerrymandering", *Political Science Quarterly,* 67, 105–10.

CHAPTER 14

THE GEOGRAPHERS' CONTRIBUTION TO REGIONAL POLICY: THE CASE OF SWEDEN

T. HÄGERSTRAND

University of Lund

It is probably pointless for representatives of any academic discipline to knock on the doors of the gatekeepers in their society and offer their services as advisors unless their approach coincides with a peculiar fit between some overriding problem of their society and the conceptual structure and empirical competence of their discipline. Such a coincidence gave economics its chance in the 1930s and again in the decades after World War II, physics had a similar experience during and immediately after that war, and biology is obviously on the march at the present time. Geography also sometimes has its opportunity and it seems that two special conditions must be present before geographers are considered capable of giving advice: there must be locational shifts on a substantial scale and also a willingness in society for planning to control or guide change. When the world is stable and/or unhampered liberalism prevails, there is probably not much for geographers to do except to maintain their competence and to train future school-teachers to know how wisely arranged the world is.

In Sweden a kind of resource geography flourished in the middle and later part of the eighteenth century. This was indeed a period of change and planning. The country had suffered severe losses in a long war with its neighbours and needed to plan for recovery and modernisation. Internal exploration, mapping the land and recording the weather and the population became major public undertakings as a base for land reforms, industrialisation and internal colonisation. The favourite topic for dissertations at the universities were geographic in kind, most of them being detailed descriptions of local areas. (Ministry for Foreign Affairs, 1974, Chap. 3.)

Change and growth actually took place at an accelerated pace in all spheres of life during the century and a half that followed the middle-class revolution of 1809. But for most of this time the prevailing climate of opinion was one of economic liberalism and planning was mostly confined to purely social issues.

Even after 1945 a strong belief prevailed in all quarters, even among the trade unions, in the competence of market forces to work out the best solutions even if locational shifts had painful consequences for many people, and planning was considered to be a rather ugly word. Under these circumstances geography was regarded merely as a boring school subject or as a source of information about exotic places.

Gradually, however, during the 1950s and 1960s a different climate of opinion developed as more and more people began to complain about the negative consequences of structural changes and the more equal living conditions throughout the country, perhaps in part because television was widening horizons. Attitudes towards planning became more favourable, and geographers and practitioners in other fields who were willing to embark on regional studies were called upon to make contribution. Sweden turned into a society in which public planning is not only accepted but requested by a broad section of public opinion. By 1972 the situation was ripe for the Swedish Parliament to adopt, without much political controversy, two closely related national plans, one a strategy for the long-term development of settlements, the other a blueprint for the long-term use of the nation's land and water resources. (Ministry of Labour and Housing, 1973.)

Swedish experience in applied research, which of course concerns much more than the regional dimension and involves many fields besides geography, could be used in several ways. One would be to look upon university research from the standpoint of science policy and to ask questions about the effects of the special allocation of funds and man-power which is being made for applied work. It might perhaps be demonstrated that large, integrated projects, which have been rather characteristic of much recent research, to a certain extent, hamper original, creative work of the kind which can be produced only by individuals who are not bound by detailed programme and irritated by dead-lines.

A second use of the experience would be to look at Swedish society from a kind of anthropological point of view and ask questions about the effects of planning and centralisation upon the enterprise, mood and conception of life among the population. Perhaps it would be revealed that the growing security and predictability of living exacted a price in terms of boredom and the lack of opportunity to be creative.

Such experiences are probably best analysed by outside observers, for it is difficult for somebody standing in the middle of events to devise an independent yardstick. But there is a third approach which is more naturally dealt with by a participant. Applied work on a broad scale in a social science discipline creates a very special kind of interaction between the society and that discipline. First, as has been noted, certain conditions have to be present in a society before a particular discipline is summoned from the university storehouse. When this has happened an interplay begins which influences both the way that society develops and the way that members of the discipline interpret its purpose and scope. This has been said many times about Western industrial society and the science of economics, and it is, and will be, equally true for every regionally-planned society and its science of geography (or whatever one chooses to call the supporting field). This kind of interplay is perhaps difficult for an outside observer to reconstruct afterwards, so this process will be illustrated from the author's experience in Sweden. Such an approach may be particularly appropriate at the present time of theoretical and methodological uncertainty. A detailed account of Swedish geographical research will be found in Allan Pred's well-informed account (1973), and the emphasis in this chapter will be on the setting within which this work has received its direction and made its influence felt.

REGIONAL PROBLEMS AND ADMINISTRATIVE ORGANISATION IN SWEDEN

A necessary preliminary to such an analysis is some background orientation on the major characteristics of the regional problems which have been identified in Sweden and on the administrative structure in which policy-making and resource allocation are performed.

The regional problems are generally of the same kind as those being experienced in most other industrialised nations; their special flavour has its origin in the physical geography and economic history of the country on the one hand and in the value premises that dominate the political thinking on the other. (J. L. Sundquist, 1975, esp. Chap. 6.)

The geographical dilemma, simply stated, derives from the vast north–south extent of the country, in combination with the small size of its population. Some conception of this extent is given by the observation that, if the country were rotated around its southern tip, its northern boundary would reach Naples in Italy. This elongated area contains not more than about eight million inhabitants.

The economic history of Sweden has left, as a legacy, an exceedingly scattered distribution of this small population. Almost up to the beginning of this century arable and pasture land were the principal natural resources, but apart from a few fertile plains of limited extent, land suitable for farming and grazing was found only in small patches throughout the country. In order to find sufficient farmland, the population had therefore to spread out over the whole area and a pattern of small villages and isolated farmsteads resulted.

When forestry began to develop as a leading industry, work in the forests became, to a very large degree, a part-time activity for smallholders. Rural colonisation extended even further into the wilderness, while early manufacturing industry grew up in the countryside, organised as it was by estate-owners who happened to find minerals or water power within their domains. These tendencies also contributed to a settlement structure made up of many small and widely-separated units.

In the present century, and particularly in recent decades, the economy has been radically transformed and, as everywhere else, this transformation manifested itself geographically in urbanisation. At first the rise of urban settlements was also a very scattered process, and people did not migrate over very long distances. But gradually the three metropolitan centres, Göteborg, Malmö and particularly Stockholm, the capital, began to leave the rest of the urban system very much behind in terms of size, incomes and provision of services, though even today, none of these metropolitan areas is very big by international standards; the Stockholm region itself does not contain more than 1·2 million inhabitants, or about 20 per cent of the national total, even when the boundary is drawn quite generously (T. Hägerstrand and S. Öberg, 1970).

The main problem is thus not to be found in the big cities, even if they have some internal difficulties of well-known kinds; the overriding problem is to overcome the difficulties arising from the vast areas of sparse population and scattered, small settlements.

Population growth has almost come to a standstill. Swedish women as a group have not reproduced themselves since 1880 and the growth which has taken place is due to the general prolongation of life and to immigration (Ministry for Foreign Affairs, 1974, Chap. 5; E. Bernhardt, 1971). On the assumption of a stable population, a continued growth of the most densely populated areas through internal migration would also mean an extension of the sparsely-populated regions. In these areas the local markets within range of daily travel are generally very small and the choice of employment is frequently very limited, circumstances which makes employment extremely vulnerable when an industry is declining or when organisational changes lead to the relocation of plant. As more and more small and medium-sized urban places stagnate and decline it will become increasingly difficult to provide employment, social services and public transport in ever wider areas of the country.

A broadly accepted value in Sweden is solidarity. This does not mean that private individuals show any more solidarity with their neighbours than in other countries. Rather, solidarity is an explicitly embraced principle in national policy which no political party would dare oppose strongly. It follows
· that re-distribution has a prominent place in policies at all levels. In practical terms this means that policies have to achieve full and secure employment for everybody who wants to go to work, an equitable distribution of real income, uniform access to public services (education, health, legal) and a good working and living environment.

In view of these principles one can hardly accept a polarisation of the population in which one part is centrally located and enjoys high incomes, secure opportunities for employment and easy access to a wide variety of services, and another part is widely dispersed, has low incomes, with insecure employment and little choice of job, and is even isolated from such elementary supply points as food shops. In many regions such a polarisation would also lead to an age-distribution which deviated strongly from the national average. The declining areas would have ageing populations to such an extent that the provision of proper care would be very difficult and costly.

It is hardly possible to appreciate the relationships between policies and background research without some understanding of how administration is organised and how political decisions are taken.

There are three levels of government in Sweden: national, regional ("lan", approximately equivalent to counties) and local (communes). The national government, which is politically controlled by the parliament ("riksdag"), works predominantly through its topical sectors, such as those for farming, forestry, industry, transport, health, education and social work. Most ministries and central boards have appointed representatives (whether single officials or councils) at the regional level, where their main function used to be to allocate state grants, make sure that the law was obeyed and give expert advice to the communes and the public.

The sectoral organisation of society goes much further than government. Industry, which is predominantly in private hands, is nevertheless very much controlled from Stockholm through its company headquarters and branch organisations. The same can be said about trade unions, other interest groups and political parties. The geographic centralisation of sectoral power has gone very far, and means that the channel of power from the top to the bottom tend to work as strings on which various specialists play melodies which are more in tune with an aggregate national perspective, clear-cut group interests and professional outlooks than with the more fixed and intertwined situations in regions and localities.

The task of looking after the cross-sectoral or "horizontal" integration of investments and operations, where spatial compromises are necessary, is undertaken at the local level, in the communes. In contrast to government at the regional level, the communes are headed by elected officials and committees. These smallest self-governing units defend their independence vigorously and a major reason for the survival of their influence is that many members of the national parliament are also local politicians or have been so. Another source of power, and one which makes integration possible, is the right of the communes to raise income taxes. In an international perspective such power is exceptional, but it is an extremely important feature of Swedish political life and a constant headache for the Ministry of Finance.

The communes have further a monopoly of power in land-use planning and building control. They are responsible for the provision of water and sewerage, local roads, schools, amenities and whatever else the elected representatives decide to spend money on in the public interest or as the law requires. They can, and do, own farmland and forest. On the other hand, the communes cannot go into commerce and industry except in relation to transport and housing; they are not even permitted to recruit industries, though they try to do so. There is also an important limit to the political independence of the communes, for the national government has the exclusive right to decide about boundary changes, a privilege which has been extensively used in recent decades.

Commerce and industry are predominantly private. Although Sweden is often considered to be a socialist country, the state owns very little industry, in fact much less than in many capitalist countries in Europe, a situation which has obvious implications for the making and implementation of regional policies and plans. The location of industry is influenced only indirectly.

Reference is also essential to the parliamentary or government commission. No major question is ever settled until it has been thoroughly examined by a commission, normally made up of representatives of the political parties and the ministries involved. These commissions receive their material from so-called experts, and it is here that university research makes its influence felt. A university cannot refuse to give leave to a member who is called upon to assist in this kind of work, which may sometimes take years.

The resulting research reports are generally published under the names of their authors as annexes to the commissions' report, so that everyone can judge how far research findings and suggestions have actually been used. Many studies in the social sciences come into being in this way and the bulk of all research relating to regional policy has appeared here. Letting research reports and suggestions from university workers stand on their own sometimes has a political function also, for they provide an opportunity to test reactions to ideas which the politicians feel are not yet ripe for serious discussion.

The reports of such commissions are then submitted to sectoral regional and local authorities, to universities and to private organisations which might be affected, and these are requested to give their opinions by a certain date. The government is thus able to test opinion, at least among professional decision-makers. Such consultation also means that reports are fairly widely read and they are often taken up by study groups which indirectly give interested laymen a say. The government then either makes a proposal or drops the matter. It is true the whole procedure is sometimes used to bury an inconvenient topic, but the process effectively demonstrates how compromise is institutionalised in Swedish society. A research worker is just one voice among many and his influence is limited to what passes through this complex sieve.

GEOGRAPHERS' CONTRIBUTIONS TO DEVELOPMENTS IN REGIONAL POLICY

As long as a national administration is dominated by the sectoral outlook it is almost inevitable that such problems as locational shifts of industry and population are dealt with in a partial way. In Sweden a labour market policy emerged in the 1950s as a strong force in attempts to deal with problems of employment arising from structural change. At first, the principal aim was to help people to move to new jobs, leaving the less productive branches to disappear or to be consolidated. Free re-training was therefore offered and migration stimulated; the state even bought empty dwellings which could not be sold on the open market.

During the 1960s it became increasingly appreciated that the principle of full employment also required industry to move to labour because some people refused to migrate. A locational policy developed which relied on many kinds of economic incentives. On the whole the machinery had a strong bias towards crisis-management; thus, the Labour Market Board functioned as a fire brigade, trying to solve day-to-day problems wherever they arose.

This never-ending battle did not seem to be satisfactory from a longer perspective. While the policy predominantly helped individuals in trouble (a desirable end in itself), it did not contribute sufficiently to the improvement of whole settlements and regions. Regional differences remained or became accentuated, and in many remote and declining settlements social life became disrupted by out-migration. Provision of both public and, above all, commercial services deteriorated.

Geographers and others argued that the settlement structure must be dealt with as a whole, with the general aim of creating throughout the country larger and more diversified labour markets and moving services of the metropolitan kind—if not of the metropolitan variety—to as many provincial centres as possible. Only by creating more equal environments for firms and people would it be possible to accommodate future technical and economic change within a distribution of population which made it easier to attain the principal welfare goals.

At the present time a philosophy which puts place before sector faces considerable difficulties. The sectoral organisation of administration, industry and politics matches remarkably well the kind of division of knowledge between disciplines which is typical of traditional learning, and it is easy for most disciplines to act as experts in the service of some closely corresponding sector. Geography, on the other hand, does not fit in well with either systematic sciences or the sectors, though this is not necessarily the fault of geography.

During the period of sectoral dominance geographers in Sweden nevertheless contributed from time to time in their capacity as experts on the location of the components of sectoral systems; for example, work was done for the school, health and transport sectors. This kind of work, however, was frequently not very satisfying to the geographer of wide interests. Furthermore, from the viewpoints of users of the environment and of taxpayers it is the combined pattern of opportunities which is important, not the internal efficiency of one or other producer system in isolation.

The main lesson that was learnt from this sectoral work was how difficult it could be to establish common views across sectoral boundaries. The freedom to give advice against the expectations of each sector was limited, and it was clear that the chosen solutions sometimes worked openly against each other.

In detail, the consequences of sectoral planning and an almost medieval communal structure were the overproduction of small, half-developed settlements and poor coordination of the sizes and location of investments in services and transport. Above all, the situation led to a kind of planning which was founded on the extrapolation of trends; every isolated decision-maker tried to estimate the sum of what all others around him were going to do. Under such conditions there is no way of deliberately breaking a trend. This situation could be avoided in a country such as Sweden where almost half of the gross investment is in public hands, but new arrangements would be required if change was to occur.

What geographers in Sweden have been doing since their first experience in applied sectoral work has been to take part in the creation of instruments and knowledge for cross-sectoral administration with the main regional goals in mind. Geographers became involved in the gradual reshaping of old institutions and the creation of new ones with the power to counterbalance the sectoral lines of command. The purpose was to turn locational policy, which hitherto had been mostly concerned with depressed areas only, into a comprehensive regional policy covering the whole country. The effort has been directed towards the institutional and conceptual *frames* for plans and decisions, and has not been concerned with detailed locational matters.

In practice, a start was made by reshaping the communal structure in order to strengthen the integrative powers at the political base level. In the old system, which originated in medieval times, rural and urban communes were kept strictly apart, but in the present century the two groups of communes developed very differently. The rural communes declined markedly in terms of population and tax-base whereas the urban commune grew. Although the smallest and weakest units had been joined to neighbouring communes as early as 1952, more than a third of the 800 rural communes had fewer than 3000 inhabitants in the 1960s; yet it was estimated that the duties communes were required to undertake, in particular through the school reform, required a population of at least 8000. (Anon., 1961.) Apart from the weaknesses of the rural communes, a further problem existed for land-use and transportation planning in the vicinity of the larger urban centres because the often dense net of administrative boundaries cut across those of functional regions.

What geographers had to offer at that time was little more than two tools: the dot map of population distribution and certain concepts borrowed from Walter Christaller's work on central place theory (1933). Such theory could help in three ways. The first was, of course, to give the new units a "natural" centre. The second, and equally important purpose was a distributional one. By amalgamating urban centres with their rural hinterland it was hoped to create units with at least a stable aggregate population; automatically, too, urban wealth would give support to less fortunate rural districts. The third purpose was to create a well-rounded spatial framework which would simplify the political issues involved in land-use planning.

After some years of intensive work the initial plans were finally implemented at the beginning of 1974. In the early 1950s there were 2500 communes; today the total number is 278, with a median population around 15,000 inhabitants. (Ministry of Labour and Housing, 1973, p. 26.)

It is clear that a reform of this scope could not be completed without complaint and conflict. The old communes had to present their own suggestions according to principles which had been adopted. The government never made an initial suggestion in the form of a map, although the expert group undertook some map experiments in order to see if the principles were reasonably sound. Research into centrality and hinterlands was a matter for local study groups. From time to time a local referendum was organised. It was interesting to note the calming influence which a population map frequently had. People could then understand that, in this sparsely populated country, there were normally not many workable alternatives, while counting people on a dot map seems to make all inhabitants equal. For all its simplicity the population map proved to be an essential tool in the political task of achieving agreement and it has continued to be so.

The second reform concerned the regional level, the 24 "lan". In the unreformed system there was a rather loose integration between the sectoral representatives of the central ministries and boards and the distribution of government funds among communes was therefore not well coordinated. Communes could play one authority off against another and legal supervision rather than initiative dominated the regional scene. Since 1970 this situation has changed. A regional unit has been established with a professional planning staff at its core and the independence of the sectors in planning matters no longer exists at this level. Full government power is invested in a body made up of laymen from the region. Half the members are appointed by the national government and half are elected by the constituent communes. There is now a meeting-point for compromises between central and local interests; at the same time an instrument exists for coordinating investments across the boundaries of the new communes.

At first glance, the geographic component in this second reform is very small; no boundary revision is involved—at least so far—and no selection of urban centres. The important point is that an institution has been created in which cross-sectoral points of view have been given power over sectoral ones. A staff also exists which is close to the decision-makers and is able to translate research findings into practical use and to carry out its own studies. These regional units offer an interesting labour market for geographers.

At the national level the situation is more complicated. Traditionally, coordination between sectors has been seen as a matter of allocating monetary resources between them, a task in which the Minister of Finance has the final word. Apart from this unquestioned device no government or parliament would be willing to accept any coordinating body other than themselves for dealing with infrastructure and population distribution in a national perspective; yet coordination at this level is perhaps even more essential for a regional development policy.

The solution adopted in Sweden so far has been to try to let regional research as such create a common conceptual frame for the policy, irrespective of sectoral competence. Since 1966 a small expert group has been at work in government, a group comprising officials from the ministries most concerned and university representatives. The task of the group is to initiate, support and summarise regional research for political and administrative use. In regular reports accounts are given of regional trends in development and suggestions are advanced about the directions in which work is needed. In addition to its research tasks the group is normally invited by commissions and ministries to give its opinion on matters which are believed to have a regional dimension of some importance (Anon., 1972.)

In order to give research in the field some initial direction the group suggested that regional development should be approached as a three-party game in which *private industry, households* and the *public sectors* (state and communes) continuously try to adjust their relative positions. In Sweden it is only the public sectors which are fully controlled by the three levels of government, and it is mainly through this potential control that a long-term regional policy can be implemented. Central, regional and local governments are responsible for 30 per cent of employment (1973, of 22 per cent in 1965) and 43 per cent of gross investment, and it is hoped that moves in the public sectors will give enough powerful signals to industry and to households for them to follow. (Anon., 1974.)

Clearly this arrangement has had a tremendous impact upon geographical research in the universities. At first, geography was almost the only field which had something to contribute, but a group of regional economists gradually emerged.

During the first period work was concentrated on questions of industrial location and such population problems as internal migration. During the second period, i.e., since 1970, much more emphasis has been placed upon the analysis of the settlement pattern as a coherent system. Another principal topic has been the study of living conditions in local labour markets of various sizes and in various locations. In the near future a closer look will be taken at the service sectors, both public and private; at the same time, efforts will be made to investigate the relative efficiency of the different political measures available.

The efforts have been successful in the sense there is now a widespread understanding of the long-term problems. Furthermore, representatives of sectors, as well as of regions and communes, have increasingly adopted the practice of looking beyond their topical or geographical boundaries. Coordination, at least inside the government machinery, is much easier than it used to be.

Since 1972 an explicitly formulated national settlement policy has been laid down by act of parliament. The size and location of all investments made by the communes and the state are coordinated to ensure that they corrrespond with the principles of the strategy. The general objective is to achieve a dispersed concentration. The most far-reaching step taken so far has been to move a large number of central government boards to the major provincial centres in order to diversify employment there. (Economic Development Committee, 1973, esp. Annex II.)

The Ministry of Finance is not very much in favour of long-term strategies of this kind, for it feels that its freedom of action is too much hampered. As a result, the aggregated national economic point of view and the disaggregated regional point of view are sometimes in conflict—they represent two widely different ways of understanding the world—and they are probably bound to be so for a considerable time to come, perhaps until geographic theory has developed something of the strength of economic theory.

THE FEED-BACK FROM WORK ON REGIONAL POLICY TO ACADEMIC GEOGRAPHY

Applications of research depend on the existence of decision-makers who are in the position to receive and make use of its findings. They need not necessarily to be able to pay for the research if an independent university system is maintained where researchers chose their own tasks. Social science in particular is asked to contribute if it can offer appropriate conceptual tools at a time when a corresponding political issue comes up. As far as geography is concerned, only very specialised branches of the discipline are called upon as long as a competitive, sectoral approach to development prevails. The pressure on the discipline to split in topical groupings is very strong, yet each of these is in strong competition with systematic sciences.

As soon as institutions dealing with cross-sectoral matters emerge, a more broadly conceived form of geography has a chance to be useful. Geographers have every reason to advocate this kind of institution, not for their own sake but in the interest of all the ordinary people who make up a society. To such people the physical and social environment does not seem to be neatly arranged into separable spheres according to the classifications of the systematic sciences. There is always a mix of all sorts of phenomena, wanted and unwanted, and these have to be dealt with in terms of a continuous sequence of connected situations. The strings of events are felt to be more or less acceptable; some groups get more of the more and other groups more of the less, and rarely because of their own choice. Even if we do not believe in the possibility of wonderful utopias we may still have reason to believe that the good and the bad events could become more justly distributed than they are at present if we try, by common effort, to keep the "production" of situations under some control. Here geography has a contribution.

Christian van Paassen is right in saying in the course of a seminar discussion in Amsterdam that geography has its strength in the study and understanding of situations. The most interesting trait of geography is that, alone among the disciplines, it is interested in the interdependence of phenomena which have nothing in common except that they come in contact because they try to accommodate themselves in the same segment of space and time. This attitude is just what is required as an aid to cross-sectoral planning.

If the concept of a situation is taken as the vantage point, the main weakness of academic geography as seen from an applied point of view is that we have not been able to handle the political dimension of human affairs very well (using political to refer not only to decision-making situations but also to outcome situations).

It is instructive to return to the Swedish example in which concepts derived from geography have affected most people directly, the reform of the communes, one purpose of which was respectable enough as seen from the principle of solidarity, viz. to transfer resources from the stronger to the weaker inside the new units. At that time we did not have a micro-geographical political theory—and we still do not have even a beginning of such a theory—which could have told us how a change in scale should have been counterbalanced by a change in internal working procedures. Today there is much complaint throughout Sweden that, since far fewer individuals per 1000 inhabitants are now involved in local political life than formerly, there is a much greater network distance between voter and elected. Furthermore, for some reason it seems that physical centralisation in the main urban centre has replaced functions which could as well have remained spread out. The new structure thus seems to have created an insensitivity to local needs which could perhaps have been avoided.

Clearly, the other purpose—to strengthen local governments in their dealings with industry and the state—seems to have been achieved. This also means decentralisation because decisions which were formerly taken at the national or regional level can now be moved down to the communal.

It is probably always the case that wherever some progress is made in one direction there is automatically a regression somewhere else; somebody has to pay and frequently not the one who can best afford it. Thus, developments in the transport sector have led to a situation where the tremendously increased mobility of 75 per cent of the population has made the remaining 25 per cent almost totally immobile.

Observations of this and similar kinds suggest that we should try to develop methods by which one could foresee the distribution of outcomes of planning and other decision over the area's population as a whole. This task is complex and fascinating. It may be that the most important features of a society are not those which are readily observable as events but rather the latent mechanisms which are at work when actions of one group open and close opportunities for some other group. Knowledge of such mechanisms would help in negotiations between conflicting interests.

The neutral study of outcomes does not lead far, however, unless we are also willing to include inventive work with institutional changes. For this we need an entirely new kind of political geography—one which deals not only with boundaries on the ground but with boundaries between groups and interests as well.

CONCLUSION

In Sweden the most influential contributions of geographers have been made in connection with the development of institutions aimed at furthering cross-sectoral planning at all levels of government in the interest of the long-term regional policy which is seen as a political necessity. Unfortunately, owing to the lack of relevant concepts and understanding, the resulting framework is in the author's opinion more centralised and bureaucratic than is comfortable. The problem is that the forms of decentralisation which are known at present entail a magnification of regional differences and perhaps also of internal social differences inside regions, developments which would be strongly at variance with prevailing values. At the moment there is no answer to this dilemma.

ACKNOWLEDGEMENT

This chapter is based on a lecture given on 9th October 1973 in the Department of Geography, University of Michigan, Ann Arbor.

REFERENCES

Anon. (1961) *Principer för en ny Kommunindelning,* Government Official Reports, 1961, **9**, Stockholm, K. L. Beckmans Boktryckeri.

Anon. (1972) *Plan International 1972,* Swedish Society for Town and Country Planning, Stockholm.

Anon. (1974) *Orter i Regional Samverkan,* Government Official Reports, Esselte Tryck, Stockholm.

Bernhardt, E. (1971) *Trends and Variations in Swedish Fertility: a Cohort Study,* Central Statistics Bureau, Stockholm.

Christaller, W. (1933) *Die Zentralen Orte in Süddendeutschland,* Jena, translated by C. W. Baskin as *Central Places in Southern Germany* (1966), Prentice Hall, Engelwood Cliffs.

Economic Development Committee (1973) *National Settlement Strategies: a Framework for Regional Development,* European Free Trade Association, Montreux.

Hägerstrand, T. and S. Öberg (1970) *Befolkningsfördelningen och dess Förändringar,* Appendix 1, Government Official Reports, 1970, **14**, Stockholm.

Ministry for Foreign Affairs (1974) *The Biography of a People. Past and Future Population Changes in Sweden: Conditions and Consequences. A Contribution to the United Nations World Population Conference,* Stockholm.

Ministry of Labour and Housing and Ministry of Physical Planning and Local Government (1973) *Planning Sweden. Regional Development Planning and Management of Land and Water Resources,* a summary, Stockholm.

Pred, A. (1973) "Urbanisation, domestic planning problems and Swedish geographic research", in C. Board *et al.* (eds.) *Progress in Geography,* **5**, 1–76.

Sundquist, J. L. (1975) *Dispersing Population. What America can Learn from Europe,* Brookings Institution, Washington.

Note
The following are the major publications of the Expert Group on Regional Development (Expertgruppen for Regional Utredningsverksamhet), Stockholm:

Balanserad Regional Utveckling SOU 1970, **3.**
Urbaniseringen i Sverige. En Geografisk Samhallsanalys SOU 1970, **14.**
Regionaleknomisk Utveckling SOU 1970, **15.**
Orter i Regional Samverkan SOU 1974, **1.**
Ortsbundna Levnadsvillkor SOU 1974, **2.**
Produktionskostnader och Regionala Producktionssystem SOU 1974, **3.**
Regionala Prognoser i Planeringens Tjanst SOU 1974, **4.**

CHAPTER 15

ACHIEVEMENT AND PROSPECTS

W. R. D. SEWELL and J. T. COPPOCK

The preceding chapters in this book have presented a selection of the contributions which geographers, acting in a variety of roles and in a number of countries, have made to various stages of public policy. Inevitably there are major omissions, notably in urban affairs and in the use of resources, in both of which there have been important contributions (as chapter 1 shows). None the less, certain common themes emerge and reflection on these contributions suggests a number of ways in which geographers can more effectively influence policy in the future.

The various chapters make clear that the formation of policy is a complex process. It is possible to think of policy making as comprising four stages: the identification of some important problem, for which there is either no policy or present policies appear to be ineffective; the formulation of a policy which will seek to solve that problem; the implementation of that policy; and the monitoring of its effects, possibly leading ultimately to a new or modified policy. Each of these stages is, of course, much more complex than this simple model suggests; policy formulation, for example, is likely to require the identification of a number of possible courses of action and the subsequent selection of one of these, possibly after a long period of consultation. Most of the chapters in this book are concerned with the first and third stages of this process, for the second stage is essentially a political one in which the contributions of any individual discipline are minimal; as the first section of the book make clear, the political system of thinking is essentially different from the academic.

There is also a variety of levels at which a geographical input to policy can be made, and the effectiveness of that input is likely to be conditioned, not only by the abilities of the individuals concerned and by the availability of appropriate concepts and skills, but also by the level in the administrative hierarchy at which it is made; for this is likely to influence both the availability of necessary information and the extent to which the contribution is known by policy makers. At one end of the scale is the policy maker himself; and at the other, the interested academic who is concerned with understanding the problems which the policy maker will ultimately seek to solve, but not himself involved in policy. In between is a variety of roles, which might be arranged in order of decreasing influence as: official advisers, chiefly senior civil servants; external advisers, whether individuals or members of advisory boards; research consultants, who undertake appraisals, investigate problems and suggest possible solutions; and unofficial critics, whether committed academics or pressure groups, who seek to influence policy making from outside. The role and place of the politician who is not a minister is highly debatable; it could be argued that he should be placed immediately below the policy maker, as here, or alternatively that he has little influence. At the lowest level, the geographer's role may be primarily in contributing to the ground-swell of discussion from which a policy may ultimately emerge or by devising some concept or skill which will be helpful in finding a solution; at the highest level a professional contribution can be made only through a general awareness of the spatial and integrated nature of a problem, which is the residual effect of a professional training. A diagrammatic representation of these various levels and stages is given in Fig. 15.1.

How effective any contribution can be will depend on the stage at which and the position from which it is made; and while the necessary condition for making such a contribution is the existence of a problem of great public concern which the skills and concepts of the particular discipline are competent to help solve, this is not a sufficient condition. There must be an awareness on the part of the policy maker or his advisers of the part that both the discipline and the individual could play, and it seems likely that this will depend in part on the channels of communication within the bureaucracy, and on the accidents of personal contact and geographical propinquity; for it seems a plausible hypothesis, at least to geographers in Edinburgh and Victoria, that the influence of individual academics will be inversely proportional to their distance from the seat of government (though such considerations are, of course, much less important once competence and reputation have been established). It is also likely to depend on the openness of government and on its receptiveness generally to outside influences. In this respect, the United States and Sweden seem to represent one end of the spectrum, with widespread public investigation by Congressional Committee and Parliamentary Commission respectively before policy is formed, and the socialist countries the other, with the United Kingdom, where discussion tends to take place behind closed doors and public debate is largely confined to an examination of the favoured solution, occupying some intermediate position. The merits of the expert group, established in Sweden to permit close contact between officials and academics in order to ensure that research is used effectively and that gaps in research which are relevant to regional policy are identified and filled, appear to warrant serious considerations by other countries.

STAGES AND LEVELS OF POLICY INVOLVEMENT

INPUTS FROM POLICY-MAKERS AND TECHNICAL ADVISORS	STAGES OF POLICY EVOLUTION			
	PROBLEM IDENTIFICATION AND STRATEGY SPECIFICATION	POLICY FORMULATION	POLICY IMPLEMENTATION	POLICY EVALUATION
POLICY MAKERS eg. Ministers	▬▬▬	▬▬▬	▬▬▬	— — —
OTHER POLITICIANS eg. Members of Parliament	ooooooooo	ooooooooo	ooooooooo	ooooooooo
INTERNAL ADVISORS eg. Senior Officials	▬▬▬	— — —	▬▬▬	— — —
EXTERNAL ADVISORS eg. Advisory Boards	■■■■■■■	— — —	— — —	— — —
RESEARCH CONSULTANTS eg. Ad hoc Advisors	■■■■■■■		■■■■■■■	— — —
CRITICS eg. Involved Academics and Interest Groups	ooooooooo	— — —	— — —	ooooooooo
UNINVOLVED OBSERVERS AND RESEARCHERS	— — —	— — —	— — —	— — —

DEGREE OF INFLUENCE ON POLICY — HIGH / LOW

CONTRIBUTIONS

Continuous	▬▬▬
Frequent and important	■■■■
Frequent but less important	oooo
Occasional	— — —

Fig. 15.1. Stages and levels of policy involvement

From the small sample of contributions in this book, several generalisations seem to emerge. The choice of topics seem to confirm the view that it is the coincidence of public concerns and disciplinary skills and concepts which largely determines the influence which a profession can have on policy; for most of the topics concern two long-established interests of geographers, the regional idea (particularly in respect of identifying regions which are meaningful to their inhabitants) and the use (and mis-use) of resources. Underlying the first is a recurrent dilemma, the conflict between policies which are devised in a national context and their application in particular localities where they are inappropriate, a failing which often arises from the lack of a spatial dimension in public policy, a deficiency which the geographer is well-qualified to remedy. Similarly there appears to be an increasing number of examples of policies failing to achieve their objectives because the structure of government ensures that they are considered sectorally from the viewpoint of a particular ministry and yet conflict with other sectorally-derived policies when they are implemented. It is in this connection, where sectoral views have to be reconciled, that the geographer's concern with the diverse phenomena which occupy segments of earth space is particularly valuable, and several contributors warn of the danger that specialisation within the profession may lead to the neglect of this traditional aspect of a geographer's training.

It is also clear that, while there is a need for case studies to increase understanding, the degree of generalisation which is possible is often limited, not only because geographical circumstances differ from country to country, but also because the structure of government and the processes of decision-making and policy formulation likewise vary; it is instructive, for example, to compare Torsten Hägerstrand's account of the concerns of regional policy in Sweden, where many problems arise from the widespread scatter of communities, which reflects both the historical and physical geography of the country (chapter 14), with Edwin Brooks' analysis of that in the United Kingdom, where problems of industrial maladjustment, unemployment and urban decay appear to dominate thinking (though in both countries similar problems arise from the co-existence of ill-coordinated policies). Perhaps the lesson of most general application to geographers who wish to see their discipline making a more effective contribution to public policy is the importance of understanding the structure of government and the processes of decision making, not only because official policy making and academic inquiry present different systems of thought, but also because effective solutions may require new administrative and political structures, particularly at regional and local levels. It is, however, ironic that, while cross-sectoral views are equally necessary in policy-making at national level, the prospects of achieving such an approach seem remote in a system of cabinet government in which ministers represent line departments.

Here perhaps is a role for a new political geography (for long the Cinderella of the subject), not only in promoting the comparative study of governmental policy-making and its spatial manifestations and consequences, but also in devising ways of predicting the likely outcomes of adopting different kinds of administrative and political regions. The drawing of administrative boundaries is a particularly challenging assignment in applied regional geography, as the various studies in this book show, though even in so small a sample there is a wide variation in the discretion given to the expert. Similarly, the administration of water resources and the control of air pollution offer opportunities to geographers to make useful contributions by analysing the consequences of establishing different kinds of regions for the implementation of public policies.

Two particular needs which have become apparent from these studies are the desirability of anticipating the requirements of policy-oriented research and the development of more adequate means of forecasting the likely outcomes of particular policies. A repeated difficulty faced by those involved in applied research has been the limited time available for the investigation, though the 1 month allowed to R. L. Morrill for the redistricting of the State of Washington is probably exceptional. Yet even a longer timetable does not allow new methods to be developed and may not even permit existing methods to be used if they have not already been tried and proved in an operational context (though it is interesting to note how often simple approaches—the use of the dot map or the basic concept of the region for example—have been important in achieving solutions). And while it is rarely possible to mount major research programmes in support of particular policies, there are certainly examples, in such diverse fields as pollution control and office relocation, of policies where inadequate understanding may result in policies which have a quite different effect from what was intended; thus, an office location policy which relies on blanket controls over office development is unlikely to lead to a satisfactory solution to the concentration of offices in capital cities, while smoke control zones may lead to distortions in the housing market.

It is self-evident that, since policies are concerned with shaping the future, forecasting, both in the wider sense of creating scenarios of likely futures and in the narrower one of predicting the likely outcome of present policies, is of fundamental importance. Geographers have shown an understandable reluctance to forecast future geographies, for it must be recognised that even forecasting for a country as a whole is difficult enough and does not have a very high success rate; yet decisions are constantly being made and policies formulated which will have major effects on the geography of the country and a major research effort in improving methods of regional forecasting would seem justified. Most models constructed so far have been static or partial models and more attention needs to be directed at the construction of dynamic models of systems and sub-systems, with particular reference to their spatial attributes. We need a much more adequate understanding of how things change so that we may better understand the consequences of altering some part of the system.

If better forecasting is to be achieved, we require a very much more adequate understanding of human systems than we currently possess. Although information about and understanding of physical systems is still far from adequate, their attainment does not present fundamental obstacles whereas we have hardly begun to secure adequate information about human systems, let alone understand them. We need a very much deeper knowledge of the mainsprings of human behaviour, of the motivations of individuals and of the discrepancies between what people say and what they do if satisfactory policies are to emerge to deal with, say, regional migration, environmental quality or natural hazards. Public participation, or at least lip-service to it, is increasingly a feature of public policy making and decision taking; yet it is not all clear how far the public understands the issues involved and whether what the public wants can be established in these ways, let alone whether such participation is likely to lead to better policies and better decisions.

In addition to forecasting in general, there are two particular aspects which would repay further work in order to improve the contributions that geographers may make, environmental impact assessment and technology assessment; both seem to merit a geographical contribution, though geographers have no monopoly of either. Since the National Environmental Policy Act of 1969 made environmental impact statements a necessary feature of major federal developments in the United States, a growing number of governments elsewhere has sought to implement similar measures, though the methodology for making such assessment is still in its infancy and both the human consequences and spatial dimensions of such impacts appear to have been neglected. The rapidity and increasing rate of technological change are now truisms, but there is nonetheless a need to examine the likely consequences of emerging technology, such as that affecting the fuel and power industries; the generation of electricity by nuclear reactors is an illustration of a highly sophisticated technology without any very adequate assessment of the likely consequences, especially for social and political relationships in the regions where plants are located.

A more effective role in public policy making requires a better understanding, both of the issues and of the ways in which policies are made. It requires both the retention of what is valuable in the old geography, especially the geographical imagination and the cultivation of the ability to see problems in the round in their spatial setting, and the development and refinement of those skills which enable us more easily to handle spatial data and to understand and predict spatial change. It requires both a willingness to think big on important issues, as with Mackinder's concept of the Heartland, while recognising that the foundations may be inadequate and the understanding imperfect, and also to be concerned with the micro-political structures within which the concerns of individual citizens are expressed. We must beware both of the dangers of being shunted into the sidings of undue specialisation and of ignoring the need for technical competence in handling complex issues. Geographers have a contribution to make to the formulation and monitoring of public policy at all stages, they are making it in increasing numbers and in respect of a widening range of issues, and they are capable of making better and more numerous contributions than they do. In seeking to do so, they must avoid the naive illusions that, as geographers, they can make policy and that they alone have the answers; they can make their best contributions in collaboration with others on topics where the man in the street (and, it is to be hoped, increasingly the politician) recognises no disciplinary or sectoral boundaries, those which affect the earth as the home of man.

INDEX